MUSIC
IN THE EDUCATION
OF CHILDREN

MUSIC
IN THE EDUCATION
OF CHILDREN

BESSIE R. SWANSON

WADSWORTH PUBLISHING COMPANY, INC., SAN FRANCISCO

45626

TO MY MOTHER,
PRIMARY TEACHER AND MUSICIAN

PREFACE

This book is addressed to all those persons who are concerned that music have its proper place in the education of children. It is designed to serve as a textbook for teachers in training and as a practical guide and source of musical information for the teacher in the classroom. School administrators, musicians, and parents will find much of interest here.

The discussions in this book show the interrelation of the musical activities of children and suggest a developmental program in activities and learning from kindergarten through the sixth grade. Singing is the activity around which teachers can best organize the classroom music program. Therefore, the discussion in Chapter Two centers on the basic topics of songs and singing voices. Simple instruments that have educational possibilities are discussed in Chapter Three and Four.

The *teaching* of singing and a special consideration of music notation are delayed until Chapters Five and Six for two reasons: (1) Simple instruments, when understood and skillfully used, can be valuable aids to teaching a song. (2) When the book is used as a college text, it will be found that the student needs a few weeks to become oriented to musical activities before he is ready to undertake the important assignment of teaching a song.

Bodily movement as a meaningful part of the music program is discussed in Chapter Seven and leads into music listening, the subject of Chapter Eight. Special consideration is given to the relationship of music to the social studies in Chapter Nine.

Explanations in this book are specific rather than generalized, and, wherever possible, musical examples are included so that the reader may test the teaching theory. Over 190 musical examples have been included; 70 of these are complete songs that may be found in the various basic school song books. Thus, in the process of learning the techniques and theory of teaching music, the reader can become acquainted with a sample of the repertoire for singing.

Three items will be particularly valuable to college instructors and teachers-in-training: (1) Following each chapter the brief section "Activities for College Classes" suggests classroom projects that are designed to encourage participation in music by the teacher-training class. For many students a practical application of the music teaching techniques is necessary for complete understanding. (2) An outline for the development of a music teaching handbook is given in Chapter One. Many of the written assignments included in "Activities for College Classes" can be incorporated into the handbook so that each student will have immediate, personally selected material to draw on in his early teaching. (3) In Appendix A will be found "Reference Material for Music Theory and Notation" to which those who have a limited understanding of music notation may be referred.

This book has grown out of the author's experience as a special music teacher and supervisor in the public schools of Visalia, California, and as an instructor in teacher-training classes at the University of Washington. She is indebted to many children, classroom teachers, musicians, and administrators with whom she has been associated. To the following persons the author would like to express special appreciation: Marietta M. Ward, Librarian at the School of Music, University of Washington, for her assistance with research; Egon Kraus, music educator from Cologne, Germany, for suggestions in the use of the Orff Instruments; Lucile Doersch, Elementary Music Coordinator in the Bellevue, Washington, Public Schools, for assistance in obtaining the photographs; Lucille Just of the Wadsworth Publishing Company for her keen editorial interest and valuable suggestions. The following music educators reviewed the manuscript in its various stages and gave valuable criticism and suggestions: Andrew M. Banse, Charlotte DuBois, Maude Garnett-Gillis, Alfred Lester Roberts, and Sylvestra Wassum.

The author is grateful to the administration of the Bellevue, Washington, Public Schools for permitting the pictures to be taken in their schools, and to the publishers of the basic song series and others who were generous in granting permission to use their copyrighted material.

CONTENTS

MUSIC
IN THE EDUCATION
OF CHILDREN

CHAPTER ONE

MUSIC FOR CHILDREN—
ITS CHALLENGES

Music has magic in it! Witness the intentness with which the freckle-faced lad plays. A boy's everyday world of Little League baseball and pocket knives has been abandoned in favor of the world of enchanting tunes.

People of all times have recognized the "magic" power of music. It was known in ancient Greece when Plato wrote, "Musical training is a more potent instrument than any other, because rhythm and harmony find their way into the inward places of the soul, on which they mightily fasten imparting grace..."[1] In the New England of 1838 the townspeople acknowledged music as a part of the authorized curriculum in the public school because through music "you set in motion a mighty power which silently, but surely, in the end, will humanize, refine and elevate the whole community."[2]

Whenever parents think of the good things in life that they would like their children to experience in school, they include music and art. Many people are not quite sure what these subjects can do for children, but they intuitively feel the need for the added dimension that these studies give to life. Teachers likewise acknowledge music and art as integral parts of the school curriculum.

The arts are not "practical" subjects in the ordinary sense. There is a difference between feeling their importance in the curriculum and spelling out their real value. Music is especially elusive. It means different things to different people. The *personal* quality of musical experience is one of its highest values, but it creates problems for the teacher who must define objectives and establish a plan for teaching music.

Those who would consider the place of music in the education of children must give some thought to the following questions. First, what is the value of music to the individual? Second, what kind of program in music should be provided for children in the elementary school? Finally, who can actively promote the proper role of music in the curriculum and in the lives of the children?

The Value of Music

To many people music is almost exclusively entertainment; for others it is also an aid in worship or in promoting patriotism. Some regard serious music as remote and divorced from life. Edwin J. Stringham says, "From its very beginnings in savage and primitive society, music has been an integral part of the daily life of the individual and the group.

4

Whether to express triumph over the enemy or thanksgiving for the harvest, the praise of heroes or the pleasures of the hunt, religious feelings, incantation against evil spirits, tenderness for the beloved or lament for the dead, music is called upon to convey and at the same time to heighten the emotional side of man's experiences."[3]

PERSONAL ENRICHMENT. Music still has the functions Stringham describes. At the same time music has become an art form that arouses feelings even when it is unrelated to another immediate experience. Thus through music one is able to extend and enrich his life beyond what is practical for him to experience directly.

In the school curriculum, music is one of the few subjects capable of bringing the pupil into contact with beauty and a broader emotional and spiritual stream of life. The school cannot define these experiences for the individual, but it can build in each child the *capacity for response* to art forms so that his life will have more richness and depth. Gaiety, tenderness, the heroic spirit, sadness, melancholy and loneliness—all are expressed in music and all are a part of a healthy, responsive emotional life.

If music is to function effectively in this expressive role throughout life the individual must have ever broader and deeper experiences with it. Character deepens as one journeys through life, and this depth perspective gives scope and meaning to his outlook on life. Music serves man in that it can express the whole range of feelings involved in the life process. The more refined aesthetic experience in music that will enrich adult life beyond that valuable to the child is dependent on his ability to hear and respond to more of what is expressed in music. The fact that all that music has to offer is not available in the same degree to the experienced and the inexperienced listener or performer is potent justification for education in music.

The questions of quality and taste invariably arise in any discussion of the arts. An extreme view, either favoring the development of *specific* taste or rejecting the necessity for *any* development of it, can be detrimental to the program in music education. There is good music in all styles and forms and music to serve many purposes. Although no exact criteria can cover the entire field, there are standards that can be applied. Among art songs, for example, judgment is made on the basis of the quality of the poetry used and the faithfulness with which the music captures the mood and ideas of that poetry. For a composition in the jazz idiom other standards prevail. According to Broudy, the ultimate justification in selection is that the "technically and formally good works of art will also achieve greater expressiveness and have a greater import for human life than the inferior sort."[4] Children need to learn to respond to beauty in sound and rhythm and to evaluate music in terms of its expressive qualities for them. Then, as they mature and their inner needs change, they will know how to find music that will serve as valid enrichment on a new level.

AN AVENUE FOR EXPRESSION. The arts provide vital forms of self-expression and recreation that people need, but from which they may be cut off because they lack experience and skills. Mechanization of work can free people for more leisure activities, but these, too, can become mechanized. Television has converted young and old alike into passive spectators. Because they have not developed resources within themselves, many people find their chief diversion in what is done *for* them.

In the visual arts significant advances have been made in helping children express their creative impulses. In appraising music in the school we find that its creative function has been glibly acknowledged but often bypassed in actual practice. Where are musical activities comparable to the free creative activities in art? In what directions can early experiences be guided so that adequate expression of mature aesthetic feelings will follow? In all music-making—singing, playing, and improvising—we find opportunities.

In the past, music educators placed much emphasis upon "appreciation." Pupils were taught "the fundamentals" so that they might eventually know the language of music and thereby be privileged to engage in the art. Undue emphasis on mastery of skills isolated the individual from an immediate realization of personal value. In many cases music as an avenue of personal fulfillment was abandoned.

In more recent years, as a reaction to the formalistic approach, music has been brought into the everyday lives of children and brightened with the slogan "Music is fun." This approach erroneously conveys the idea that fun is the chief end of music. It is true that in the early years music-making should be of a type requiring little skill so that children can participate in simple, satisfying ways. However, in presenting music as an immediate source of enjoyment, many teachers find themselves unable to develop a long-range program that assures growth in skills and insights. Pleasure and satisfaction in the use of music in a creative capacity throughout life is dependent upon the development of musical skills to a functional level. If the simple approach remains the *only* level of contact, boys and girls are deprived of the opportunity to grow into a more mature relationship with music. Music is enjoyable but its greater values can never be realized if it is experienced solely on the childhood "fun" level.

Musical activities have definite social value for those who participate in group music-making; individual musical activities have many other personal values. These will be brought out in the study of more specific aspects of the program.

A Program with Many Facets

An individual makes use of music in two ways: he may listen to it or he may produce it. It is generally acknowledged that music offers more to those who participate actively than those who merely listen. There are many ways to make music, and individuals may find one form of participation more natural than another. Thus, a teacher planning the music program must include many activities to interest children of varied talents and varied backgrounds.

SINGING AND PLAYING INSTRUMENTS. In the elementary grades the music program often is organized around singing because this is the mode of musical expression closest to the individual, and to it the other activities may easily be related. The child may sing his own tunes or he may choose a folk melody or a composed song to serve as a vehicle for his expression. Singing is literally "the music of the people." Through it children can readily express their feelings and share the feelings of others.

All sorts of simple instruments have been adapted for use by children. They have an important place in the music program for improvising, for accompanying singing, and for the practical study of music. Children often develop dynamic, rhythmic chanting patterns, using the voice and combinations of rhythm instruments. Original melodies grow out of opportunities to play simple melody instruments, and the desire to play a known melody can lead to an understanding of music notation. Some older children with talent and interest can be encouraged to study the standard orchestral instruments.

MUSIC AND MOVEMENT. Children express themselves directly and effectively through movement. Teachers have learned to encourage children to use bodily movement as a response to music. Children do more than merely run, skip, and gallop with the music; they use these natural movements to express what they hear in the music. Impersonation and dramatization serve a similar purpose and may be used with songs as well as with instrumental music. Through movement children learn to listen to music in order to follow its rhythm; they learn to hear and to interpret progressively more detail in its melody and form.

CREATIVITY IN MUSIC. In a broad sense, creativity is a part of all the other musical activities. When children, through bodily movement or in color and design on paper, express what they hear, they are responding creatively; when they produce desired musical effects with instruments, or when they sing a particular song in a special way, they create a mood.

Adults too often impose their standards on children. They demand that the child develop skills before he has a chance to discover that he can express something from within himself through his own simple type of music. Elementary teachers must first be concerned with promoting situations in which children may explore and use music in their own natural ways. Children can be induced to experiment with voices and instruments to satisfy their instincts to manipulate and to make sounds. More important, they can find ways to express their joy or sadness, their feelings of aggression or loneliness. Watch a group of children producing rhythmic sounds with a drum or with their feet. Observe a first grader picking out a melody on the small xylophone. Listen to a child singing at his work and you will hear the creative music of children.

More specifically, creativity in music means the composing of melodies. Elementary children are quite capable of undertaking this activity, sometimes as a group project but often as an individual pursuit. Here, with a little guidance, the gifted child can find an avenue of fulfillment. There are diverse types of creative temperament, and no textbook will explain how they are best aroused and implemented. In Mozart were combined a superb natural talent for music and a facility for expressing it. When he sat down to write his compositions they were often completely worked out in his mind. On the other hand, Beethoven struggled mightily, even with many of his simpler creations, but he often struck out in entirely new directions in music. All creative people range between the temperamental extremes of these two types. The teacher may sense such diversity within a class of children, and somehow must bring out the best in both by different approaches.

LISTENING, A BASIC ACTIVITY. A child learns to listen as he sings and plays instruments. He must listen if his interpretations of music through bodily movement are to be rhythmic and expressive of the music. In addition, the only way to evaluate and enjoy one's own musical creations is to listen to them as they are performed. All of these activities aid the child in the important project of learning to listen, which is the chief musical activity of the majority of adults. Hence, although listening experiences are discussed in the last sections of this book, they are, in a sense, first in importance in any consideration of music.

LEARNING MUSIC NOTATION. The medium of musical expression is organized sound. Notation is a visual representation of the sound of music but it is not the art itself. Only after a person has had such extensive experience with music that seeing the notation actually promotes an inner *hearing* of the music can "notes" and "music" be considered analogous.

The child's introduction to music is through its sound; then gradually its notation may be presented to define and support what the ear perceives. This is the normal development of any musical concept:

1. It is experienced by the ear; e.g., one may hear and sing the "amen" at the end of a hymn.
2. It is identified to the ear; one recognizes the "amen" as a common chord progression that often functions in this capacity.
3. Its notation is related to it; one sees the "amen" chords in notation, he learns how they are formed, their relationship to each other, etc.

The discussion of the music program in this book is designed to follow a developmental pattern. First, the childhood activities of singing, playing instruments, and moving to music are outlined. In conjunction with each activity are shown ways of leading children to a deeper understanding of music through a functional use of its notation. With the teacher's help, children can learn to express themselves through music and to respond to the expression of others. Eventually with proper guidance the children will see printed symbols as a visual representation of the sound of music.

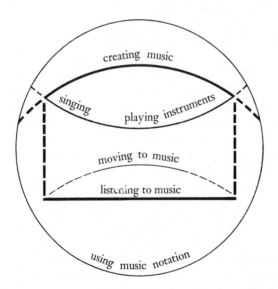

The diagram illustrates the activities that must be considered separately and in combination in a study of music for children. Through experience with all of them children will grow in their ability to use music as an avenue of personal fulfillment in their daily lives.

Who Is Responsible for Music Teaching?

Education in the elementary school is developed on the basis of a close relationship between a teacher and his pupils. In current practice many elementary schools are organized around the "self-contained" classroom, in which one teacher is responsible for all aspects of the education of the children assigned to him for the year.

Many teachers are quite skillful in teaching reading, arithmetic, the social studies, and other such subjects; but when all teachers are expected moreover to provide for the children significant experiences in art, music, and other specialized fields, many feel less than qualified in one or more areas. Does this limitation diminish the value of the plan? What can be done to strengthen the self-contained classroom with regard to the teaching of music?

THE NEED FOR THE CLASSROOM TEACHER. It is true that not all elementary teachers have sufficient skill to meet, unaided, the needs of *all* children in *all* fields of education, although the possibilities for success are greater at the primary level than at higher levels. The music program is no exception to the rule that the educating process should be built around the individual needs and abilities of the children, which are best known by the classroom teacher.

Music educators responsible for the program believe that (1) the active interest of the classroom teacher is essential to the promotion of an adequate program of music in the elementary school; and (2) music in the classroom should not be isolated in one period during the day as it is when the special teacher carries on the program alone. Music is an integral part of life and it should function in this capacity in the classroom.

The teacher needs music in his life as much as children need it. By participating in the arts, one achieves self-esteem and personal satisfaction. Almost in self-defense, however, because he fears that music is only for the talented, a person who has little experience with it may claim complete inability and lack of interest. Yet a few successful experiences with music can grip such a person with enthusiasm. Any teacher can find that there is something in music for him and some way in which he can share music with the children in his classroom.

How is it possible to provide a program in music to which the classroom teacher contributes his intimate understanding of the children as well as his own personal interest and presence, and yet make real understanding and skill in music also available? Music educators have found that a good program in music can be achieved through the active participation of two people: the classroom teacher and the music specialist (helping teacher, supervisor, consultant, or counselor).

MUSIC TEACHING A COOPERATIVE PROJECT. The music specialist serves as a resource person, a technical advisor, and an assistant to the teacher and his pupils. How much time the specialist spends in any one classroom depends on the skill and musical background of the individual teacher and the generosity of the school administration in providing enough specialists to fill the need. Under optimum conditions, he works in the classroom with the teacher and pupils as often as seems necessary to provide a well-balanced program in music. In some cases the specialist may keep a regular, once or twice weekly appointment with a teacher and his class. Other teachers are so capable musically that a monthly conference, to which the specialist brings requested resource material and suggests new techniques, is sufficient assistance. Under this plan, the music program for the class utilizes all the skill and understanding the classroom teacher is able to bring to it. Over a period of time the music skills of the teacher may be strengthened, and the specialist may find that a greater part of his assistance gradually can be withdrawn.

It is true that the system does not yield the best results in every classroom. Some teachers do not care enough about music to work amicably with the specialist, and some specialists are highly qualified as musicians but do not have the necessary qualities of leadership to do the job. Complacent administrators, whose only concern is a token gesture toward providing music in the school, may stand in the way of an effective program.

All of this brings us back to the classroom teacher himself; the great challenge of the music program to him must be that, regardless of who does the major portion of the music teaching, his interest in music and his skill as a teacher are indispensable to a vital music program in his classroom. Whether he has sufficient musical background and skills to provide *all* the leadership his children require, or whether he must call for assistance in specified areas, the responsibility for music in the classroom remains his. He must prepare himself in whatever ways he can to meet this challenge.

High praise is given those who achieve flexible, creative teaching. This is the result of three conditions:

1. An understanding of those taught (their needs and abilities).
2. Enthusiasm for and appreciation of the value of the subject being taught.
3. Skills and the knowledge of techniques to bring the above together.

A student can develop the first condition by observing children and communicating with them, and the second by participating in musical activities. To have rewarding experiences with music is of extreme importance, for it is the teacher's personal convictions that provide the real incentives for his music program.

The third condition may more easily be delineated in a book. The program in music education proposed here suggests many approaches and uses for music. As the prospective teacher works with it he can develop his own musical skills and gain insights into ways in which music can be brought to children. This background is basic to the teacher's training, and yet we know that a school music program cannot be set up merely from a book, nor can the program of one teacher be adopted as a whole by another; every teacher is under some obligation to do what he finds particularly applicable to his situation. As long as he keeps his objectives in sight, his techniques may be as varied and creative as he is able to make them.

Organization of a Music Handbook

The music program recommended in this book is both generalized and idealized; it is designed to suggest approaches to be used by those who have little skill and experience, and yet to present a challenge to those who are already well trained in music. The teacher must tailor a music program that he will be able to carry out. Those plans, however, must have a certain breadth and scope. Although the teacher may be quite limited as he begins teaching, he will grow in his ability to deal with music in the classroom, and he will find others to assist him in achieving his goals.

Supervisors are often surprised to see teachers working from year to year without any organized plan for music, and without making notations of the materials that were most useful in their past years of experience. If music teaching is taken seriously, it must be based on sound planning and continuity. The following suggestions for the organization of a music teaching handbook can contribute toward these ends. The teacher should list a limited amount of personally selected materials for use during the early days of teaching, and he should also establish a form to serve as a cumulative experience record of music materials used from year to year.

The development of the handbook should take place as each aspect of the music program is considered during the term. Many of the suggestions in "Activities for College Classes" at the end of each chapter should be incorporated into the handbook.

BASIC ORGANIZATION. A three-holed loose-leaf binder holding $8\frac{1}{2}'' \times 11''$ paper should be organized into six sections, using tabs or dividers. The following pages suggest content that may be useful. The important thing is that the student compile it in such a manner that the result will be valuable to him, with his particular talents. It is expected that material will be added in all sections. If the student is *sure* that he will teach kindergarten or first grade, he will want to select materials with this specific grade in mind. However, many young teachers find it more realistic to plan a music handbook for two or more grades, or to make a general handbook to be adapted later to any teaching situation. The decision should be made by the user of the handbook.

Section I. *The Teacher and the Program*

A. An evaluation of the student as a music teacher should be written at the end of these studies. At that time the student will have been testing his native abilities and growing in experience and musical skill for several months; what can he expect of himself as a beginning teacher? He should list specific strengths and weaknesses, being frank and fair in his appraisal, because it will determine to some extent the materials he will use, the techniques he will be able to employ, and the kind of assistance he will seek.

B. A check-list giving the general outlines of the music program the prospective teacher hopes to provide should be compiled. The following headings give suggestions:

  1. I hope to bring to my pupils these benefits:
  2. In planning the total program, I want to keep these points of organization and balance of activity in mind:
  3. I will need specific assistance in these areas:

Section II. *The Singing Activities* (to be completed after study of Chapters Two, Five, and Six)

A. An introductory check-list will help the beginning teacher to remember the important aspects. In order to be specific, he should use such headings as the following:

  1. Simply stated, my objectives in singing are these:
  2. Important reminders about my own teaching of songs:
  3. References and materials that will be especially helpful:

B. A list of songs should be started. A separate page can be prepared for each topic that will be useful at the teaching level selected (e.g., autumn, holidays, American Indians, animals, etc.). This is only the beginning of a collection; therefore two or three good titles under each topic will be sufficient. The right-hand side of the page should be reserved for teaching notes. These must be brief, serving only as a reminder of the character of the song and its possible use when the teacher can no longer recall the melody or words. As he begins to teach he will find this column very useful, so ample room should be left for additional comments.

The grade level selected will have some bearing on the song topics and will determine the song books used. Two or three basic song series as well as other supplementary sources should be included in the planning. The source of the song should be given in a short code,* followed by the page number. The key and first tone of the song are indicated in another column, so that when the song is memorized the teacher will know the key without having the song book in hand.

If the song as it appears in the book seems too high, it is wise to indicate a transposition, as shown in the tune-up column for the third song in the example given. A song in a minor key should be marked as shown in the fourth song. The tune-up code gives the pitch to be sounded on the pitch pipe or piano (the location of "do") and the syllable on which the song begins. All of this will be understood after a study of Chapter Five.

TITLE	SOURCE	TUNE-UP	TEACHING NOTES
"Bow, Belinda"	ECh-64	F-do	Singing game in line-dance formation. Very easy and tuneful.
"Scraping-up Sand"	MIOT-64	C-do	Play-party song suggesting fundamental mv'ts in drama. Appealing to boys. May use some rhythm instruments. Tonal pattern: "Good-by, Liza Jane" mi-mi-re-re-do.
"Where is Thumbkin?"	KBk-51	G-do (tr.F-do)	Finger-play; good to capture interest. Easy to sing, repetitious, charming. Tone call: "run away."
"Silver Moon Boat"	ABC II-173	D-mi (B minor)	Minor mode, five-tone song but not pentatonic in the usual sense. Stress melodic flow and feeling. Use fingers, hands, and arms to express "word pictures" found in song. Enrich with finger cymbals.

Section III. *Playing Instruments* (to be compiled while studying Chapters Three and Four)

A. An outline of the important points in children's use of instruments will help in planning and developing a significant program.

---

* See Appendix B for a list of codes used in this book.

B. Following the form suggested in the preceding section, and again on separate pages, listings should be made of songs or other compositions that may be enriched or accompanied by instruments. On each page, space can be left for later addition of other titles. There will be some cross references to songs included in Section II.

C. Melodies that children may play on bells should be listed; sample material should be prepared.

D. Older children will be able to make rhythm orchestrations. Suitable compositions may be suggested.

Section IV. *Moving to Music* (to be compiled while studying Chapter Seven)

A. In a brief outline of the purposes of the activity, varied approaches can be shown, along with sources for further information.

B. Following the form suggested for topical songs, several songs that may be enriched through bodily movement should be listed. The songs should exemplify a variety in types of movement. Brief notes can accompany each.

C. On another page, piano or recorded compositions that suggest variety in types of movement should be listed. The right-hand half of the page can be reserved for sources (books or recorded numbers) and teaching notes.

Section V. *The Listening Program* (to be compiled during the study of Chapter Eight)

A. An outline should state the objectives, important teaching techniques, immediate sources of information and other materials.

B. Compositions and teaching notes should be listed for use with the grade selected. Pictures and suggestions of related activities may be included.

C. Specific compositions that can be used in other ways should be listed:

    1. Background music for resting or activities:
    2. Art inspiration:
    3. Study related to a particular musical topic (instruments, musical form, rhythm, composers, etc.):
    4. Correlation with social studies units:

    As far as possible, these titles should be drawn from material that will be readily available. Sources (books or record numbers) should be included.

Section VI. *Creative Aspects*

A. A philosophy of promoting creativity should be developed, and teaching techniques to be employed can be described. As a reminder of the many situations in which creativity may be promoted, the student should list specific activities for each of the following areas: singing, playing instruments, moving to music, and listening.

B. Examples to be accumulated:

    1. Songs the student has composed or assisted in composing:

    2. Rhythmic names, jingles, and rhymes to be chanted, sung, or improvised on:

    3. Short appealing verses that might provide children of this grade possibilities for melody writing:

It is hoped that each teacher will find significant ways through which to develop the spirit of exploration and creativity in his pupils. He should remember also that creativity is a way of life that is not limited to poets and composers, but that extends to teachers as well as to their pupils.

Not every classroom teacher is capable of single-handedly providing the rich program of musical experiences his pupils should have. However, the challenge must go out to him to discover children's musical needs and capabilities and to see to it that music has its well-deserved place in their education. To that end this book is addressed to the general classroom teacher of the elementary grades.

CHAPTER NOTES

1. Plato, *The Republic.*
2. Edward Bailey Birge, *History of Public School Music in the United States* (Boston: Oliver Ditson Co., Inc., 1928), p. 47.
3. Edwin John Stringham, *Listening to Music Creatively* (Englewood Cliffs, N.J.: Prentice-Hall, Inc., 1943, 1946), p. 1.
4. Harry S. Broudy, "A Realistic Philosophy of Music Education," in *Basic Concepts in Music Education,* ed. Nelson B. Henry. The Fifty-seventh Yearbook of the National Society for the Study of Education (Chicago: University of Chicago Press, 1958), p. 84.

OTHER REFERENCES

Andrews, Frances M., and Clara E. Cockerille, *Your School Music Program* (Englewood Cliffs, N.J.: Prentice-Hall, Inc., 1958). Chapter 4, "Elementary Music Teachers."

Mathews, Paul Wentworth, *You Can Teach Music* (New York: E. P. Dutton and Co., Inc., 1953). Chapter 1, "You Can Teach Music," and Chapter 2, "—but I Know What I Like!"

Morgan, Hazel Nohavec, editor, *Music in American Education,* Music Education Source Book Number Two (Washington, D.C.: Music Educators National Conference, 1955). Chapter 1, "Music in General Education," and Chapter 5, "Music for Elementary Schools."

Mursell, James L., *Music and the Classroom Teacher* (Morristown, N.J.: Silver Burdett Company, 1951). Chapter 1, "Why Music for Your Children?"

Myers, Louise Kifer, *Teaching Children Music in the Elementary School,*

Second Edition (Englewood Cliffs, N.J.: Prentice-Hall, Inc., 1956). Chapter 1, "Music in the New School," and Chapter 8, "The Classroom Teacher."

Sheehy, Emma Dickson, *There's Music in Children*, Revised and Enlarged Edition (New York: Henry Holt and Co., Inc., 1952). Chapter 7, "Music and the Classroom Teacher."

CHAPTER TWO

SONGS AND SINGING VOICES

Singing is an important part of any school music program. Teachers should be concerned not so much that children become great singers, but that they become *enthusiastic* singers. In singing, children should find a very personal way to express themselves and another means through which they may be touched by beauty.

The essential concern of the teacher is (1) how children learn to sing and (2) what and when they sing. The teacher will need to know what characteristics he may expect to find in these voices, and how he can help each child develop a more satisfactory singing voice. He must know in what situations children like to sing and what kinds of songs they find easiest and most appealing. A varied repertoire and opportunities for singing, both in the classroom and in other groups, must be provided.

These and related questions will be discussed in this chapter. Here also songs of many kinds are reprinted to be sung and evaluated. A list of the basic school song books and a code to identify the sources of songs used as examples throughout this book are included in Appendix B.

THE CHILD VOICE EMERGES

The idea that singing is for all children is not new. In *Creative Music for Children* (1922) Satis Coleman expressed it very well when she told of her observations of a singing school for baby robins which took place in her garden in the early summer. Relating this to her considerable experience in teaching music to children she said: "I believe that any child, who would begin relatively as early, and sing as much as those robins sang, with a simple and correct pattern ever ready for him to imitate, would be able to sing well and accurately no matter what his lack in musical inheritance might be."[1]

Children learn to speak and sing, as do robins, in imitation of what they hear and in response to an inner urge to express themselves—the chief differences being that few children have an extensive and early contact with song, and that in the average human situation singing is not necessary for communication, nor is it encouraged. As a result, some kindergarten and first grade children do not sing, or their singing is not recognized as such, when they first come to school. Many of these children will learn to sing merely by associating with those who do and by experiencing a pleasant singing situation. Others, unfortunately, may be classed as "non-singers" or "monotones" until they encounter a wise teacher and an environment in which their voices may emerge.

Variations in Children's Singing

Some people account for the wide variation in children's singing skill by referring to "ability" or "talent," but a great many other factors are involved. Donna Jean, at two and one-half, sang as easily as she spoke, perhaps more easily, because her singing was not necessarily tied to words. Nor was she limited to known melodies! Occasionally a recognizable song fragment emerged, but more often she crooned her own tunes, using whatever word patterns and ideas came to her at the moment. She was an effervescent child who easily gave expression to her moods and whims.

Perry, her eight-year-old brother, had never been heard singing. He did not lack a musical environment, for his mother was extremely musical. She had one of those unique, naturally beautiful voices; singing seemed to be a special gift, and Perry intuitively knew that he did not have it. Music was *too* important in his family. His own cautious temperament prevented him from singing until third grade experiences convinced him that other people sang, though not in such a special way as did his mother. Thus, we see that a child's temperament, his need for expression in sound patterns, his confidence as well as his environment and his vocal inheritance are important factors influencing singing practices.

If singing is considered an extension of speech, one can readily understand why there is such a wide range of ability among kindergarten and first grade children. It is influenced by the same factors that affect the development of speech. Because singing is very closely associated with the emotions it is readily affected by psychological problems.

VOICE RANGE AND FLEXIBILITY. The term "monotone" is an unfortunate one that should never be used, for it implies that the individual sings or speaks on one level with no pitch variation. Some people assume that, in such cases, no vocal development is possible. Out-of-tune singers may be more accurately described as "conversational singers," who "sing" much as they speak. This condition can be found in children who have not yet become aware of the possibilities of their vocal mechanisms. Others may not have perceived that singing is a combination of changes in pitch as well as in word rhythms. People differ in sensitivity to pitch. Those who are most sensitive tend to sing without instruction when they discover the flexibility of the vocal mechanism. Others may need to have their attention directed to pitch levels before they begin to notice the details in melody, just as some need a guide to point out details in visual design in order to appreciate what is there.

Greater use brings wider range and flexibility to the voice, just as exercise and training build skills and coordination in other muscular activities. Some kindergarten and first grade children have a vocal range from middle C to D or E above the octave.

Others are limited to four or five tones centering around F or G.

This fact has some bearing on the songs selected for young children. It has been observed that groups of nursery-school and kindergarten children employ chants similar to those heard in cultures uninfluenced by music of Western civilization. A limited middle-of-the-voice range is used, and a tonal center is established on one pitch level. From this point the voice drops a minor 3rd and may then rise to the tone a full step higher than the tonal center.

The pattern is heard in many variations.

Young children who have never sung can most easily be helped if their first songs incorporate the tonal range and intervals that children sing most naturally. Kindergarten and first grade teachers must expect a wide variation in singing skill among children when they first come to school. No one factor is responsible for this wide range. Additional discussions of reasons why children do not sing may be found in the Ginn Company *Kindergarten Book*[2] and in *There's Music in Children*[3] by Sheehy.

TONE QUALITY IN CHILDREN'S VOICES. The quality of the child voice is another variable, dependent on such factors as experience, available vocal examples, and physical structure. Not only do children imitate what they hear but they elaborate on it and explore their own sound-making mechanisms; some are more curious and exploratory than others. Since children imitate rather realistically the high whine of a siren or the deep whistle of a steamboat, the teacher should expect that the singing voice might be capable of considerable variation; it is produced by the same mechanism. Within musical limits such variation in vocal tone quality is desirable, for singing should be expressive of many ideas and moods.

We should not *always* expect children to conform to the traditional concept of the child voice—that it is high, light, and flutelike. This quality is ideal for certain songs, and the teacher should promote it through the mood and feeling to be expressed in these songs, rather than because it is the only quality ever heard in the child voice. The English folk song, "Lavender's Blue," is such a song. It should be sung brightly, in a very dancing mood. No heavy cowboy voices here, please!

LAVENDER'S BLUE

From *Our First Music* of A SINGING SCHOOL Series, 1941. Copyright Summy-Birchard Publishing Company. Used by permission.

Similar, yet different in character, is "Away in a Manger" (MRC-78, OFM-226, MTD-119),* which requires the sweet, floating quality characteristic of lullabies.

Some children emulate a more vigorous voice quality, which is suitable for exuberant songs. Their enthusiasm for such songs may be an important factor as they learn to use the singing voice. The sea chantey, "Up She Rises" (MTD-84), game songs, and folk songs such as "Knock Along Brother Rabbit" (ECh-29) are excellent examples of rhythmic songs that should be sung with as much enthusiasm as possible.

UP SHE RISES

From *Music Through the Day.* © 1956, Silver Burdett Company.

* See Appendix B for key to code of song books.

Classroom Singing Situations

Under favorable conditions most children enjoy group singing in the classroom. With younger children it is more an experience of "feeling" than of hearing; the teacher should not expect conformity to melody and rhythm by all pupils. Only after ears have been trained to listen and when the beauty of a *particular* melodic line is appreciated will fine unison singing begin to emerge.

Considering the individuality of each child, his lack of experience in cooperative activity, and his lack of singing skill, it is nothing short of amazing that a kindergarten or first grade teacher achieves any sort of unified singing response from the group. Yet, in spite of obstacles, group singing is a tradition in the early years. It is a satisfying experience because it captures the spirit in an unusual way. When conformity to a particular melody and rhythm is achieved, it is chiefly through response to mood and feeling.

These facts develop a case for individual and informal small-group singing as an early experience, for until a child has sung he can hardly be expected to master the more difficult task of singing together with others. Consequently, the classroom teacher must look for varied times and places to foster individual singing during the school day. In the kindergarten many of the informal periods when children work alone or in small groups might be used to promote individual singing. As children build with blocks, play at housekeeping, paint, or color, they should feel free to sing and croon.

In this informal singing, a song need not be complete; phrases, repeated tone calls, make-up songs, and chants are natural and satisfying. The important thing is that the child sings because he feels free to do so, and this continued vocalization leads to greater facility in the use of the voice. The teacher, of course, gives encouragement and a good example when it may be beneficial. As other activities progress, the teacher may sing with a small group, accompanying them on the Autoharp or the piano; children will be encouraged to share new or original songs with the class.

Informal activity periods are less frequent in the first grade, because more time is given to reading, numbers, and writing. To promote informal individual and small-group singing, the teacher can use moments before school, after school, and at recesses, as well as during the classroom activities periods. Often as he stands talking with a few children, he will notice and encourage singing. For this purpose the children's original chanting songs or short folk songs are appropriate; some of the following may be sung anytime, anywhere, with complete informality: "Go Tell

Aunt Rhodey" (AS II-14), "All Night, All Day" (MTD-35), "Mary Wore Her Red Dress" (AFlk-130), "Jimmy Rose He Went to Town" (SGro-58), "Handy Spandy" (KBk-70), "The Wind Blow East" (AFlk-66), and "Gretel, Pastetel" (MRT-26).

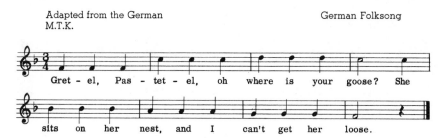

GRETEL, PASTETEL

Adapted from the German
M.T.K.

German Folksong

Gret - el, Pas - tet - el, oh where is your goose? She
sits on her nest, and I can't get her loose.

"Gretel, Pastetel," from *Music Round the Town* of the New TOGETHER-WE-SING Series, published by Follett Publishing Company, Chicago, Illinois.

Observe how readily other verses concerning the everyday interests of children may be added to this song: "Nancy, dear Nancy, oh where is your coat?" etc.

For the child who has no natural inclination to sing, larger group activities may stimulate an interest or an unconscious first participation. Singing games, action songs, and finger-plays are appealing to most children and encourage participation. Some children respond to ideas and picture images, and therefore storytelling and descriptive songs are important. Pupils may sit in a semicircle around the teacher as he talks and sings; they in turn join in. The teacher must bear in mind that individual and small-group participation, as well as singing by the entire class, should exist to meet the needs of every child.

What To Do About Out-of-Tune Voices

There are many ways to help children find their singing voices. Children who are generally inattentive may not sing well because they have never learned to listen. The teacher must capture their interest by selecting appropriate songs. In the kindergarten and early first grade, the chief approach should be through a good singing example set in many easy songs. These songs should be in a small, middle-of-the-voice range and so appealing that the children will sing spontaneously. One such song is "Who's That Tapping at the Window?" (AFlk-52)

WHO'S THAT TAPPING AT THE WINDOW?

Virginia

From *American Folk Songs for Children*. Doubleday & Co., New York, 1948. Re-printed by permission of the publishers from Dorothy Scarborough, *On the Trail of Negro Folk-Songs* (Cambridge, Mass.: Harvard University Press, 1925, 1953).

THE USE OF TONE CALLS. Children who are unable to sing an entire song should be encouraged to repeat short song fragments or tone calls. When a child recognizes his success in singing one or two tones, he will have established a concept about singing in tune that will enable him to repeat the process with longer melodic fragments. Song-related tone calls are especially valuable because they can be used as a natural part of the song learning process and need no separate motivation. "My Dog Teddy" (OFM-17) is a song that many children like.

MY DOG TEDDY

Words and music by
Floy A. Rossman

From *Our First Music* of A SINGING SCHOOL Series, 1941. Copyright Summy-Birchard Publishing Co. Used by permission.

The last motive in the song is a fine tone call:

Its characteristics are these:

1. It has unity and completeness in itself and thus is satisfying to sing.
2. It is a melodic pattern found in many simple songs.
3. It lies in the most advantageous range of the child voice.
4. It has rhythmic interest but is not difficult to sing.
5. Other names may be used to capture personal interest, e.g., "My dog Blackie," "Sandy," etc.

When first singing the song for the children, a teacher may make a game of this simple tone call. One small group after another may sing it, imitating the teacher, who uses dogs' names suggested by the children. Individual children may sing it, imitating the teacher or another child. When the song is learned, individuals may sing their choice of names after the group has sung the song together. All of this with the objective that this song fragment will be sung in tune, and that the children will discover how it sounds and how it feels to sing it so.

If it is not advisable to have a particular child sing alone, he will be given an opportunity to participate within a small group singing a tone call. Many children are eager to sing alone, and hearing them often arouses a less competent singer to try also. In such cases the teacher must arrange that the tone call that the child attempts is very easy and that it has been heard correctly several times before the weak singer has an opportunity to try it. Following such an attempt, approval and encouragement must be forthcoming.

Tone calls from many songs must be used. For some children singing success will come only after several months of trying. The process demands considerable ingenuity and imagination on the part of the teacher. A pleasant "game spirit" must prevail so that the children do not become tense or anxious in any way but can give full attention to the melodic fragments they are singing.

The following are suggested as further examples of tone calls taken from familiar primary songs:

"Rig-a-Jig-Jig" (see page 40):

Heigh - o,   heigh - o, ___ heigh - o. _____

"Are You Sleeping?" (see page 84):

ding, ding,   dong.   Bro - ther   John.

"See, Saw, Margery Daw" (MRC-30):

See,   saw,   Mar - ger - y   Daw.

Very often the ending phrase makes the most appropriate tone call because it has a sense of unity and completeness in itself. It must, however, be short and have rhythmic interest. It is important that it be sung rhythmically. The discussion and examples in "Tone Plays and Phrase Repetitions," pages 39 to 42 of *American Folk Songs for Children*,[4] are helpful. *The Kindergarten Book* and *Book One* of MUSIC FOR YOUNG AMERICANS[5] give song fragments in the form of one-tone and two-tone calls.

OTHER REMEDIAL TECHNIQUES. Some children are "conversational singers" because they do not have established concepts of what singing a *particular* melody really is. Occasionally the teacher should sing with "la" or "loo" the first phrase or two of a song the children know; a singing game such as "London Bridge" or "Mulberry Bush" may be used. The children may be asked to identify it and in turn, as individuals, in small groups, or as a class, sing it back to see if they can make it identifiable without the words.

In the privacy of the music corner, as he picks out his favorite song on the bells, many a child finds the necessary quiet concentration that enables him to match the melody of the bells with his own voice. Thus another beginning for singing is found in a situation removed from the singing group. Such freedom for individual work is important and requires special planning on the part of the teacher.

Other techniques can be used to establish the singing voice in children: Satis Coleman said that "to speak in a singing voice with abandon, without having to conform to a set song, is a great help in freeing the voice." She suggested practicing utter freedom in vocal sounds and holding conversations on one tone, later moving to two tones, using a higher tone on the word to be emphasized.[6]

Some teachers use tone games with high and low sounds in order to increase flexibility in the voice. Children imitate the rising sound of the siren, the ring of a bell, the cuckoo of a clock, or the call of an animal.

One fall day during play period, the boys and girls ran to the fence to watch the high school band practicing for the football game. The children were enthralled with the look and sound of the various instruments and returned to the classroom full of excitement and interest. Such enthusiasm was not to be suppressed, and the teacher became a willing listener as various children described the scene and gave their interpretation of the sound of the instruments. The trumpet, the drums, the trombone, and tuba were the most discussed and imitated.

These children kept the scene in mind for several days and worked to create vocal sound effects that would satisfactorily represent these instruments. During this period the teacher encouraged individuals and the group as a whole to try the various sound effects. The project was a valuable experience in producing, listening to, and evaluating vocal sounds.

INDIVIDUAL HELP. In the second and third grades good results may come from individual voice instruction. By this time, children have learned to accept special help in several areas of their school studies. The type and extent of the special help to be given in singing depends on the child and the teacher.

From his kindergarten days, Robert had a husky speaking voice and was not able to sing. In spite of customary remedial measures in the first and second grade classrooms, he showed no improvement. During Robert's third grade term the music consultant gave him special private work because he seemed interested in improving his singing voice. First they read character lines from children's stories: e.g., "What did the wolf say when he came to the door of the first little pig's house?" Robert had a good voice for the big wolf; and the consultant encouraged him to make it sound even bigger and deeper. "How did the little pig reply?" This was more of a problem, but, given an example, Robert soon produced a high, frightened-little-pig reply.

Now that he knew how to change his voice, Robert experimented with other dramatic recitations. After a few lessons the music consultant showed him how to sustain any of the pitch levels of his newly flexible speaking voice into a singing tone. Robert understood the process and began to experiment with his voice and to practice sustaining tones at various levels. He soon found that he could match tones and sing tone calls correctly in the class singing lesson.

Frequent opportunity must be given boys and girls to sing alone, in pairs, or in small groups, for this will build individual confidence and enable the other members of the class to listen objectively to voices of various qualities. The teacher, however, should avoid the practice of having groups with better voices chosen to sing so often that they feel the superiority of their ability. Plan variety in small-group singing so that the poor singer may occasionally have the pleasure of singing with two or three of those who have better voices. Children are aware of differences in voices, but they accept them and are as enthusiastic as the teacher when an individual makes some improvement.

Voices in the Intermediate Grades

Those concerned with the music program of the intermediate grades must continue to develop the singing voices of boys and girls. If the previous training has been adequate, the singing as a whole will be quite satisfying, but there usually are some voices that need individual attention.

After the fourth grade, the vocal tone is more brilliant. The *practical* range for *all* voices in general classroom singing is about the same as that for the primary grades, but with good training many children are able to sing several tones higher or lower:

Vitality and energy are essential to good singing and, fortunately, most children have an abundance of both. Good singing is the result of clarity in enunciation and adequate breath support which gives the phrase its continuity. When pupils are enthusiastic about singing, breath support is no problem because the muscular framework is strong and flexible. If interest wanes, bodies sag in the chairs and tone quality deteriorates. In the intermediate grades breath support is achieved only indirectly through (1) good posture, promoted as far as possible through interest and enthusiasm, and (2) the message of the song—how it should be sung to achieve an expressive melody.

Precise enunciation of words is important. Children can be careless or simply untrained in proper habits of enunciation. A flexible use of tongue and lips is necessary for clear speaking as well as for good singing. Singing is intoned speech, and unless the words are understood it does not fulfill its intended function. The teacher's example and insistence upon clarity of speech will aid in the development of good singing.

THE BOY'S VOICE. Although the range and general quality in the voices of elementary school boys and girls is essentially the same, psychological factors occasionally result in more vocal problems among the boys. Problems may arise because singing voices were not well established in the primary grades. As they grow older, boys are less interested in developing a high singing voice; they would rather believe that their voices are low and "manly." At puberty the boy's vocal cords lengthen and thicken so that his voice drops in pitch. During the fifth, sixth, and perhaps seventh grades, prior to the change in voice, he has his last opportunity to sing in the high register. At this time his soprano voice tends to develop more brilliance than the girl's and, when properly trained, may have a range even higher than that given above. When these two facts are appreciated by the boys, there is usually little difficulty in promoting interest in the development of the unchanged voice.

On occasion a teacher will encounter boys in the sixth grade who appear to be experiencing a change in voice. The boys may be older than other members of the class. The class also may include boys who have not earlier learned to use their high singing voices and who at this age have no inclination to do so. The teacher's problem then lies in helping them learn to sing in a lower limited range, knowing that within a year or two the normal lengthening of the vocal cords will permit them to extend the range downward. A practical range for these voices is:

Obstacles to the development of these voices are that the normal singing range for the class does not include all of the low notes, and that almost every sixth grade song goes above this range. Three suggestions are made:

1. The teacher should encourage and sing with the boys whenever the song goes within their range.
2. Occasional songs with a short range should be transposed and sung in the lower octave by these voices and in the higher octave by the normal voices.

GO TELL AUNT RHODEY

Early American Song

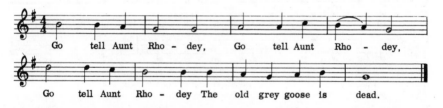

Go tell Aunt Rho - dey, Go tell Aunt Rho - dey,

Go tell Aunt Rho - dey The old grey goose is dead.

From Beattie, Wolverton, Wilson, and Hinga, THE AMERICAN SINGER, Second Edition, *Book Two*. American Book Company, publishers. Used by permission.

"Go Tell Aunt Rhodey" (AS II-14), when sung in the Key of A, has this range:

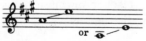

"Polly Wolly Doodle" (AS VI-147) in the Key of A has this range:

3. Some melodic sections of songs may be sung by these lower voices while the others sing harmony parts. The verse of "Liza Jane" (AS VI-153) is an example.

LIZA JANE

Traditional   Old American Song

Transposed from C

From Beattie, Wolverton, Wilson, and Hinga, THE AMERICAN SINGER, Second Edition, *Book Six*. American Book Company, publishers. Used by permission.

There is no easy solution to the problem, for there may be only one or two such voices in a classroom. However, when the range of the voice has been determined, the teacher or music consultant can usually find some suitable singing material and ways to help the individual achieve some vocal satisfaction.

GENERAL REMEDIAL WORK WITH VOICES. Some teachers are able to work with an entire fourth grade singing class in such a way that individual voices will improve. Focusing attention on the sound of short phrases and tonal patterns from the song is a valuable technique. However, in these grades it becomes increasingly necessary that those who do not sing in tune be given special private assistance. Work with groups of three or four students can be very successful. It may be undertaken by the classroom teacher in noon or after-school hours. Usually twice-weekly lessons (ten to fifteen minutes in length) over a period of two or three weeks will begin to yield results.

One music consultant gradually worked this type of service into her weekly visits to the various schools. Because the children enjoyed music and liked the consultant, an offer of a "private lesson in singing" became a hoped-for privilege for good as well as poor singers. The classroom teachers usually selected the three or four in greatest need of assistance.

The consultant liked to use the piano, although it was not absolutely necessary. The pupils would bring their song books, and the first question asked would be "What song do you like to sing?" She knew that poor singers are most readily successful on middle-of-the-voice folk-type songs. Songs like "Polly Wolly Doodle" or "Go Tell Aunt Rhodey" were chosen in preference to the more difficult "Star-Spangled Banner" or "Old Folks at Home." When the song had been agreed upon, the consultant started right off with "Let's sing it!" She sounded the tonic chord and first note, and all began with enthusiasm. The result was more spirited than accurate and often came out in as many keys as there were singers. At the end of a phrase or two, before enthusiasm lagged, all were stopped and the consultant would say to the singer who seemed to have the most promising voice, "You were doing very well. Let's hear you sing it."

The pupil then sang alone or with the aid of the consultant in whatever key seemed to fit his voice. Usually he managed to sing the song quite recognizably for one or two phrases. "That's fine. Now, Jimmy, you sing along with Tom on the same song, just the first phrase." Having found the best singer in the group, she asked others to sing with him. It was important that these children have success in singing at least one phrase, and therefore the song often was not used in its entirety at this time. If the group succeeded in sounding a whole phrase accurately together, they were asked to repeat it and listen to the sound; some were asked to listen as others sang together. "Was everyone on the same tune?" If a small amount of success was recognized, another favorite song might be used in the same way. The chief objective was to work on a phrase or two to get it going together in the most appropriate key for the voices. Encouragement was essential. After the pupils were successful in singing the melody in a lower key, the consultant might move up a whole step to see who could sing it at a higher level: "You sang it exactly right there. Now try it in this key."

If one or two of the voices were so inflexible that they did not get on tune at all, the consultant would try another approach: "When an airplane pilot flies 'blind' he has to follow a radio signal. They call it 'getting on the beam.' You have to get your voices 'on the beam' in order to learn to sing. This is the tone of the radio beam; see if you can match it." The consultant often found that C above middle C

was a good "radio beam" tone. Sometimes those who could not match lower tones proved to be good "pilots" at this level. If the singers did not hit the tone immediately, they were asked to slide up to it like a siren. At other times a lower tone was used and, once contact was made with the "radio beam" tone, this became the first tone of a song;

became

"Oh, I   went   down   south,   for to   see   my   Sal"____

The pupils should be given simple things to practice: making siren sounds outdoors, matching "radio beam" tones with each other and listening carefully to match the pitch pipe tone when the class tunes up to sing a song. If melody instruments are available, the number notation may be written out for the phrases of the songs that the students sing correctly; in their free time they can then practice matching tones as they play the melody on the bells.

The classroom teacher who can give this remedial work himself, or who knows what the consultant is working toward, will know what to expect of less skilled singers during the classroom singing time. He will see that care is taken in the tuning-up process so that all may have a chance to match the key tone; he will see that one or two simple songs in an appropriate but limited range are included in the song selections so that the newly developing voices will have a better chance to sing in tune; he will provide these opportunities but he will not call attention to, nor embarrass by too much attention, those who are trying to get their voices in tune.

OUTSTANDING VOICES. Occasionally an intermediate pupil may possess an unusually beautiful voice that floats free and true without any apparent effort. When such a voice is discovered the teacher may be concerned about its proper development. Private lessons and any special training of the voice itself must be delayed until the singer is fifteen or sixteen years old. However, the general musical education of such a child should be promoted so that he will be in a position to use his voice to greatest advantage when it does mature. He should be encouraged to sing and to develop a repertoire of folk and other songs which he enjoys sharing with others. In order to develop his musicianship he should study a musical instrument during his intermediate years. The piano is a most practical instrument for a singer to know, but musicianship can be improved through the study of other instruments.

A musically gifted child should have broad experiences in listening, so that he develops an intuitive sense of good musical expression. All of the classroom activities in music will combine to give this child basic understandings upon which he may later develop more specific music skills in accordance with his needs.

Singing Experiences Beyond the Classroom

THE SINGING ASSEMBLY. In schools where an assembly hall is available, pupils from all classes often come together biweekly or monthly to sing songs they have learned in their classrooms. The thrill of many voices singing together gives this activity its major appeal. Such an activity can serve as an objective for work in the classroom. Teachers and student leaders may get together each month to decide what new songs will be used in the following assembly. The music consultant will need to see that music is available to each class and that all classes have a satisfactory means of learning it.

In selecting these songs, musical appeal is highly important. These points should be considered:

1. Simplicity in melody and rhythm is best for large-group singing.
2. Younger children are not able to sing all of the songs suitable for older voices. For this reason, the assembly singing should often be limited to intermediate grade singers.
3. When a school houses a large number of classes on one grade-level, satisfying singing experiences may be had by singing songs closely related to classwork at that level.

Assembly singing is traditionally accompanied by the piano. If the group is very large, a single piano may not be loud enough to support the entire group. Some songs, especially those sung in harmony, are best sung unaccompanied. Carefully planned assembly singing can serve as an extension and enrichment of the basic music program in the classroom.

SPECIAL CHORAL WORK. Special choral groups, led by a trained director, should be available for pupils who have a particular interest in singing. Such singing enriches their musical experience and also prepares them for choral work in the high school, church, and community.

The music consultant or a skilled teacher may organize such a group. Membership should be open to all fifth and sixth grade students on the basis of interest and, to some extent, singing ability. Whatever selection seems necessary should be done with due consideration for the needs as well as talents of individuals who are interested. Fourth grade students might be included, although some prestige is achieved by limiting membership to the older children. Sixty voices will provide a good-sounding group capable of singing three parts.

A choral group should meet two or three times weekly to make satisfying progress. It should not be a substitute for classroom music. Rehearsal within the school day is the most desirable arrangement. However, it may be necessary to practice before school or at noon. After-school rehearsals are not recommended because boys and girls are tired. A compromise may be made by extending the 30- or 40-minute rehearsal into a school session for 15 minutes in the morning or after lunch.

Membership should be selective as well as elective. The voices selected should be clear and flexible with a reasonably wide range. Voices can be auditioned individually or in groups of two or three. Since children sing more easily and naturally a song they know well, choose a song such as "America, the Beautiful" (OLS-189) to be sung in two different keys that reveal the range of the voices.

AMERICA, THE BEAUTIFUL

Katharine Lee Bates   Samuel A. Ward

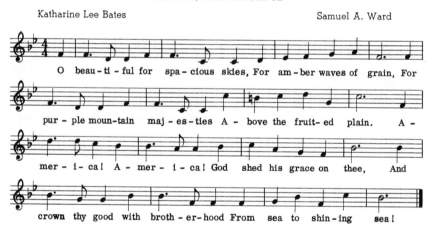

The range in the Key of B♭ is

and in the Key of E♭ is

Those singing easily in the higher key should be considered for the high part in three-part singing.

In the United States elementary school choirs traditionally sing many of their songs in two or three parts. Part-singing can be beautiful when the boys and girls are sufficiently experienced to listen to the total effect and to stay in tune. It is most effective when unaccompanied. In some schools, however, emphasis has been placed on part-singing to the exclusion of unison singing. A select group of children's voices singing a lovely art song or a suitable sacred song in unison is a musical treat for any audience and provides a genuine thrill for the performers as well. Let the director strive for a balance of experiences for these young singers and avoid the error of asking them to sing consistently difficult arrangements in which they fail to realize the full musical appeal of the song.

An audience is a challenge if performances are well spaced and do not become the chief purpose of the choir's existence. Some teachers think only in terms of public performance and fail to see the real values of the choir:

1. To provide an enriched singing experience for talented and interested pupils.
2. To acquaint singers as well as audience with a more artistic and varied repertoire of songs than is ordinarily sung in the classroom.
3. To develop musicianship through expressive singing.
4. To develop skill in reading notation through contact with a greater variety of music.

It is important to give all of the children an opportunity to sing in a performing group. In a massed choir all children in specified classes can be brought together to rehearse and polish selected compositions. If the songs are studied and memorized in the individual classrooms, the large-group rehearsals can be limited to three or less. One such project a year, planned for simplicity, can be very beneficial. If multiple parts are to be sung each class should present a balanced group. The real ends of music education are not served when different parts are learned in different rooms and combined only in the mass group. Children who are accustomed to hearing the harmony in their classrooms will understand the composition from a musical point of view and will be more sensitive singers in the large organization.

THE REPERTOIRE FOR SINGING

One of the striking observations a visitor may make in a kindergarten or first grade classroom is of the genuine, direct response that the effective teacher receives from the children. The boys and girls are carried away by the simplest story or discussion about things they have experienced. Likewise, children seem charmed by many songs. But is the appeal actually in the song itself, or is it in the setting the teacher creates for it? There is no doubt that many poor songs will "go over" temporarily with children, merely as a result of external motivation. For this reason, there is diverse opinion among teachers on what is an appealing song for children of a certain age. The most valid criterion for judging a song's worth to children is whether or not they sing it for themselves in situations not motivated and directed by the teacher.

Children use their singing voices in three important situations:

1. They sing in groups when engaged in some physical activity. Improvisation may go into this singing, and a mere fragment of a song may be repeated over and over in a chanting manner. Songs with simple melodies and strong rhythms best serve this need.
2. They sing to themselves as they go about their own private activities or lie in bed for a nap. This singing is more crooning; it has a broader range in melody and may include parts of the wistful quiet songs the child knows.
3. They share songs with parents and the family when these songs are strongly appealing to them and to the family group.

Generally speaking, a teacher might expect that a song he likes will have appeal for the children. This, providing he has not selected the song with some special motive in mind, such as to exemplify good manners, safety, or a trip to the zoo! Songs composed especially for didactic purposes often lack grace, are soon outgrown, and have little meaning outside the specific situation in which they were originally used.

What Is a Good Song?

A good song is essentially a simple song that the child may sing with pleasure outside the classroom. Each song must stand on its own merits, but the following characteristics may be important in different songs:

1. The melody is easily remembered and interesting enough to sing without the words.
2. The song prompts a definite rhythmic response.
3. The text fits the rhythmic scheme and melody line.
4. The message and feeling of the text is well mated with the message and feeling of the music.
5. The text may be nonsensical, repetitious, tender, or heroic, but it is not "preachy" or written to educate.
6. The melody is in a comfortable singing range for the average child's voice.

Let us examine a song, related to second or third grade social studies, to see how well it meets these requirements. Perhaps at some point in a farm unit a pupil, attracted by the lively drawing of the cow in the song book, suggests that "The Dairy Maids" (MRT-22) would be an appropriate song. The subject ties in with the unit study, although dairy maids are hardly the modern way of getting the milking done! There is nothing really informative in the song, and so it will remain in the repertoire only if it has genuine appeal.

THE DAIRY MAIDS

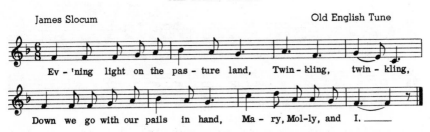

James Slocum

Old English Tune

Ev - 'ning light on the pas - ture land, Twin - kling, twin - kling,

Down we go with our pails in hand, Ma - ry, Mol-ly, and I. ____

"The Dairy Maids," from *Music Round the Town* of the New TOGETHER-WE-SING Series, published by Follett Publishing Company, Chicago, Illinois.

But what gives the song its charm? The gently swinging rhythm and the repetitious, easy-to-remember melody so typical of folk tunes are largely responsible. This is the sort of song to which dairy maids, or anyone else, could walk along quite happily, la-la-ing the melody. For these reasons, "The Dairy Maids" meets the melodic and rhythmic requirements (1 and 2) for a good song.

The words are in the same quiet mood as the melody. They have the pleasant repetitious quality found in the melody, and their rhythm fits the musical rhythm. There are no problems here; this is a delightful song in a very comfortable singing range.

THE VALUE OF FOLK SONGS. Beatrice Landeck is convinced that folk songs should be the basic song material for young children:

After much experience with children and music, I came to rely almost entirely on folk songs. I've found in them colorful language, vivid imagery, humor, and warmth. They never seem to be outgrown. You hear them sung by adults with as much enthusiasm as by children.
One reason American folk songs have such an appeal for children is that every child senses their vitality. Folk songs reflect every emotion from joyousness to despair. They may bounce up and down on the nonsense level or tread a stately pace.[7]

The songs selected for use in the classroom should represent many moods and feelings to provide each child with music appealing to him, and to enable the group to express a wide range of emotion through singing. Folk songs offer variety as well as genuine reflection of human feeling. In some the emotional content is the chief factor: The love and concern which is felt for baby brother or sister is expressed in the Southern lullaby, "Everybody Loves Baby" (FGB-57).

EVERYBODY LOVES BABY

Southern Lullaby

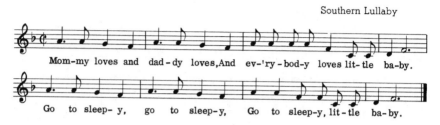

Mom-my loves and dad-dy loves, And ev-'ry-bod-y loves lit-tle ba-by.

Go to sleep-y, go to sleep-y, Go to sleep-y, lit-tle ba-by.

From *The First Grade Book* of OUR SINGING WORLD Series, Enlarged Edition. Used by permission of Ginn and Company, owner of the copyright.

What a comforting feeling for a child to know that "All Night, All Day" (MTD-35) someone is watching over him. Such a song as "I Wish I Were a Little Bird" (SGro-19) will enable the child to express some of his innermost feelings to "be" a carefree bird or a fish who would "swim 'way down in the sea." This type of song will serve the child in his private thinking and crooning even more significantly than in group singing at school.

In other songs the topic is of such small significance that any words, or no words at all, would do. The infectious rhythm or irresistible melody carries the song along. "Rig-a-Jig-Jig" is found in many collections of children's songs. It gallops and dances along in such a delightful fashion that every child, young or old, loves to sing it.

An analysis of its melodic content reveals that much of this song consists of the intervals found to be natural to the singing of children, i.e., a minor 3rd and the upper neighboring tone. It is not surprising that children sing it so readily.

RIG-A-JIG-JIG

Singing Game

As   I   was walk-ing down   the street, Heigh-o,   heigh-o,   heigh-

Transposed from E♭

From *Singing Together* of OUR SINGING WORLD Series, Enlarged Edition. Used by permission of Ginn and Company, owner of the copyright.

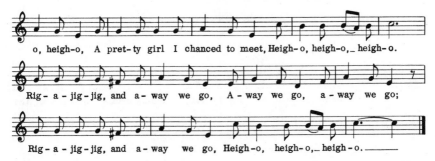

o, heigh-o, A pret-ty girl I chanced to meet, Heigh-o, heigh-o,_ heigh-o.

Rig-a-jig-jig, and a-way we go, A-way we go, a-way we go;

Rig-a-jig-jig, and a-way we go, Heigh-o, heigh-o,_ heigh-o. _____

A good song need not necessarily have much of a melody: "Old House" (MIOT-83) is chiefly a chant, but it has an impelling rhythmic pattern. The rhythm of the melody seems to be determined by the inherent rhythm of the words. For this reason, although when seen in notation the rhythm may look complicated, it is not difficult to sing.

OLD HOUSE

American Folk-Game Song
Collected by John W. Work

Old house. Tear it down! Who's going to help me? Tear it down!

Bring me a ham-mer. Tear it down! Bring me a saw._ Tear it down!

Next thing you bring me, tear it down! Is a wreck-ing ma-chine. Tear it down!

From *Music in Our Town* of MUSIC FOR LIVING Series, Silver Burdett Company, publishers. Used by permission of John W. Work.

This type of song enriches children's musical experiences both because it has such a vigorous, unusual rhythm and because it is built on a minor chord and gives a new experience in sound.

SONGS COMPOSED FOR CHILDREN. A good song need not be a folk melody. "The Funny Clown" (S&R-102) has all the qualities of a good song. The melody can be whistled or hummed with much satisfaction, and the lively rhythmic swing carries it along. Although it is limited to a five-tone range and is repetitious, the short sequences descending in 3rds at the

THE FUNNY CLOWN

E.A.B.

Ellen Arnott Bates

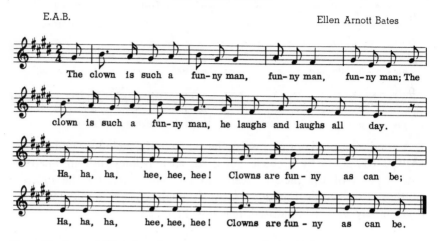

The clown is such a fun-ny man, fun-ny man, fun-ny man; The

clown is such a fun-ny man, he laughs and laughs all day.

Ha, ha, ha, hee, hee, hee! Clowns are fun-ny as can be;

Ha, ha, ha, hee, hee, hee! Clowns are fun-ny as can be.

From *Singing and Rhyming* of OUR SINGING WORLD Series, Enlarged Edition. Used by permission of Ginn and Company, owner of the copyright.

end of the first phrase are characteristic of children's singing. The words are simple and repetitious and yet just right for the subject and the tune.

Although a lovely song, related to a subject of interest to children, may be an inspiring addition to the repertoire, the teacher should resist the temptation to use a poor song just because the text is appropriate to the topic at hand. Many teachers have composed, or have written down songs composed by their pupils, as a creative outgrowth of a unit of study. These are admirable creative products in the atmosphere in which they were inspired and took form. It is desirable that teachers compose music or inspire and guide their pupils in composition.

Unfortunately, when the majority of these songs are removed from the situation that inspired them, they lose their initial value as creative achievements and do not measure up as lasting song material. It is not necessary that all the songs used be folk songs, but the fact that a song has existed long enough to become a "folk song" indicates that it has vitality beyond its original use.

Basic school music textbooks have been published for many years, and with changes in the teaching emphasis, the selection of songs has changed. The prospective classroom teacher should become well acquainted with the series of books used in the school system in which he expects to teach. For those who do not know what books will be available to them, it is recommended that a general use be made of the several series listed in Appendix B. Accompaniment books and recordings are also listed.

Songs for the World in Which
Children Live

Believing that children enjoy songs related to their own daily interests in the home, with the family, or among school friends and neighbors, editors of many of the basic song texts have organized song material around these topics. If the song itself is good, the fact that the subject is of immediate concern to the children will make it even more welcome.

SONGS OF PERSONAL INTEREST. The child from five to seven is the center of his own universe; his interests and concerns do not range too far. He will be delighted with such a simple, repetitious song as "My Birthday Is Today" (FGB-83).

MY BIRTHDAY IS TODAY

Lilla Belle Pitts

From *The First Grade Book* of OUR SINGING WORLD Series, Enlarged Edition. Used by permission of Ginn and Company, owner of the copyright.

If there is a new baby at home, as there is with so many children of this age, it is "my baby." Thus "Pinky Winky Baby" (KBk-47) and other similar songs represent a topic close to the kindergarten or first grade child and will appeal to the baby's entire family!

Story book characters have sung themselves into the hearts of young children for many generations. Mother Goose characters such as "Humpty Dumpty," "Little Jack Horner," and "Three Little Kittens" will find a place in the repertoire. Other characters from folklore like "Oh, John the Rabbit" (AFlk-100, Ech-63) and "Old Molly Hare" (AFlk-99, see next page) soon become friends when children sing about them.

PATRIOTIC AND HOLIDAY SONGS. As the class becomes more proficient in singing, the repertoire will expand in several directions; art songs as well as folk songs should be included. Among the important songs heard in the community are the patriotic songs, Christmas carols, and songs of thanksgiving. Many of these have become traditional in the United States, and children can sing them along with their families. However, some of them

OLD MOLLY HARE

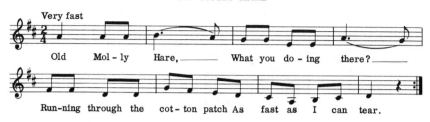

Old Mol - ly Hare, _____ What you do - ing there? _____

Run-ning through the cot - ton patch As fast as I can tear.

From *American Folk Songs for Children*, Doubleday & Co., New York, 1948. Reprinted with permission.

lack the simplicity of folk songs; they are wide in range and more difficult to sing. When it seems appropriate, the younger children may experience such songs by hearing others sing them, by hearing recordings, or by singing only the refrain.

Young children do not need many patriotic songs. "America" and "God Bless America" are two of the easiest and will enable the children to join in at any community gathering. In the third grade "America, the Beautiful" can be learned. Other songs have been written or arranged for children, such as "There Are Many Flags in Many Lands" (S&R-7, NMH III-74) and "Our Own Dear Country" (MTY-89). Fourth graders can begin to learn "The Star-Spangled Banner." In the fifth grade other patriotic songs are learned as a part of the study of United States history.

Christmas brings a wealth of traditional songs, and some questions about how many of these have a place in the public school. Teachers in different communities find different answers. If a song is a thing of beauty and a joy to sing, it may be used regardless of its cultural or religious heritage. However, many of the carols are too difficult musically for children and too deeply religious in text for school use.

"Away in a Manger" is a traditional children's song found in many music series texts (MTD-119, KBk-80, FGB-92, MRC-78). Other less well-known carols are suitable for children. The jolly Swedish carol "Now It's Christmas Time" (FGB-98) and old English carols such as "Christmas Is Coming" (MTY-53) and "I Wish You a Merry Christmas" (SOOW-82, MRC-79, MTY-65, MIOT-142) are delightful and easy. "O Come, Little Children" (AS II-78, S&R-90, MNLA-153), "The Friendly Beasts" (MRT-88, AS III-82, MIOT-146) and "O Christmas Tree" (AS II-80) seem particularly appropriate carols for children. Two spirituals, "Mary Had a Baby, Yes, Lord" (ECH-103) and "A Band of Angels" (SGro-54), make unusual additions to the Christmas repertoire. Some current holiday songs may be used if they are musically good.

I WISH YOU A MERRY CHRISTMAS

Cornish Folk Tune

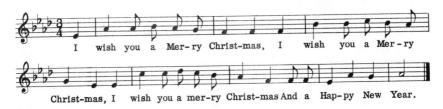

From *Singing on Our Way* of OUR SINGING WORLD Series, Enlarged Edition. Used by permission of Ginn and Company, owner of the copyright.

Carols and customs from Sweden, Mexico, and many other countries can broaden the appreciation of Christmas as well as give a basis for an acquaintance with people in other lands. "Christmas in Other Lands" is a rewarding theme around which almost any size play, pageant, or tableau may be developed.

In addition to the Christmas celebration, a teacher might consider the Jewish December Festival of Lights, as children are led to share an appreciation of traditional songs of holidays that receive less public attention. "Song for Hanukah" (ECh-102, MRC-73), "On This Night" (MTD-118), and others are available in the basic song books. *A Treasury of Jewish Folklore*[8] by Ausubel is an aid to the teacher in his search for interesting material about the Jewish faith and customs.

Thanksgiving may be highlighted by appropriate songs. The verse titled "A Thank-You Prayer for Thoughts and Things,"[9] by Elizabeth McE. Shields, has been set to music in "Heavenly Father" (FGB-90) and with other melodies in other sources. Also, the old English round, under the different titles "Choral Grace" (MTY-43), "Song of Thanks" (MRC-71), or "Thankfulness" (MTD-113), seems especially appropriate.

SONG OF THANKS

Old English Round

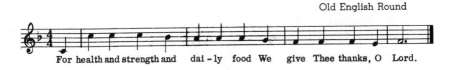

By kind permission of J. Curwen & Sons Ltd., 24 Berners Street, London, W.1.

Third grade children may learn "Come, Ye Thankful People, Come" (NMH III-39), "Swing the Shining Sickle" (MNLA-149, MTY-50),

"For the Beauty of the Earth" (MTY-51), and other traditional harvest songs that are a part of the American heritage. There are a number of "turkey" and "pumpkin" songs, but very few of them have genuine musical worth.

Easter is a holy day, rather than a holiday, and as such is even harder to deal with in the public schools, where all faiths are represented, than is Christmas. Songs that treat of Easter as a time of waking earth and flowers are usually quite acceptable.

ART SONGS. Songs that have been composed so artistically that the music conveys the meaning and feeling equally with the text are considered art songs. There are many famous art songs by Schubert, Brahms, Grieg, and others, which are too difficult for children to sing, although they may be heard in the listening program.

Among the art songs that primary children can learn to sing are Brahms' "Lullaby" (MTY-136), "Cradle Song" by Mozart (MTY-74, NMH III-156), "Little Man in the Woods" and others from Humperdinck's children's opera, *Hansel and Gretel* (MTY-21), and "Sweet and Low" by Barnby (NMH III-139, MM-29). Intermediate grades will enjoy many more, and the repertoire of a select choir should be rich in such songs. The beauty of these songs will bring a quality to the music program that cannot be had from folk songs alone. A number of these are available on the recordings that accompany the books.

"COMMUNITY" SINGING. Because it was felt that the schools had an obligation to help boys and girls become acquainted with the music used in the community, teachers in the elementary grades have included patriotic, community, and camp songs in the singing repertoire for many years. Such old favorites as "Swanee River," "Down by the Old Mill Stream," "Sailing," "Old Black Joe" and others were considered basic community repertoire. In looking through the school music books today one fails to find these old favorites. Does the omission indicate that taste in "community" songs has changed or that community singing as it once was known is no longer an important activity among our people?

We think both factors are involved. People sing together in smaller groups at home and on picnics, more often than in community gatherings. The repertoire has changed, although the standard patriotic and holiday songs are still sung. In some communities the music of a particular national group is more important than songs that might be considered typical of the American heritage. Many of Stephen Foster's songs, once considered basic repertoire, are encountered chiefly in the study of the musical heritage of our country. Most people are acquainted with them but few know the words so well that they can be sung in their entirety.

When young people sing around the camp fire they are more likely to sing the interesting folk songs of other countries such as "The Happy Wanderer" (VOA-13) and "Zulu Warrior" (MAW-77) than "Camptown Races," "Down by the Old Mill Stream," or "Tenting Tonight." For young people these latter songs do not have the associative, sentimental appeal they had two generations ago.

SINGING WITH THE SOCIAL STUDIES. Second and third grade social studies center in part around the farm and the community. Although some of the songs based on people and activities are musically worthwhile, many more lack the desired qualities. It would not be practical here to list all of the good ones; we can only urge the teacher to sing the song several times to test its value before teaching it to the children.

Since some primary classes study American Indians, authentic Indian songs have been included in various texts. These tend to be modal in quality, and so a different musical sound is experienced when they are used in the classroom. It is much better that children have an opportunity to sing authentic songs of these peoples, when simple, appropriate examples can be found, than that they merely sing songs which are composed *about* the Indians. The latter may lack musical quality, and they do not project the imagery and feeling of the ethnic groups. MUSIC FOR YOUNG AMERICANS, *Book Three*, pages 32 to 38, *Our Songs*, pages 77 to 81, and *Music Now and Long Ago*, pages 87 to 90, present groups of songs which may be used in a general study of Indians.

It is not necessary to limit the singing of ethnic songs to those times when a social studies unit is in progress. Peoples all over the world have similar activities and their songs can be shared by children here merely because they are appealing. "Indian Lullaby" (NMH III-8) and "We-Um" (S&R-72) are both lullabies with the characteristic quality of Indian melodies.

WE-UM

Cherokee Indian Lullaby

We-um, we - um, we - um, we - um, We-um, we - um, we - um, we -
um, we - um, We - um, we - um, we - um, we - um.

"We-Um" from *Grammar School Songs* by Charles Farnsworth. Charles Scribner's Sons, publishers.

Folk songs from other countries will enrich the singing repertoire. Recent basic song books include original texts for some folk songs. The teacher who can pronounce the words correctly should use the original language for interest and for the cultural enrichment that it brings to the singing program. Because young people pick up words and phrases easily, childhood is the ideal time to learn a language. Some elementary schools teach foreign languages and folk songs are an important part of the project.

At the intermediate level songs related to the social studies become very important. Numerous references will be made to such a correlation of material throughout this book. In Chapter Nine some consideration will be given to the organization of units of study based on such topics.

ACTIVITIES FOR COLLEGE CLASSES

A. Written Assignments

1. From any basic song book select two songs that require different tone quality as discussed on page 23. Describe briefly your feeling about the song and the character of the singing that would be appropriate.

2. In four songs find tone calls that fulfill the characteristics of a good tone call. Write these tone calls out in staff notation.

3. Choose two contrasting songs that you find appealing. On the basis of the criteria in the section "What is a Good Song?" analyze the songs.

4. Select two or three good songs related to each important singing interest of children in the grade you hope to teach. List the songs under topical headings for use in your handbook as suggested on pages 13-14 of Chapter One.

5. Study the content and make-up of three basic song books designed for one particular grade. Compare and evaluate the books in terms of their song material. What percentage of the songs are good? What variety of song material is there? How many are folk songs, and how many are arranged or composed for special purposes?

6. Make a list of essential heritage songs for children in your community. In a class discussion, be prepared to defend the inclusion or omission of specific songs.

B. Classroom Projects

1. Select a partner and carry on a brief singing conversation on any topic. Use only one or two tones but be sure that everything is said in a singing tone.

2. Read aloud contrasting character lines from a story such as "The Three Little Pigs," "Chicken Licken," "Goldilocks." Experiment with different voice qualities and depths to portray the several characters.

3. Be prepared to sing two informal folk songs, such as are listed on page 25. In these, what phrases do you find that are captivating and easy to sing in an informal manner? Invite the college class to join in the singing on these phrases.

CHAPTER NOTES

1. Satis N. Coleman, *Creative Music for Children* (New York: G. P. Putnam's Sons, 1922), p. 103. Reprinted by permission.
2. Lilla Belle Pitts *et al.*, *The Kindergarten Book*, OUR SINGING WORLD Series (Boston: Ginn and Company, 1959), "Teaching Suggestions, I—Vocal Expression," pp. viii to xi.
3. Emma Dickson Sheehy, *There's Music in Children*, Revised and Enlarged Edition (New York: Henry Holt and Co., Inc., 1952), pp. 62-65.
4. Ruth Seeger, *American Folk Songs for Children* (New York: Doubleday and Company, Inc., 1948), pp. 35-42.
5. Richard C. Berg *et al.*, MUSIC FOR YOUNG AMERICANS, ABC Music Series (New York: American Book Company, 1959), *The Kindergarten Book*, pp. 141-143, *Book I*, pp. 174-175.
6. Satis N. Coleman, *op. cit.*, pp. 100-105. Reprinted by permission.
7. Beatrice Landeck, *Children and Music* (New York: William Sloane Associates, Inc., 1952), pp. 52 and 55. Copyright 1952 by Beatrice Landeck. Reprinted by permission.
8. Nathan Ausubel, *A Treasury of Jewish Folklore* (New York: Crown Publishers, 1948).
9. Mary Alice Jones, *Prayers for Little Children* (New York: Rand McNally and Co., 1937).

OTHER REFERENCES

Mathews, Paul Wentworth, *You Can Teach Music* (New York: E. P. Dutton and Co., Inc., 1953). Chapter 3, "The Common Sense Way to Singing."

Mursell, James L., *Music and the Classroom Teacher* (Morristown, N.J.: Silver Burdett Company, 1951). Chapter 6, "Singing."

Sheehy, Emma Dickson, *Children Discover Music and Dance* (New York: Henry Holt and Co., Inc., 1959), Chapter 4, "Singing."

Timmerman, Maurine, *Let's Teach Music* (Evanston, Ill.: Summy-Birchard Publishing Company, 1958). Pp. 113-114, "Suggested Supplementary Song Sources."

See Appendix B for listing of song books and records in the basic music series.

CHAPTER THREE

THE USE OF
RHYTHM INSTRUMENTS

From the earliest times man's music making has included the use of instruments. In almost all ethnic groups, chanting, singing, and dancing have been accompanied by them. Children are fascinated by sounds of all sorts; their natural tendencies to touch and to manipulate make the use of simple instruments a vital part of any program of music in the schools. Singing and sound-making with instruments go together. Only after the teacher understands the place of simple instruments in the music program is he in a position to teach songs and promote the varied program recommended in this text.

Simple percussion instruments (those that are struck to produce the tone) are standard equipment in the kindergarten. Although their use by older children is accepted they are found less frequently in other classrooms for they still are suspected of being toys rather than musical instruments. It is true that under certain circumstances they serve as toys or noise-makers, but if handled properly simple percussion instruments have undeniable value in the elementary music program.

Although all instruments may play rhythm, the group ordinarily classed as "rhythm instruments" sound only one pitch and so are incapable of playing a melody line. In the percussion section of the symphony orchestra a number of these are standard equipment: tambourine, triangle, castanets, drums of various kinds, cymbal, gong, maracas, claves, and others. Small copies of these have been adapted for children. Multitoned percussion instruments (xylophone, glockenspiel, piano, etc.) are included among "Melody Instruments" in Chapter Four.

Recommended Instruments

Many times a teacher eagerly begins to collect rhythm instruments for use in the classroom. He may have such enthusiasm for the project that the principal and other staff members become enthusiastic and money is allocated for the purchase of such instruments. Disappointment ensues when, after a few weeks of use, the head of the drum grows flabby and there is apparently no simple way to recondition it. Soon the paper on the sandblocks is torn, the teacher is too busy to re-cover them, and these are discarded along with the drum.

Any musical instrument planned for active use must be durable enough to last for a long time, and it should be possible to replace easily the worn parts, so that the instrument will sound with its original good tone. A drum, to be more than a decorator's item, must have a head that is sturdy enough to be struck repeatedly with a padded mallet. After two or three years of active use, it may be necessary to replace the drumhead, but at a small part of the original cost.

The quality of sound in the instruments is also important. If there is anything that will keep the instrumental program in the "toy" classification, it is the use of instruments with poor and indistinctive sound. Many teachers, for lack of funds, have provided home-made substitutes for instruments. This practice is not to be condemned, if the substitute has fine tone quality. In fact, almost any group of children can benefit greatly from a project in which they explore quality of sound in metal and wood objects in an attempt to find substitutes for instruments not otherwise available to their classroom. Other projects may have less musical value:

Shakers and "maracas" are made out of small cans partially filled with pebbles, beans, or other material, fitted with handles, and painted. Large light bulbs covered with layers of papier-mâché, struck sharply to break the glass inside and then decorated, have been popular "maracas."

"Drums" are made of brightly painted oatmeal boxes, coffee cans, and other cylindrical containers, and fitted with rubber or cloth drumheads. "Tambourines" are made of pie tins or paper plates to which bottle caps are attached. The chief values of this project lie in (1) the interest which it creates in rhythm instruments, by providing each child with his own instrument, and consequently a temporary, keener interest in playing rhythmic accompaniments; and (2) the experience in constructing and decorating the items.

Such a project does not yield durable instruments, and the sounds produced are more those of noise-makers than of distinctive musical instruments. Therefore, their use in the classroom is limited. If they are constructed, the teacher should capitalize on the interest they promote and use them temporarily in as musical a way as possible.

A BASIC GROUP OF RHYTHM INSTRUMENTS. When a teacher plans to obtain rhythm instruments for his classroom he should know that (1) if a complete set of instruments is not available immediately, he may gather a basic group first and then accumulate the remainder over a period of time; (2) some home-made instruments are more durable and have better tone than those which are bought.

Instruments basic to primary musical activities are described in the following paragraphs. After that, additional desirable instruments are listed. Finally, the more authentic folk type is suggested as the distinguishing feature of rhythm instruments used in the intermediate grades.

Drums. Every classroom should have at least one drum and, where possible, two or more of contrasting size. A tunable, 14-inch modern dance drum or "side" drum is a light-weight, versatile instrument. If the rim does not extend above the drum head, the hand can produce interesting variety in tonal and rhythmic effects. Primitive drums with skin heads are available in many sizes from the small hand drum to the large ceremonial drum that rests on the floor. These are durable and have a splendid tone but they are quite expensive and therefore may not be available to the average classroom.

A less expensive drum with a reasonably good sound may be constructed with these materials:

1. *A wooden barrel, keg, or pail, 10 or 11 inches in diameter.* This should be quite sturdy, open at one end and with a smooth rim or edge over which the drum head material is stretched. If the barrel is old and dry, soak it for several hours so that the tacks may be driven in more easily. The larger barrel results in a drum with a deeper tone.

2. *Hide or gum rubber for the drum head.* Scrapped rawhide, chamois, or old bass drumheads can be used if they are soaked in water until they are pliable enough to be stretched over the drum. Formerly old automobile inner tubes were used, but the neophrene rubber now found in them does not have the stretching quality necessary for a drum head. Commercial, pure gum, sheet rubber, 1/16-inch thick is probably the best rubber available for this use. Buy a square slightly larger than the diameter of the barrel; by the time it is stretched it will have ample edge for tacking.

3. *Upholstery tacks with large heads.* Drive these in about an inch from the edge of the rubber or hide. Put three tacks in rather close together, and then pull the drumhead across the opening and drive in three more tacks. Working on alternate sides around the drum, putting in a group of tacks will prevent the material from tearing.

The life of the drum will be longer if the hand or a *padded* drum stick is used to strike it.

Rhythm sticks. In the symphony orchestra or in a Latin-American orchestra the claves is a pair of resonant wooden sticks, which are struck together. Rhythm sticks are their counterpart among the primary rhythm instruments. The most resonant tone is made when they are held loosely in the hands as they are tapped together. These may be purchased, but the home-made version is simple to make, much less expensive, and just as satisfactory.

Buy 3/8-inch doweling in a lumber or hardware store. Cut it into 12-inch lengths and stain any desirable color. For a lighter sound, use 1/4-inch doweling. Each classroom can use three or four pairs of both sizes.

Triangle. The 5-inch triangle with striker is adequate. For quality in the sound the commercially-made triangle is best, but a large nail struck with another nail will produce a similar tone. The triangle or nail must be suspended by a short piece of twine so that the tone will ring freely. Two or three triangles are necessary for bell and other tinkling effects.

Sandblocks. Two or three pairs of sandblocks are useful. Those available commercially are generally too small and not durable. Long-lasting sandblocks with an excellent sound may be made with

1. Two half-sheets of fine emery cloth (9″ × 5½″).
2. Plywood (two pieces 3″ × 9″).
3. A 4-inch piece of ¾-inch scrap lumber for a handle.

The construction is simple. Nail the handle in place with short nails driven through from the plywood side. Draw the emery cloth smoothly around the plywood base and thumbtack on the top side. Do not glue it down because it makes a better sound when merely drawn tightly around the wood base.

Coconut shells. Nothing makes a better sound for galloping and trotting horses than hollow halves of coconut shells tapped together. Two pairs are recommended. To prepare them, drain the milk from a coconut, cut it evenly in half, and scrape out the meat. When the shells are dry, they may be scraped and polished.

Sleigh bells. It is best to buy medium-size bells that are attached to a handle. Three or four of two different sizes are enough.

With the above group of instruments the teacher will have variety and will be able to promote very worthwhile instrumental activities. It is desirable, of course, to have a greater selection of instruments. As the budget allows, some of the following may be added:

Tambourine. Home-made varieties are rarely adequate in quality of sound. It is worth the money to buy a good quality instrument. Two or three 7-inch tambourines are sufficient.

Tone blocks. Two sizes of these are very useful for clock sounds. The tone block is tapped with a small wooden mallet. The commercial variety is recommended.

Cymbals. One pair of small 7-inch cymbals is enough. Even the commercially made small cymbals leave something to be desired as far as tone quality is concerned.

Gong. This is a more expensive item, but one which will provide climaxes and dramatic effects. It should be suspended, struck with a padded mallet and allowed to vibrate freely.

Maracas. One or two pairs of the commercial variety is recommended. It is worthwhile to buy a better quality instrument, for the handles of the cheaply made kind come off. Teachers have made quite good sounding maracas out of dried gourds that have been cut open, cleaned and shellacked inside, and re-sealed with a small amount of fine rattling material inside (rice, shot, etc.). If the gourds have been buffed on the outside they may be painted and lacquered in colorful Mexican designs.

Quiro (gourd rasp). One of these will serve special purposes from time to time. It is played by rhythmically stroking a light stick over the notched area. This is quite easily made by filing notches in the side of a large dried gourd and shellacking the instrument.

Castanets. Orchestral castanets on a handle are used by children. They have a loud tone and one pair is sufficient.

Finger cymbals. Two pairs will provide special effects as needed.

Bells. Any small bells are useful.

FOLK INSTRUMENTS AT THE INTERMEDIATE LEVEL. Although authentic rhythm instruments from different countries are useful in the primary classroom, they play a more important role at the intermediate level. Prestige is given this work when such instruments are used. Instead of rhythm sticks, substitute claves, the authentic Cuban instrument. Buy these, or make substitutes with hardwood doweling 9 inches long and 1½ inches in diameter. Tambourines should be larger than those used in the primary grades. Maracas, castanets, quiro or other types of rasp are especially valuable with Latin-American songs.

Triangles, cymbals, or gong may be used occasionally for specialized effects and, when possible, should be of the standard orchestral size. If such instruments are not available, pupils may explore the potential of different metal objects that, when suspended and struck, make sounds of an acceptable quality. Drums may be of varied types, but the bongo and conga drums are of particular interest to children this age. Latin-American and West Indian songs are included in the new basic song books so that there is a real reason for having such authentic native instruments. Bongo drums are a pair of small drums, one higher in pitch than the other, bound together so that one player can sound them with both hands as he holds them between his knees. Very intricate rhythms can be played on the bongos. A conga drum is much lower in pitch because it is longer. It may stand on the floor, tilted at an angle so that the sound is free; or it may be held between the legs as the player sits on the floor and plays it with both hands.

Home-made versions of bongo drums can be made of short lengths of cardboard tubing taken from the inside of linoleum rolls or by bolting together two small butter kegs, the open tops of which have been covered with goatskin. Some firms sell the complete materials for bongo drums, and these are assembled by the purchaser. Home-made substitutes for conga drums can be made of fiber waste pipe which has been cut in lengths up to 26 inches. The application of goatskin drumheads and tuning procedures are described in detail in *Make Your Own Musical Instruments* by Mandell and Wood.[1]

As pupils become acquainted with people of other cultures they become interested in the typical instruments, e.g., drums and rattles of the American Indian, Chinese woodblocks and gong, and Hawaiian uli-uli and drums. The construction of such instruments makes an excellent art and crafts project for intermediate grades. *Drums, Tomtoms, Rattles,*[2] which describes the construction of primitive instruments for modern use, is one of the best sources of information for such a project.

The Exploration of Sound and the Enrichment of Songs

Important objectives of the instrumental program are to develop sensitivity to different tone colors and qualities in instrumental sound, and to establish basic concepts of pitch, dynamics, and duration of tone. Therefore, children must have opportunities to experiment with the instruments. Children's natural interest in sound should be cultivated to the end that they discover differences:

1. Instruments such as the drum have a booming sound, while the triangle has a tinkling, bell-like sound.
2. The drum has a low tone and the triangle has a high tone.
3. Some drums have lower tones than others.
4. The tones of triangles, cymbals, and drums resound for a longer period of time than the tone of the rhythm sticks.
5. Instruments may be played in more than one way with varied effects.

This is only a sampling of many musical discoveries to be made. In this work some teacher-guided group experimentation is possible, but much individual, free exploration should be arranged.

In many classrooms, activity centers are established, and music has its center where instruments are kept. Since sound-making and listening are the basis for exploration, there are limitations on acceptable times for the activity. Some small groups may use the instruments before school, after school, or during recesses and activity periods. During good weather, the more durable instruments may be taken to a specified location out of doors.

In the kindergarten the teacher can guide the free exploration by limiting the number of available instruments. Drums are often the first instruments placed in the instrument center. As an introduction, the teacher may arrange a demonstration-discussion in which the pupils show and tell what they know about the instruments. He may suggest ideas that would lead the children to explore the instruments further. Later, when some interesting discovery is made (a new combination of instruments or a new and effective way of playing an instrument), the teacher may wish to bring it to the attention of the entire class. In *There's Music in Children*,[3] pages 18 to 26, Emma Sheehy gives interesting examples and suggestions for this use of the instruments.

A CLASSIFICATION OF SOUNDS. Although in the beginning a classification of the effects produced is not important to children, two or three years of work with the instruments should lead them to a summarization of the representative sounds:

1. Short, dry sounds can be produced by:

   rhythm sticks   *skin head drum*
   tone blocks   *coconut shells*
   sandblocks—short, quick stroke   *tambourine*—tapped
   quiro—quick stroke   *castanets*

2. Sustained, dry sounds are produced by:

maracas—shaken   *quiro*—stroked slowly
sandblocks—rubbed slowly together

3. Sustained tones with greater resonance are produced by:

larger drum with skin head   *tambourine*—shaken
drum with rubber head

4. Tinkling sounds, higher in pitch, are produced by:

triangle—tapped   *finger cymbals*
cymbal—tapped lightly with hard
  stick

5. Ringing sounds of longer duration are produced by:

triangle—struck repeatedly and ra-   with a padded mallet and al-
  pidly at one corner (for a louder   lowed to vibrate freely
  tone, the striker can be rung re-   *sleigh bells*—shaken for the de-
  peatedly around the entire inside   sired duration
  of the triangle)   *gong*
cymbal—crashed together or struck   *bells*—allowed to vibrate freely

TECHNIQUES IN ENRICHING SONGS. Group exploration of sound and
rhythm can be an outgrowth of selecting suitable instruments for use with
songs and rhythmic activities. In the kindergarten and first grade, instruments as well as hands and feet are used to create sound effects as they
are needed with particular songs. Several small pairs of rhythm sticks
tapped rapidly and lightly or many fingernails clicking on desk tops
or on paper provide excellent rain-on-the-roof effects! Sandblocks make
train sounds. Pupils should be guided to experiment, to listen and decide
what produces the sound desired in a particular song. "Jingle, Jingle
Johnny" (KBk-140) suggests the use of triangle or bells:

JINGLE, JINGLE JOHNNY

Peter Thornton   German Folk Tune

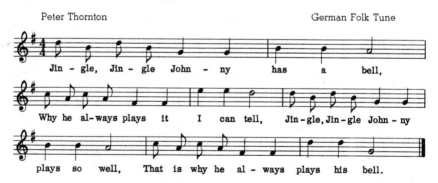

Jin - gle, Jin - gle John - ny   has   a   bell,

Why he al-ways plays   it   I   can tell,   Jin-gle, Jin-gle John - ny

plays   so   well,   That is why he al - ways plays   his   bell.

From *The Kindergarten Book* of OUR SINGING WORLD Series, Enlarged Edition. Used by
permission of Ginn and Company, owner of the copyright.

These instruments may be sounded in a steady rhythm throughout the song or played only at the end of each phrase. The children may wish to try it both ways. Some of the following songs suggest the use of instruments for sound effects:

"Who's That Tapping at the Window?" (AFlk-52)
"Jingle at the Window" (MTD-17)

"By'm By" (SGro-18)
"Transportation" (AS I-27)

Marching songs like "Yankee Doodle" demand a steady drumbeat or use of rhythm sticks or sandblocks on the metric beat.

YANKEE DOODLE

Traditional

When the drum sounds the steady 1-2 beats, it follows the rhythm of the marchers' feet. Rhythm sticks might play on the metric beat in the verse of "Going to Boston" (SGro-78) or they may furnish the steady ticktock in "The Clock" (KBk-125).

The melody rhythm is sometimes played. Often, after the children know a song thoroughly, it is the easiest response, for they merely follow the rhythm pattern of the words throughout all or part of the song. In the folk song "Chickama Craney Crow" (ABC K-70) rhythm sticks may follow the melody rhythm whenever the words "Chickama, chickama, craney crow" are heard.

CHICKAMA CRANEY CROW

Southern Folk Song

From Berg, Burns, Hooley, Pace, and Wolverton, MUSIC FOR YOUNG AMERICANS, *Kindergarten Book.* American Book Company, publishers. Used by permission.

went to the well to— wash my toe; When I came home, one

chick-en was gone! Oh, Chick-a-ma, Chick-a-ma Crane - y Crow!

Since tinkling sounds seem most appropriate for "angels," children might use them to follow the melody rhythm in "Band of Angels" (SGro-54) or "The Angel Band" (MIOT-48).

Such simple enrichment of songs can be quite worthwhile at both the intermediate and at the primary level. Although the techniques are essentially the same, the older pupils are more interested in the effects produced than in the use of the instruments for their own sake. "Down the Stream" (SED-128) is a Yosemite Indian melody that can benefit from the addition of a drum.

DOWN THE STREAM

Derrick Norman Lehmer Collection   Miwok Indian Song

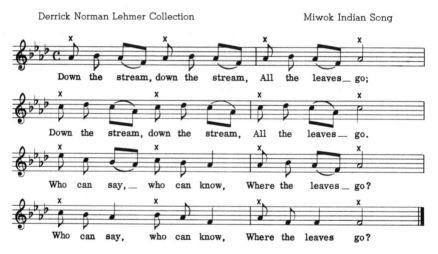

Down the   stream, down the   stream, All   the   leaves_ go;

Down the   stream, down the   stream, All   the   leaves_ go.

Who   can   say,_   who   can   know,   Where the   leaves_ go?

Who   can   say,   who   can   know,   Where the   leaves   go?

From *Singing Every Day* of OUR SINGING WORLD Series, Enlarged Edition. Used by permission of Ginn and Company, owner of the copyright.

To maintain the feeling of dignity and wonder expressed in this song, use only one deep resonant drum playing the first and third beats. Start softly, crescendo to the third phrase of the song and diminuendo toward the end, letting the drum continue fading away for two measures after the voices conclude.

Simple instruments should be used as an enrichment in the singing program. Be sure that each song has its own appeal and is not selected if its sole merit is that it offers an opportunity to introduce the instruments.

A Study of the Elements of Rhythm

The use of instruments in the singing program should lead to a study of the basic elements of rhythm. In addition to the metric beat and the melody rhythm, the accent and special rhythm patterns can be discovered and studied by older children.

THE METRIC BEAT AND THE MELODY RHYTHM. The essential concept to be developed in this study is that the durational values of tones in the melody line are related to the basic metric framework that underlies the melody. The metric beat is on-going at a certain tempo and in a particular pattern of pulses. Sometimes a melody consists of short rhythmic patterns that may be repeated; in contrast, another melody may be long-lined and more smooth-flowing in character. If children are to understand rhythmic notation, their experiences should be designed to point up the varying relationships of melody rhythm and metric beat.

The rhythm instruments are especially appropriate for this study because they are easy to play, and when instruments with contrasting sounds are used, the different aspects of rhythm are clearly defined. During their early experiences children play by ear one element at a time (the metric beat or the melody rhythm). Which of these is heard most readily depends on the nature of the composition and the rhythmic experience of the children. As a result of extensive experience, pupils from the second or third grade upward will be ready to study the relationship between these elements of rhythm.

To demonstrate the relationship between the metric beat and melody rhythm in "Yankee Doodle" or any other strongly rhythmic song, the teacher might follow this procedure:

1. Have one instrument, perhaps a high-toned drum, play the steady metric beat as the children sing the song.
2. Sing again, this time having rhythm sticks sound the melody rhythm, which is the rhythm of the words.
3. A third time establish the metric beat as sounded on the drum (be sure it is going well), then have the singers and those playing the sticks add the melody rhythm.
4. Repeat the process and urge the children to listen to both sounds. If those playing the sticks know the melody rhythm well, perhaps the singing can be omitted so that the two elements of rhythm can be more easily heard.

Songs that have strong rhythms, such as marches and dance tunes, are best for such rhythm study. It would be entirely inappropriate to accompany a lullaby or an art song with rhythm instruments. We must not lose sight of the fact that music is expressive and that it must always be studied in ways that will help the children feel its message.

Rhythmic song-chants are studies in the relationship of metric beat and word rhythm patterns. Primitive chants, such as those of the American Indian, lend themselves to interesting uses of rattles and drums. The primitive use of rhythm instruments is startling and dynamic. If possible, the pupils should hear recordings of such chants and songs. *The Columbia World Library of Folk and Primitive Music*[4] and *Folkways*[5] recordings are excellent sources for ethnic music. The following songs can be quite authentically combined with instruments: "Breezes Are Blowing" (MNLA-89), "Brothers, Let Us Dance" (S&R-49), and "Work Song" (ABC III-34).

WORK SONG

Dakota Indian Song

From Berg, Burns, Hooley, Pace, and Wolverton, MUSIC FOR YOUNG AMERICANS, *Book Three*. American Book Company, publishers. Used by permission.

In this Dakota Indian song, drums can play the steady metric beat while rattles follow the rhythmic pattern of the chant.

The teacher can help the children notice that the important words in a chant coincide with the heavy beat (the accent) in the metric rhythm. The pupils may also explore jingles and short poems to determine how they swing and which are the important words. An understanding of this principle will be of help when they wish to create melodies for original or selected poems.

PLAYING THE ACCENT. Playing a rhythm instrument on the accented beat is appropriate for songs such as "Old Mister Elephant" (AS I-80). The sound of a deep-toned drum on the first and third beats of each measure intensifies the feeling of the elephant's swinging walk. Playing the accented beat is a more difficult technique that should be developed

OLD MISTER ELEPHANT

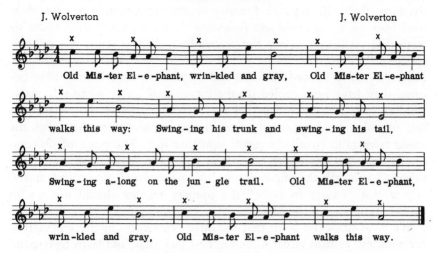

J. Wolverton   J. Wolverton

Old Mis-ter El-e-phant, wrin-kled and gray, Old Mis-ter El-e-phant walks this way: Swing-ing his trunk and swing-ing his tail, Swing-ing a-long on the jun-gle trail. Old Mis-ter El-e-phant, wrin-kled and gray, Old Mis-ter El-e-phant walks this way.

From Beattie, Wolverton, Wilson, and Hinga, THE AMERICAN SINGER, Second Edition, *Book One*. American Book Company, publishers. Used by permission.

after the children have learned to respond with ease to the metric beat and the melody rhythm. In this song, bodily movement on the accented beat assists the player in sounding his instrument.

In developing an understanding of accent, it is well to work from the metric beat. "The Bridge of Avignon" is available in many of the song books:

THE BRIDGE OF AVIGNON

Translated   French Singing Game

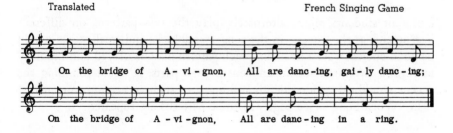

On the bridge of A-vi-gnon, All are danc-ing, gai-ly danc-ing; On the bridge of A-vi-gnon, All are danc-ing in a ring.

A few of the children can play the metric beat on the rhythm sticks, counting with the beat, "one-two, one-two," while the class sings the song. Following this, the drummer is instructed to play only the "ones." The counting helps him to find the accent; if he has no difficulty, count-ing aloud soon may be dispensed with. Another way to help children clap or play on the accent is to have them move the hand or drum stick rhythmically in the opposite direction on the unsounded beat. Thus their total response is rhythmic and following the meter, yet if they count silently they will sound only the proper beat. At this stage, the children speak of rhythms that "swing in twos" or "threes." They know this because they have learned to listen and respond to meter rather than because they have been drilled on the meaning of meter signatures. After children have had much experience successfully playing the metric beat and accent in combination, the teacher should show them that when the music "swings in twos" the meter signature is $\frac{2}{4}$. The point of observation is only that the upper number in $\frac{2}{4}$, $\frac{3}{4}$, or $\frac{4}{4}$ shows how the "music swings." Although the pupils should have much experience with $\frac{6}{8}$ meter, as one that "swings in twos," the primary teacher should not try to explain its notational complexities.

We must stress the point that the early experiences in rhythm analysis are aural rather than visual. Children first feel, hear, and learn to respond to the separate elements of rhythm; then they listen for a combination of two or three of the elements and learn to play any of them at will. Most third grade pupils readily learn to play the melody rhythm, metric beat, or accent at will if they have had, in the first and second grades, extensive experience using the instruments as song enrichments to play one element at a time.

DISCOVERING RHYTHM PATTERNS. Playing the melody rhythm of a song such as "The Bridge of Avignon" can lead to the discovery of rhythm patterns. In this song there are two patterns:

Different students might alternately play the two patterns on different instruments as they occur in the song (sandblocks and small sticks would be good choices). At a later time each pattern may be played continuously to form a rhythmic accompaniment in two parts. A drum sounding the accent would give added depth and unity to such an accompaniment.

In "Work Song" (see page 62) these patterns are repeated:

Third graders can easily create an accompaniment by playing either or both on different toned instruments repeatedly as an introduction and during the song.

Often a single specialized rhythm pattern provides the most suitable accompaniment for a song. Such patterns are not selected arbitrarily, but are integral to the rhythmic scheme of the song for which they are suggested. For example, in "Rig-a-Jig-Jig" (see page 40) coconut shells may be used throughout for the galloping rhythm:

This is a more advanced use of the instruments, for the player sometimes must respond relatively independently of the metric beat or melody rhythm heard in the song. Some second and third graders may be able to play such patterns. If this rhythm pattern is played as an introduction for two measures before the singing begins, the player will establish a security that will permit him to continue it more successfully throughout the song. This technique may be used with any of the following songs:

"Mister Banjo" (ABC III-97):

"Circus Riders" (MRT-63):

"Snow-White Little Burro" (S&R-150):

"Roving Cowboy" (MNLA-54):

"Bongo Drums" (ABC II-167):

Folk songs and reel tunes of the American frontier, as well as European dancing tunes, can be accompanied by clapping, foot-tapping, and rhythm instruments. The metric beat or accent may .be tapped with toe or heel or played on a deep-toned instrument; the melody rhythm may be played by lighter-sounding instruments.

PLAYING AFTERBEATS. After they have had much experience with such elemental rhythmic responses, intermediate-grade boys and girls may begin to clap and play the afterbeats, a common form of rhythmic participation in reels and dance songs. "Sandy Land" (MAOC-24) is a relatively simple song that may be treated in this manner.

SANDY LAND

American Singing Game

Make my liv-ing in Sand-y Land, Make my liv-ing in Sand-y Land,

Make my liv-ing in Sand-y Land, La-dies, fare you well.___

"Sandy Land" from *Music Across Our Country* of the New TOGETHER-WE-SING Series, published by Follett Publishing Company, Chicago, Illinois.

In order to play the afterbeat successfully, the children must hear and feel the downbeat. Often the spectators at a square dance tap a foot on the downbeat and clap on the afterbeat.

$$\frac{2}{4}$$

| 1 | & | 2 | & |
| tap | clap | tap | clap |

The ability to play afterbeats successfully will strengthen the students' preparation to play more complicated syncopated patterns. Children can learn to play afterbeats at a moderate tempo and then increase the speed as demanded by the dance. To maintain continuous rhythmic movement, let the hands move outward on the downbeat. If instruments are used, a deeper-sounding instrument can be played on the accent with a short dry-sounding one on the afterbeats.

In ¾ meter the accent may be played on one instrument and two afterbeats on a different toned instrument as in "Waltzing with Anya" (SIH-41).

WALTZING WITH ANYA

Katherine S. Bolt   Bohemian Folk Tune

When An - ya joins in the dance, Light as a

bird she floats, Sway - ing to sweet vi - o - lins

From *Singing in Harmony* of OUR SINGING WORLD Series, Enlarged Edition. Used by permission of Ginn and Company, owner of the copyright.

Play - ing their gold - en notes. Twirl - ing, swirl - ing,

None is so love - ly as she._____ Twirl - ing,

whirl - ing, An - ya is waltz - ing with me._____

Play a high-toned drum on the accent and a tambourine on the second and third beats of each measure. To sustain the dotted half notes, rap on the first beat and shake the tambourine on the second and third beats. In the early experiences with such a pattern it may be necessary for the children first to play the continuous metric beat in combination with the accent and then *count* but do not *sound* the "ones" as they learn to play "two-three" as afterbeats.

LEARNING WRITTEN NOTATION FOR RHYTHM. After the children respond well to the basic elements of rhythm and understand the relationship between them, the teacher may begin to present rhythmic notation, using first those songs for which pupils have supplied the rhythmic accompaniment by ear. The following steps, with some variations, are suggested. "The Bridge of Avignon" will serve as an example (see page 63 for notation).

1. The class sings the song with a previously developed instrumental accompaniment, rhythm sticks on the metric beat and sandblocks playing the melody rhythm (omit the accent played by the drum).
2. The child playing the metric beat is asked to continue as the teacher makes short vertical lines on the chalkboard to represent the beats he is sounding.
3. A child is asked how to count a metric beat that swings in twos. He says "one-two, one-two." The teacher numbers the strokes on the chalkboard.

4. The class then sings, and sandblocks sound, the first phrase of the song. From experience, the children are well aware that the melody sometimes moves quicker than the metric beat, sometimes slower, and sometimes right along with it. In this song they have previously dis-

covered and played by ear two rhythm patterns (see page 64) that are an integral part of the melody rhythm.

5. With rhythm sticks sounding the metric beat and sandblocks playing the melody rhythm, the teacher draws long and short lines (blank notation) to represent the melody rhythm under the metric beat on the chalkboard:

6. With rhythm sticks sounding the metric beat, the children clap and sing the melody rhythm as the teacher or a child points out rhythmically what has been placed on the chalkboard.

The first phrase or two of other known songs that swing in twos, threes, or fours may be worked out in similar fashion. Blank notation for specific rhythm patterns may be placed on the chalkboard. In the American folk song "Go Tell Aunt Rhodey" (see page 31) we find the simple repeated pattern which in blank notation would be:

The following patterns from "This Old Man" (MRT-122) can be treated in the same manner:

For further experience children may make an analysis of the rhythm in names and old sayings: The words should be chanted repeatedly until the syllabic rhythm can be heard in relation to the metric beat and can be clapped freely and correctly, then it may be written in blank notation on the chalkboard:

$\frac{2}{4}$	1		2			$\frac{4}{4}$	1		2		3		4	
	Rich	ard	Brown				Rose		mar	y	Jack		son	
	El	la	Wil	son			bu	sy	as	a	bee			

The children should rub the palms of their hands together in the rhythm of the words so that they feel the note lengths and thus learn to make the blank notation themselves.

At a later date rhythmic notation can be explained more fully so that it includes measure bars and the standard notation for rhythm:

1. Establish the familiar blank notation for a song the children know well and have accompanied with rhythm instruments. "Bridge of Avignon" will be used here as an example.

2. Tell the children that, since the metric beat swings in twos, the notation is divided by bar lines which come just before the "one" beat. Place heavy bar lines in the notation.

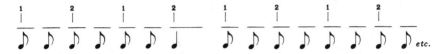

3. Under the blank notation draw in notes for the melody rhythm (see above). Have the children sing and clap this rhythm as it is pointed out on the chalkboard, then find the same rhythmic notation in the song book.

4. Show the children how the relative value of eighth and quarter notes in this pattern can be counted:

1 & 2 & / 1 & 2 — / 1 & 2 & / 1 & 2 & /

The spacing of the rhythm pattern is important when it is written on the chalkboard. Since the notation represents duration of sound in time, this duration must be shown by the note spacing as well as by the kind of note used if the children are to comprehend it readily. The metric beats must be evenly spaced and the melody rhythm accurately placed in relation to them. At the fifth and sixth grade level pupils should be given a practical method for reading more complicated rhythm notation. The teacher who has an understanding of the method of rhythmic analysis given in Appendix A will be able to impart some of that information as more difficult patterns are dealt with in song literature.

At several stages in the program of rhythm study, the children may be encouraged to create original rhythm patterns. Echo clapping, wherein the teacher or a pupil claps a short rhythm pattern and others imitate, can be a useful means of developing rhythmic freedom and skill. A splendid motivation for promoting the use of rhythm messages is found in the Young People's Record 15006, *Little Indian Drum*. In this song-story "Red Fox," the Indian boy with a little drum, sends a message to his father, who answers on his big drum. When the pupils have learned the essentials of rhythmic notation, they may wish to notate their own "drum talk" and combine it with story writing as a creative project.

It is to be expected that children will create many more rhythm patterns than they will be able to write correctly. They will learn that notation is never adequate unless it conveys the intent of the composer. However, the free spirit that enables children to explore and create is of prime importance. The understandings basic to correct notation will develop gradually and must grow out of many different experiences with rhythm.

MORE ADVANCED USES OF RHYTHM PATTERNS. Folk songs from Italy, Spain, and central Europe make interesting uses of rhythm. Latin-American songs are filled with uneven dotted rhythm patterns of the habanera and the syncopated patterns of the tango:

At first these special rhythm patterns are experienced as they are found in the melody of the song. The words of "Tinga Layo" (MN&F-126) support the pattern and make it possible for the students to play it.

TINGA LAYO

Calypso song from the West Indies

From *Calypso Songs of the West Indies* by Patterson and Belasco. Copyright 1943 by M. Baron Company. Used by permission.

As the children learn this song, they may accompany it with bongo and conga drums, claves and maracas. At first the claves might be played on the metric beat and the conga drum on the accent. As the melody becomes familiar, bongos and maracas may play the melody rhythm with maracas sustaining the half notes with a shake. After this is successfully carried out, the teacher should help the children discover and isolate the typical rhythm patterns. These may be placed on flannel board or chalkboard for observation. The particular characteristics of the rhythm patterns are brought out by playing them against the metric beat, which is sounded on another instrument:

These patterns may then be played continuously over and over, one on the bongo drums and the other on the maracas as the song is sung. To avoid doubling of parts, simplify the first pattern:

A conga drum may be added on the accents or played continuously:

Most intermediate pupils need many simple experiences before they are ready to play continuous complex patterns. Playing one pattern at a time will suffice in the early stages. Rhythm instruments can provide introductions and codas as well as accompaniments. Combinations of the accent, metric beat, afterbeats, or specialized rhythmic patterns from the melody may be used. Specific suggestions for introductions and codas are made in many of the basic song books.

After students have had considerable experience, they may wish to create their own interesting rhythm combinations using two, three, or four different instruments. Earlier experiences should be with simple ²⁄₄ or ³⁄₄ meter. Later more advanced combinations such as the following may be created:

1. Establish the metric beat with the claves.
2. Add a habanera rhythm with the maracas.
3. Furnish an accent with the conga drum.
4. Top it all with a lively bongo pattern:

It is valuable to improvise, adding instruments one at a time until a satisfactory combination is achieved. Then the questions may arise: "What are we doing?" "Can we put it down in notation?" Thus, skills grow, both in responding freely to rhythm and in understanding rhythmic notation. The film "Percussion, the Pulse of Music"[6] is an excellent one to show to intermediate grades as an introduction to improvisatory use of rhythm instruments.

The Study of Musical Form and Instrumentation

In working out instrumental accompaniments for their songs children learn to listen and to analyze in order to reflect the particular qualities of the music in their playing. It is but a short step from the more advanced work in enriching songs to the creation of rhythm orchestrations for recorded music. Children can learn to listen for contrasting sections and changes in the recorded instrumentation that suggest changes in the rhythm orchestration. An understanding of the tone qualities of the rhythm instruments, skill in playing them, and skill in responding to the elements of rhythm are necessary before this more advanced work is undertaken.

OLD AND NEW CONCEPTS OF THE RHYTHM ENSEMBLE. Up to this point the "rhythm band," which in the past has been such an important activity in kindergarten and first grade, has not been discussed. If one considers the musical objectives that are to be achieved through the use of rhythm instruments, and the type of activity needed to achieve those objectives, it can be seen that the kindergarten or first grade is too early for beneficial *mass* use of the instruments. In the traditional rhythm band, promoted at this early age, we see practices that are in direct opposition to the approach to rhythm instruments recommended in the early pages of this chapter.

1. Young children are individualists who have not yet learned to work together. To put a rhythm instrument into the hands of every child is to promote indiscriminate sound-making rather than to develop sensitivity to the tone quality of the various instruments.

2. In a rhythm band the children are required to learn *how* to play

the instruments simultaneously with *when* to play them in the orchestration.

3. When an orchestration is predetermined by the teacher, as it must be at this level, the children must learn the various parts by rote. Their response is not prompted by an understanding of the elements of rhythm and musical form.

4. While the project may strengthen the children's automatic response to certain elements of rhythm, bodily movement is a much more effective way to develop such response.

5. Generally, only a few especially talented children are ready at this age to participate in the rhythm band. Their talents are exploited and "stars" are developed while the majority of the children have little opportunity to benefit from a more educational rhythm instrument program.

There is a place for an organized ensemble of rhythm instruments from about the third grade level upward. Rather than using a predetermined orchestration, children of this age can work out their own arrangements on the basis of their understanding of rhythm and their skill in the use of the instruments. Out of experience in arranging comes an understanding of musical form and instrumentation with further experience in discriminating listening.

Early emphasis can be given to the importance of listening for changes in instrumentation by working with a composition such as the first section of "March Past of the Kitchen Utensils" from *The Wasps* by Vaughan Williams (A in M, III-1).* Throughout this section a deliberate marching accompaniment is carried by the bass instruments. This could be played in the rhythm orchestra by selected drums. The accent at the end of each 8-measure phrase suggests a bold crash of cymbals. The instrumental contrast is in the melody, which is carried alternately by trumpet and piccolo and by violins and bassoon. To reflect this change in instrumentation the children should select different rhythm instruments. The brassy quality of the trumpet might be suggested by finger cymbals on the melody rhythm and triangles on the accents of each measure. In contrast, the violin-bassoon sections might suggest the use of drier sounds such as rhythm sticks or tone blocks.

For early study in musical form, the entire composition, "March Past of the Kitchen Utensils," might be used. (The *Teacher's Guide*[7] to the ADVENTURES IN MUSIC record series will be a great aid to the teacher in analyzing the music.) The composition has three large sections which can be labeled *A, B, A*. Within the first *A* there are five 8-measure phrases,

---

* See Appendix B for identification of record albums.

each further divided in two parts. The latter *A* is similar, but with only three 8-measure phrases. Section *B* is a sharp contrast in rhythm, mood, and use of instruments. It has five phrases, each only four measures long.

To label the sections in the composition and to remember what instruments are selected to play the different parts, the teacher and pupils should, as a result of their listening, discussion, and experimentation, develop on the chalkboard an outline such as the following:

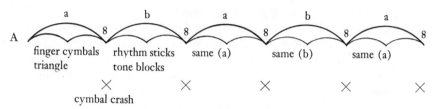

A

a	b	a	b	a
finger cymbals	rhythm sticks	same (a)	same (b)	same (a)
triangle	tone blocks			

cymbal crash

metric beat throughout: drums

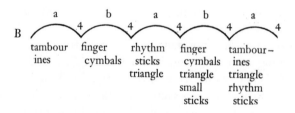

B

a	b	a	b	a
tambourines	finger cymbals	rhythm sticks triangle	finger cymbals triangle small sticks	tambourines triangle rhythm sticks

metric beat throughout: sandblocks
special heavy accents throughout: drums

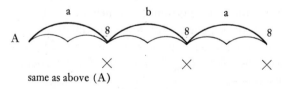

A

a	b	a

same as above (A)

Other compositions that might be used for an initial study of instrumentation and musical form are "Happy and Light of Heart" by Balfe (Rhy II), "Waltz" No. 1 by Brahms (Rhy II), and "Rataplan" by Donizetti (Rhy B).

WORKING OUT AN ORCHESTRATION. Once the children understand how the rhythm instrument arrangement should change with the form, instrumentation, and character of the music, more advanced work can be undertaken. The orchestration is not pre-planned by the teacher, but he must be so well acquainted with the music that he is able to guide the children as they make observations and determine their orchestration.

Making one orchestration may take three or more periods of work. During the first session the composition is heard, its general form is sketched out, and perhaps a rough idea of the orchestration for the first section is developed. Between lessons, some students who are particularly interested may give some thought to the project. If the music is recorded and a record player with headsets is available, individuals may hear the music several times and be prepared to make recommendations at the next lesson.

The composition chosen for rhythm orchestration must be appealing as a piece of music in itself and yet be suitable for the particular class to work with competently. Its rhythmic characteristics must be appropriate for use with rhythm instruments. The rhythm of some compositions is too intricate, or there are syncopated passages and such rapid fragmentary figures that children are not able to play them. Compositions with interwoven contrapuntal lines do not lend themselves to this use. The addition of rhythm instruments is entirely incompatible with many compositions having slow, smooth-flowing melodic lines.

The following compositions will provide worthwhile musical experiences and may lead to some very interesting rhythm orchestrations: "Viennese Clock" from *Háry János* by Kodály, "Dance of the Moorish Slaves" by Verdi (Rhy III), "The Clock" by Kullak (Rhy III), and "Amaryllis" by Ghys (Rhy B).

A creative project, designed to develop musical taste and discrimination, cannot be imposed on the pupils; it must be guided so that experience in the activity itself is the real teacher. Good judgment on the part of the teacher is essential. At one extreme, too many instruments may be played so loudly and poorly that the result is very unmusical. On the other hand the teacher may be so sensitive about tone quality and volume that the children are given no freedom to explore the sound possibilities for themselves. The instruments should never be played so loudly that they obscure the recorded music. A dynamic balance can be found between recording and instruments that permits a sense of freedom in playing.

The instruments suggested in the listing on pages 53 to 56 provide a reasonably well-balanced ensemble. Not all of the children need to play instruments at the same time. Emphasis should be on the music and the appropriate orchestration created rather than on the mass playing of instruments. Pupils should take turns so that everyone will have an opportunity to play the various instruments.

Listening to the music, discussing the form and notating on the chalkboard the possible uses of instruments, trying out each idea to hear the effect, and deciding upon the orchestration to be adopted are the important activities. As in any other creative session, the teacher needs to be skillful in developing the chain of ideas so that many pupils contribute suggestions and participate in the experimentation. The great difference between the program suggested here and that of the old school "rhythm band" is one of musical and creative values. If the music is appropriate and worthwhile, if the approach is exploratory and furthers the understanding of musical concepts, then ensemble playing of rhythm instruments can be a valuable experience.

COMPOSERS' USE OF RHYTHMIC EFFECTS. Some composers have made continuous specialized rhythm patterns a basic ingredient in orchestral compositions. Children can play these rhythm patterns with the recorded music even when the development of a rhythm orchestration is not an objective. "Spanish Serenade" by Bizet (Rhy VI) has castanets as the outstanding percussion instrument. Sixth-grade students may play the basic rhythm pattern heard throughout much of the composition:

If castanets are not available or if the playing technique is not sufficiently developed, pupils may play the pattern on claves, with alternating hands on the knees or on dry-sounding drums.

"Bolero" by Ravel has the following rhythm patterns which are easily heard:

The upper pattern can be played on high and low drums. Since the lower pattern moves very rapidly, pupils will be more successful if they use maracas or bongo drums so that both hands may be used alternately.

In the "Habanera" from *Carmen* (Act 1) by Bizet, this rhythm pattern may be played almost continuously throughout:

"Aragonaise" from *Carmen* (Act 4) may be accompanied by these patterns:

"Ritual Fire Dance" by Falla is brilliant and exciting. Pupils need to direct their attention to basic rhythms in order to play the following patterns with different toned drums. Experimentation for appropriate tone quality and dynamic level is important.

Haydn's *Symphony No. 101* is titled "Clock" because the second movement, Andante (Lis V), has a clock-like effect produced by the pizzicato rhythm of the lower strings and bassoons. Likewise, *Symphony No. 8* by Beethoven has in the second movement a metronomic rhythm which may be played on tone blocks or rhythm sticks.

Other compositions may be used but the basic rhythm patterns must be obvious and continuous enough to permit the children to hear and play them with satisfaction. Pupils should not only direct their attention to the basic rhythm, but should hear the melodic flow and improvisation above it. Through this activity the pupils become acquainted with some of the world's most colorful music.

Here is a means of exploring music that will appeal to all, if intelligent guidance goes with it. The instruments provide a convenient way to point up rhythm in the music. However, from the beginning and throughout, they must serve as an enjoyable means of experiencing music. If the technical studies become so pedantic or overemphasized that the expressive factors are beat right out of the music, then the project is in vain.

The use of rhythm instruments quite often is very successfully established in the primary grades. It can only be hoped that more intermediate classes may be given an opportunity to explore these interesting musical activities. The teacher must continually draw rhythm to the attention of the pupils. They should learn to create and to respond to increasingly complex patterns. They must learn the music symbols which represent rhythm. Consistent use of chalkboard and flannel board is necessary to show the relationship of metric beat, accent, and rhythm patterns. Gradually the approach must be shifted from explanation and the development of concepts about such symbols to the interpretation of them as they are met in new musical material. Only then will the students begin to be independent music makers.

ACTIVITIES FOR COLLEGE CLASSES

A. Written Assignments

1. Write rhythm notation for the names of four people. Select names with different rhythm patterns.

2. Hear the record "Little Indian Drum" and, using "drum talk" with story writing, create another short episode in the life of "Red Fox."

3. Create a rhythm orchestration for one short recorded composition. Diagram it and state why you suggest specific instruments for certain effects. What might the children at a particular grade level learn about music as a result of the experience?

4. Find songs to exemplify the several ways in which rhythm instruments may be used. Make brief notes for two songs under each heading. Include under handbook Section III-B.

5. Select one Latin American song that could be appropriately accompanied by rhythm instruments. Decide how you would use the instruments, and explain as was done for "Tinga Layo."

B. Classroom Projects

1. Make some basic rhythm instruments outside of class. A drum, rhythm sticks, and sandblocks would be a good beginning. Give careful consideration to the tone quality. Bring the instruments to class so that the instructor and other students may evaluate your results and benefit from your experience.

2. In a small group, prepare to sing a song and use rhythm instruments as suggested in the written assignment No. 5.

3. In a small group, improvise an original combination of rhythm patterns using at least three different instruments. Prepare to play your example.

CHAPTER NOTES

1. Muriel Mandell and Robert E. Wood, *Make Your Own Musical Instruments* (New York: Sterling Publishing Co., Inc., 1957).
2. Bernard S. Mason, *Drums, Tomtoms, Rattles* (New York: A. S. Barnes and Co., Inc., 1938).

3. Emma Dickson Sheehy, *There's Music in Children,* Revised and Enlarged Edition (New York: Henry Holt and Co., Inc., 1952), pp. 18-26.
4. *The Columbia World Library of Folk and Primitive Music,* compiled and edited by Alan Lomax (New York: Educational Department, Columbia Records).
5. Folkways Records, 117 West 46th St., New York 36, N.Y.
6. "Percussion, the Pulse of Music" from *Music for Young People* series, National Educational Television, Audio-Visual Center, Indiana University, Bloomington, Ind.
7. *Teacher's Guide* to ADVENTURES IN MUSIC (A New Record Library for Elementary Schools) prepared by Gladys Tipton and Eleanor Tipton, © by Radio Corporation of America, 1960.

OTHER REFERENCES

Coleman, Satis, *The Drum Book* (New York: The John Day Co., Inc., 1931).
Morales, Humbert, *Latin American Rhythm Instruments* (New York: H. Adler Publishers Corp., 1954).
Orff, Carl, and Gunild Keetman, *Music for Children, I—Pentatonic,* English adaptation by Doreen Hall and Arnold Walter (Mainz, Germany: B. Schott's Söhne, 1956; Associated Music Publishers, Inc., N.Y.). See "Studies in Rhythm and Melody," pp. 66-87.
——, *Music for Children* (recording), Angel Records 3582 B.
——, *Music for Children* (film), Contemporary Films, 267 West 25th Street, New York 1, N.Y.

See Appendix B for listing of companies supplying rhythm instruments.

CHAPTER FOUR

USING MELODY AND HARMONY INSTRUMENTS

One of the best ways for children to develop understandings about melody and harmony is through playing tuned instruments. These may range from tuned glasses, bells, and small xylophones to the piano and standard orchestral instruments. In early playing experiences it is important that the instruments be of simple construction and demand little skill in playing. Then the freedom to play rhythm on untuned instruments will carry over into the playing of tuned instruments.

Children should do much of their playing in conjunction with the singing program. Instruments can help enrich the singing activities, develop the ability to listen and to discern different pitches and combinations of tones, and promote interest and skill in interpreting simple melodies and tonal patterns from the printed score. In addition, children can be led to create melodies and sound effects through individual as well as group experimentation and study. Children in the intermediate grades can combine melody instruments and singing to produce harmonic effects. The Autoharp also provides an easy approach to harmony.

THE MELODY INSTRUMENTS

The xylophone and glockenspiel are classed as percussion instruments because they are struck with mallets. They are also called keyboard instruments because the tone bars are arranged in the same order as the piano keyboard. Some of them may be simplified so that as few as three tones are used.

Instruments of the xylophone type have wooden sound-bars and those of the glockenspiel type are made of metal. The larger sizes are chromatic; that is, they sound the tones represented by both black and white keys on the piano, and therefore can be played in any key. Smaller instruments that sound only eight or ten tones of the diatonic scale are used in many classrooms. Some teachers have successfully made their own xylophones out of hard wood. Detailed instructions for the construction are found in special sources such as *Creative Music in the Home*.[1] Construction kits are available for diatonic xylophones and glockenspiels; they contain tuned bars for which teacher or pupils make the framework.[2]

The instruments with metal bars have a bell-like quality. They are most useful in early singing-instrumental work. The set of one-octave diatonic bells is in the Key of C, sounding an octave above:

Because of the small number of tones, it is less expensive than other types, but its use is limited. A German firm[2] produces a diatonic glockenspiel with a tonal range:

The alto glockenspiel sounds as written here and the soprano glockenspiel sounds an octave higher. These instruments have greater potential for use because the tone bars are removable, and alternate B♭ and F♯ bars can be inserted so that the Keys of F and G major may be used. This expands the playing possibilities of the instrument considerably. Such an instrument may also be used with the F and B or other tones omitted so that a pentatonic or other limited scale is obtained.

Resonator Bells are tuned metal bars, each of which is mounted on a separate block of wood. These form the chromatic scale when properly arranged, or they may be rearranged to form any single scale or selected group of tones. They are more expensive than some other bell types but also are more versatile.

All melody instruments should be correctly tuned because the children must become accustomed to the correct sound relationships of the tones in the scale. Cheap, carelessly tuned toy instruments do not serve the purposes of music education. Instruments played in combination must be tuned to the same pitch.

Many children enjoy playing individual hand-bells, each of which has a handle and may be rung separately. If these are well tuned, they are useful for young children exploring tone and pitch relationships. The children may be able to play a few tunes on them, but the bell instruments that are struck with small mallets are easier to play rhythmically, and they have a more direct relationship to the piano keyboard.

Some teachers substitute tuned glasses if the other bells are not available. If the glasses ring well and are accurately tuned, their quality is pleasing, quite mellow, and easy to match with the voice. Eight-ounce glasses may be tuned in the Key of C; to get the complete scale, smaller glasses should be used for the higher tones. If the glasses are to be played regularly, the water line can be marked on each glass to indicate the scale step it represents so that the children can keep them in order and filled correctly for the designated pitch. Older pupils should share in the scientific experiment that determines how much water is needed in each glass; the more water in the glass, the lower the pitch.

Song Enrichments

A simple example of the use of bell instruments in early singing experiences is provided in "Hickory, Dickory, Dock" (MTD-21, FGB-164).

HICKORY, DICKORY, DOCK

Mother Goose   J. W. Elliott

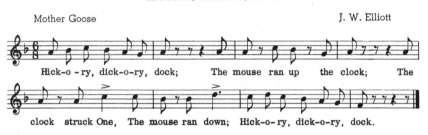

From *The First Grade Book* of OUR SINGING WORLD Series, Enlarged Edition. Used by permission of Ginn and Company, owner of the copyright.

A child may play a glissando up the bells after "the mouse ran up the clock" and a downward glissando at the end of the song. This embellishment will objectify *up* and *down* on the bells. Bells mounted on a frame may be held vertically so that the children may more readily understand the low and high concepts and think in terms of stair steps as they play toward the top of the bells. Later they should play from low to high in a left to right movement.

INTRODUCTIONS AND CODAS. Fragments of melody may be played as introductions or codas that add interest to the song. These provide experience in playing the instruments and working with specific combinations of tones. As an introduction to "Are You Sleeping?" (MTY-76), younger children may sound the key note (G) on the bells a specified number of times to represent the hour of day at which "Brother John" should arise. The same tone may be struck several times as an ending to the song.

ARE YOU SLEEPING?
(Frère Jacques)

French Round

"Are You Sleeping?" from *Music Through the Year* of the New TOGETHER-WE-SING Series, published by Follett Publishing Company, Chicago, Illinois.

John?   Morn - ing bells are   ring - ing,   Morn - ing bells are
vous?   Son - nez les   ma - ti - nes,   Son - nez les   ma -

ring - ing,   Ding,   ding,   dong,   ding,   ding,   dong.
ti - nes,   Din,   din,   don,   din,   din,   don.

Older children may create an introduction or a coda by playing the tonic and dominant tones in a pattern such as this:

The same technique may be used for other songs in which clocks or bells are the topic, such as "Oh, How Lovely Is the Evening" and "Bells Are Ringing" (MTY-67).

Imaginative pupils and their teacher can find many things that suggest introductions for songs. "Jack and Jill" (FGB-82) may be preceded by playing up and down the "hill" on the bells.

JACK AND JILL

Mother Goose   Paul Forde

Jack and Jill went up — the hill to fetch a pail of wa - ter;

Jack fell down and broke his crown, and Jill came tum-bling aft - er.

Transposed from Key of D

From *The First Grade Book* of our singing world Series, Enlarged Edition. Used by permission of Ginn and Company, owner of the copyright.

If Key of C diatonic bells are used, sing and play in the Key of C as shown. With Resonator Bells, the teacher may build the scale in D and sing in the original key.

Some second and third grade song books suggest introductions, codas, and special effects. A very appropriate introduction and a coda are given for "White Coral Bells" (MRT-93). With "There Was A Crooked Man"

(MIOT-18) it is suggested that a crooked scale be played as an introduction:

etc.

TONAL PATTERNS WITHIN SONGS. As the children become more accustomed to playing the bells and develop skill in playing rhythmically, they may begin to play by ear simple scale or chord fragments that occur in the songs. The entire song "One Two, Buckle My Shoe" (SOOW-40) is based on a scale line. As the group sings the song, one child may play this melody line up the scale and down in time with the singing. In the Scottish folk song, "Dundee, Dundee" (ABC II-120), the interval of a 5th occurs four times and may be played when the children sing that portion of the song.

DUNDEE, DUNDEE

Scottish Folk Song

From Berg, Burns, Hooley, Pace, and Wolverton, MUSIC FOR YOUNG AMERICANS, *Book Two.* American Book Company, publishers. Used by permission.

Generally, early song enrichments are confined to the scale or two- and three-toned patterns that are easily remembered and played by the children. Some primary songs are in the Key of C, and when the small diatonic bells are used children will have no difficulty learning to play the enrichment parts. Resonator Bells may be set up in any scale or combination of tones, so that in the early years pupils do not need to be concerned with key signatures, sharps, and flats, and yet may play in the key most suitable for singing. When the larger chromatic bells or piano is used, the teacher may make a keyboard diagram of the position of the tones to be played with a particular song. The pattern in "Dundee, Dundee" would be shown:

Three points should be made in regard to group singing with the bells:
1. The children should take their pitch from the bells if they are going to sing with them.
2. Very rarely are the bells so tuned that they may be used in combination with a recording of a song.
3. Bells are easily covered by the voices. When the entire class sings with the bells, the children must sing lightly and listen carefully so that they stay in tune.

Playing Melodies

Children as well as adults enjoy playing familiar melodies. If the teacher is able to remove some of the technical obstacles, children can pursue this activity with continuous satisfaction. It is best to begin with songs having a limited number of notes. There are a few appealing songs with just three tones; many songs use only five or six tones. When Resonator Bells or other adjustable instruments are available, just the tones in the song may be arranged in the proper order. Children then can play rhythmically by ear without having to search for the necessary tones.

PENTATONIC SONGS. Many melodies are based on scales other than the major scale (seven tones) that we hear so often. Fortunately, some of these melodies find their way into school song books and offer tonal variety. The pentatonic or five-tone scale is very easy to play (see Appendix A). Although we often think of it as an Oriental scale, it is the basis of many children's chants as well. Music educators in Germany have made extensive use of keyboard instruments, and have done much work with the pentatonic scale. Simple children's chants that are sung and played by ear on five-toned glockenspiels or xylophones provide the early song material for this work. "Ring Around a Rosy" is an example of a four-tone chant based on the pentatonic scale.

RING AROUND A ROSY

Children's Singing Game

This song may be played on the black keys of the piano beginning with Db or on bell instruments in which the tones are arranged as follows:

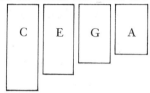

"The Farmer in the Dell," "Mary Had a Little Lamb," "Hush, My Baby" (SOOW-56), and "Old MacDonald Had a Farm" can easily be played by ear on five-toned bells or glasses. The advantage of using this scale, in addition to the limited number of tones, is that as children mature they can easily improvise counterparts for simple pentatonic songs they know.

USING KEYBOARD DIAGRAMS. When an adjustable instrument is not available children must learn the position of the necessary tones in relation to the total keyboard pattern. The MUSIC FOR YOUNG AMERICANS series uses small keyboard diagrams to show what keys are to be used in a particular song. "The Shoemaker" has just three tones; when the children know the song and can locate the notes on the instrument, they can play the melody by ear.

From Berg, Burns, Hooley, Pace, and Wolverton, MUSIC FOR YOUNG AMERICANS, *Book Three*. American Book Company, publishers. Used by permission.

The use of keyboard instruments in combination with such a diagram is an important step in developing an understanding of note position on the keyboard. First the child notices the black key combinations in alternating patterns of two and three, then he learns to find a note "to the left of two black keys" or "to the right between three black keys," etc. Later these positions are related to notes on the staff, and letter identification is established.

The teacher should think in terms of acquainting children with the arrangement of the keys and their relationship to the musical staff rather than of "teaching piano" per se. A functional use of piano and bells, the desire to explore, to improvise, and to play known melodies by ear are valuable activities. A number of the basic song books suggest interesting uses of the keyboard and the following songs are examples of types that are easy to play:

"The Bee and the Pup" (SED-31)
"The Blacksmith Sings Merrily" (ST-67)
"The Cuckoo Clock" (MAOC-162)
"Go Tell Aunt Rhodey" (AS IV-49)
"Johnny Boker" (MN&F-115)
"A Joyful Thing" (MN&F-164)
"Lightly Row" (ST-148)

"Little Carl Must Go to Rest" (SED-70)
"The Old Gray Goose" (MAOC-108)
"The Piper of Hamelin" (AS V-19)
"Put Your Little Foot" (AS IV-71)
"Whistle, Daughter, Whistle" (OLS-8)

USING NUMBER NOTATION. Another approach to keyboard instruments is through number notation, which assists children in playing simple, familiar melodies. Diatonic bells are used first and the melody is played by ear with the number notation serving as a visual guide to the correct bars, which have corresponding numbers. Gradually skill is developed, for the ear demands that the child learn to play the song as rhythmically and accurately as he and the class sing it.

As a result of this experience, the child begins to notice scalewise melodies, how they sound and how they are played on the bells. Intervals within chords become a part of his playing as well as his singing repertoire, and the relationships of the tones become more understandable to him. Again, this is not an isolated activity. It is related to the other uses suggested for the bells in this chapter.

Number notation for known songs should be prepared on tagboard sheets or in a special, heavy-paper notebook. The teacher who is able to write his own number notation can provide a bell part for any song that is suitable for his class.

Many teachers use the diatonic bells in the Key of C for this work; if Resonator Bells are available, any scale may be arranged. Third grade children who have had a year or more of experience playing songs on the small set of bells may begin to play the same melodies on the chromatic bells in the Keys of F and G, partially by ear and partially with reference to the numbers. The earliest songs used should have an easy rhythm and a predominance of scale movement in the melody:

"My Little Ducklings" (MRC-21)
"Mary Had a Little Lamb" (SOOW-14)
"Here Come the Monkeys" (MIOT-98)
"Baa, Baa, Black Sheep" (FGB-155)
"Go Tell Aunt Rhodie" (MIOT-19)

"This Old Man" (SOOW-7, MRT-122, FGB-44)
"A Play Song" (MTD-22)
"My Fiddle" (ABC K-50)
"The Happy River" (FGB-127)
"Gretel, Pastetel" (MRT-26)

When the diatonic eight-tone bells are used, the original notation of the song need not be in the Key of C, but all of the tones must lie between the low and high tonic notes of the key in which it is written. The necessity for this limitation will be clear as the teacher notates a song or two. As a first step, he goes through a song and numbers each note according to its place in the scale in which it is written:

GRETEL, PASTETEL

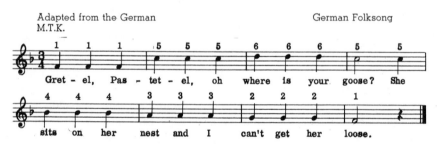

"Gretel, Pastetel," from *Music Round the Town* of the New TOGETHER-WE-SING Series, published by Follett Publishing Company, Chicago, Illinois.

Having determined the correct numbers, he writes out the text on the tagboard sheet, putting each phrase or each double phrase on one line, because children will pause at the end of the line and it is better that their pause coincide with the phrasing. Words, numbers, and bar lines should be given and, in addition, the rhythm may be suggested by rings around the tones that move rapidly or dashes after tones that are sustained. This is essentially a simple notation, and therefore no attempt is made to give it the completeness of the standard notation. In the beginning the children play it by ear as well as from the numbers.

1	1	1	5	5	5	6	6	6	5 -
Gret-	el,	Pas-	tet-	el,	oh	where	is	your	goose?

5	4	4	4	3	3	3	2	2	2	1 -
She	sits	on	her	nest,	and	I	can't	get	her	loose.

Few songs exactly fit the tonic-to-tonic range and when the children learn how to play from number notation they will be eager to try many songs. Some special considerations will make it possible to include a few more songs in the eight-tone bell repertoire.

A song in the Key of F may be played on C-scale bells if the range lies between middle C and the C above, and if the fourth tone of the scale (B♭) is not in the song. "The Mulberry Bush" and "John Brown Had a Little Indian" are examples. In such cases the number notation for tones below the tonic is indicated with a line below them and a new numbering system is assigned to the bells with the "number-one" note on the key note, F. A folded piece of tagboard can be set up behind the bells as a marker for the tones of the scale to be used.

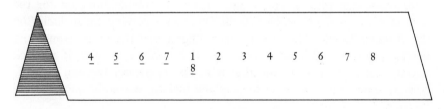

We are training ears to hear characteristic patterns in the scale and it is important that the tonic note which is the "home tone" and point of repose of the song always be specified as "1."

1	1	1	1	-	3	5	5	3	1	-
Here	we	go	round		the	mul-	ber-	ry	bush,	

3	2	2	2	2	-	1	7	7	6	5	-	-
The	mul-	ber-	ry	bush,		the	mul-	ber-	ry	bush;		

1	1	1	1	-	3	5	5	3	1	-
Here	we	go	round		the	mul-	ber-	ry	bush,	

3	2	-	2	5	6	7	1	-	-	1	-	-
So	ear-		ly	in ————		the	morn-			ing.		

When diatonic bells with alternative F♯ and B♭ tones are available, number notation may be used successfully for even more songs. The pupils will need to know that the change of tone bar is necessary and where the number-one note is located.

As they play and replay their favorite songs, the children will memorize the number notation and the intervals in the melody. They should then be encouraged to play the melodies on the piano at school or at home. All that needs to be done for songs in the Key of C is to show the children that C, the number-one note, is the white key just to the left of the two black keys in the middle of the piano keyboard.

TRANSITION TO STAFF NOTATION. When a child in the late second or early third grade can play several songs written in number notation for the Key of C, he is ready to have some experience playing his melodies on the chromatic bells. The teacher may suggest that the number-one note be changed to F and he may show the child where F is. "Baa, Baa, Black Sheep" is a good song to use if it is in his repertoire. He will immediately discover that, in order to play the melody correctly, he must use B♭ for the number-four note.

$$\begin{array}{c|cccc|cc|cc|cc|c} \frac{4}{4} & 1 & 1 & 5 & 5 & 6\,6\,6\,6 & 5 & - & 4 & 4 & 3 & 3 & 2 & 2 & 1 & - & etc. \end{array}$$

After playing several of the songs he knows in both keys he will be well aware of the fact that when the "home tone" is on F, the fourth step of the scale is B♭. Having this sort of keyboard experience with several songs and learning to hear and sing tonal patterns in their singing activities will prepare third grade children to play simple melodies directly from the staff notation in their books. At first only the easier phrases of songs in the Key of C are used, just as they were played by ear to enrich songs in the first and second grades. Then songs in the Keys of F and G may be played, because the children will understand the function and necessity for the sharp or flat note. These are good songs for early reading experiences:

In the Key of C:

"Theme" (S&R-167)
"The Frog" (MNLA-113)
"Christmas Is Coming" (MTY-53)

"Down in the Meadow" (ABC III-45)

In the Key of F:

"Out Among the Fir Trees" (S&R-151)
"Stars" (MNLA-142)

"Why Cats Wash After Eating" (ABC III-87)
"Choral Grace" (MTY-43)

In the Key of G:

"What a Happy Day" (S&R-166)
"A Churning Lilt" (MNLA-103)

"Winter Rain" (MTY-79)
"My Burro" (ABC III-116)

In all of their work with melody instruments the children should have much opportunity to play individually. Learning to play an instrument is a personal thing; a child cannot experiment and learn by doing as the entire class waits and watches. Children should have opportunities to explore both rhythm and melody instruments privately in the music center.

Number notation may be introduced in the latter part of the first grade. One or two lessons with a very familiar song will make the process clear. A few children can follow the teacher's example in relating the number notation to the numbers on the bells. Then they will be ready to practice by themselves during their free time with the bells and the notation set up for them in the music center. If a pencil with a rubber eraser is used instead of the wooden mallet, the tone will be so soft that it will not disturb the other children. Periodically the teacher should ask individuals to play for the class the songs they have learned.

Exploratory and Creative Uses

In their eagerness to teach "music," teachers should not neglect to let children discover the sound and functional characteristics of musical instruments. Useful musical insights can be gained by investigations that do not damage the instruments. Children may discover that the instruments made of metal have a more sustained, ringing tone (longer duration) than the xylophones, which are made of wood. They can notice that the longer bars have a lower pitch than the shorter bars on both types of instruments, and that pitches of the strings on the piano, psaltery, Autoharp and violin are determined by both length and thickness. In tuned glasses the height of the column of water affects the pitch of the tone.

The piano is a magnificent instrument to investigate, to learn what makes the strings vibrate, how many strings are struck by one hammer, how the high tones sound, the rumbling quality of tone produced by the lowest string, what the pedals do, etc. Chapter 3, "The Piano," in *There's Music in Children*[3] gives excellent suggestions of how young children may use the piano in unusual and satisfying ways.

FIRST STEPS IN MELODY WRITING. In early free creative uses of the melody instruments children should work with only the two tones, E and G, or the three tones, E, G, A, which provide the basic intervals in their natural chanting songs. They may chant and clap short jingles such as "Busy as a bee," "Try, try, try again," etc., and then play the same rhythm on the three-toned instrument, experimenting with different combinations of the available tones. This work reveals the value of adjustable instruments that can be held vertically. With these, children more readily understand the concept of high and low in pitch and, because the tones can be limited, the skills developed in the use of rhythm instruments lead directly to rhythmic playing on melody instruments.

Such an approach provides a valid avenue for creative music on the part of young children. Guiding principles for the teacher are:

1. Help the children find freedom in creating tunes based on the rhythm of a very short jingle or chant. (Sound the metric beat and syllabic rhythm through clapping or rhythm instruments before any attempt is made to sound the rhythm on the melody instrument.)
2. Help the children learn to sing back and show with hand levels the pattern sounded on the melody instrument. (This is a development of the ear, voice, and tonal memory.)
3. Train the children to remember and play back the pattern created.

Short class lessons can easily be carried on along with other singing activities, and, later, individuals may work in the music center during their free time. A valuable discussion of the correlation of singing and playing in creative work is given in *Creative Music for Children.*[5]

Considerable improvisation on a limited number of tones should precede the use of notation. As the children mature and tonal memory, skill, and independence in responding rhythmically develop, this work can be expanded in three directions:

1. Add a fourth tone (C), and later, a fifth tone (D), which completes the pentatonic scale. When the children are completely free in their improvisation with the pentatonic scale they can use the first five tones of the diatonic scale and, finally, the complete scale.
2. Use longer chants such as "A penny saved is a penny earned" and "To market, to market to buy a fat pig," etc. Examples are given in *Music for Children—Pentatonic.*[4]
3. Older children can learn to add accompaniments with other instruments as suggested in the reference above and later in this chapter.

Bell instruments that are mounted on a frame and can be related to the lines and spaces of the staff are especially useful in the primary grades. A flannel board with adjustable vertical bells attached to the left side enables children to play and notate their own tunes as well as tonal patterns found in their songs. When the tone bars have the letter names stamped

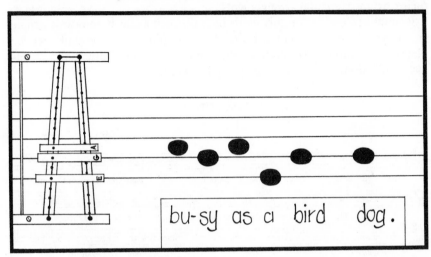

bu-sy as a bird dog.

on them, the names of pitches as well as staff lines and spaces are readily learned. In this creative work the words below the staff serve two purposes:

1. They establish a rhythmic basis for improvising.
2. They help the children understand the left to right placement of the notes to show duration in time as contrasted to the up and down placement of the notes that indicates pitch level.

After pupils have gained facility in creative melodic activities such as the above, they may make up words and longer melodies for subjects of interest to them. Individuals may notate their songs and present them to the class for consideration. If the pupils in all of their musical experiences have developed an understanding of the basic principles of musical form, rhythm, and melody, they are able to make a constructive evaluation of such original works.

Skill is developed through repeated attempts and through the insight gained with each experience. The teacher can promote creative activities in his classroom by being generous in his encouragement and at the same time training children to be objective in their evaluations. Pupils must be challenged to try again, to compose and evaluate many melodies.

PLAYING COUNTERMELODIES. Growing out of the song-enrichment activities and an understanding of notation, simple countermelodies may be played by third grade students. Essentially, these are bell parts that go all the way through the song but do not follow the melody itself. The introduction and coda suggested for "Are You Sleeping?" on page 84 may be developed into a counterpart that is played repeatedly as the song is sung. Many basic song books show countermelodies for bells, but teachers who understand simple harmony can guide students in creating their own instrumental arrangements.

Rounds are useful for this work because their basic harmony is simple and repeated in a definite pattern. An easy phrase of a round may be played continuously throughout the song. "The Bell Doth Toll" (SIH-199) lends itself to a variety of uses with instruments.

THE BELL DOTH TOLL

Three-part Round

Transposed from Key of F

From *Singing in Harmony* of OUR SINGING WORLD Series, Enlarged Edition. Used by permission of Ginn and Company, owner of the copyright.

1. In an early acquaintance with the song one pupil playing the bells can join the singers on the "bell part" (last phrase) when the voices arrive at that point.
2. The last phrase may be used as an introduction and continuous counterpart throughout the song.
3. The complete melody is not difficult and the children can easily learn to play it.
4. After the melody is well known, older pupils may be encouraged to improvise a rhythmic variation on the melody. Many rhythms are possible and the only limitations are the tones used. The following are simple rhythmic variations:

5. Another variation can be made by changing the melody through embellishment. One possibility, using passing and neighboring tones, might be:

Other easy, well-known melodies may be treated in like manner. Such experiences develop rhythmic and melodic flexibility and can lead to important understandings about the composer's art of variation.

Songs based on the pentatonic scale are useful for early experience in the creation of counterparts because almost any combination of the five tones makes an acceptable sound and improvisation can go on without a knowledge of harmony. In addition to songs listed on page 88, "The Moon Ship" (S&R-108), "Trot, Pony, Trot" (MTY-32) and "My Corn Is Now Stretching Out Its Hands" (MNLA-88) are in this mode.

MY CORN IS NOW STRETCHING OUT ITS HANDS

English words by Ralph Hess   Papago Indian Song

From *Music Now and Long Ago* of MUSIC FOR LIVING Series. © 1956, Silver Burdett Company.

Either of the following patterns might be played repeatedly as a counterpart for "My Corn Is Now Stretching Out Its Hands."

The Italian term for such persistent, repetitious melodic-rhythmic passages is *ostinato*. Other ostinato patterns may be improvised and will be most effective when played an octave higher than the melody. For this song, use the glockenspiel or the Resonator Bells arranged in a pentatonic scale built on F. The black keys of the piano or upper tones of the chromatic bells in the pentatonic scale based on G♭ can also be used.

In a similar manner, "Ring Around a Rosy" (see page 88) might be sung or played while an ostinato is improvised on the five tones, C, D, E, G, and A, in the higher octave. Examples for such work with this and other songs is given in *Music for Children—Pentatonic*.[4] In the system outlined there, the combination of basic melody and ostinato played on contrasting instruments is important. Usually the glockenspiel plays the higher, brighter part and the xylophone plays the middle-range melody.

Recorder-type Instruments

The recorder or fipple flute is a classic among wind instruments. It is made of wood, has a two-octave range and a pleasing tone. Much music was written for it during the late Middle Ages, and its use in ensemble playing is being revived. Of the several sizes the soprano recorder is most used in the elementary music program.

Instruments similar to the soprano recorder, but molded of plastic and much less expensive, have been used for many years in the public schools, The Song Flute and the Tonette are limited in range to a ninth and are quite easy to play.

The teacher who intends to use such instruments in the classroom should learn to play them in order to understand the problems involved and to more effectively guide the pupils. If he can go beyond the plastic instruments and learn to play a recorder, he will be able to enrich the music program further and show the children an avenue for musical exploration which they can enjoy for a lifetime. An instruction book is helpful in learning to play the instruments and in organizing an approach to be used in the classroom. In *Melody Fun*[6] by Buchtel the material is designed to combine singing with the playing of the Tonette or Song Flute. This approach should be the basis for the use of these instruments in the classroom music program.

As with the keyboard instruments the recorder-type instruments are useful because they specifically define tonal relationships. When the melody moves along the scale, the fingers move consecutively; when the melody skips a third, two fingers are raised, etc. Keyboard instruments generally are preferred because the child can sing as he plays. However, some benefits can be derived from recorder-type instruments if they are used wisely in conjunction with the singing program.

The Tonette and the Song Flute are most widely used in the fourth grade although they have been used successfully in both earlier and later grades. The following approach will enrich the singing program and will teach children to play the instruments:

1. Teach the children to play selected portions of songs they know and sing well. The ear then will serve as a guide and a goad to the fingers forming the pitches on the instrument.

2. It takes considerable finger coordination to cover all of the holes successfully and thus obtain a good-sounding middle C, which is the lowest available note. This tone is also the hardest to sound in tune. The first melodies played should use only the upper tones of G, A, and B, which can be made with only one hand on the tone holes. As skill is developed, lower tones may be added. (See the progression suggested in *Melody Fun*.[6]) Many basic song books contain melodies or fragments that employ only a few tones; these may be used when the children are learning to sound their instruments.

"Careless Shepherd" (MN&F-45)

"Gifts from Over the Sea" (MN&F-104)

"Hanging Out the Clothes" (MAOC-20)

"Jingle Bells" (chorus) (SED-140)

"Spring Garden" (SED-147)

"Winter Has Come" (SED-137)

3. When the pupils are able to play familiar melodies by ear, select simple songs and fragments to be played directly from the notation. Later these songs will become part of the singing as well as the playing repertoire.

4. Combine singing with playing of obbligatos and counterparts found in the song books, or assist the children in working out simple arrangements.

Success in playing an instrument depends on practicing the skills. When a singing-playing program is undertaken, all children in the class should have an opportunity to learn to play simple melodies, but a major portion of the classroom music time should never be given over to drill on technique. Pupils should be so motivated and the work set up in such a manner that they will practice and improvise in their free time. Some will develop greater skill than others and will become the natural leaders in this activity. When the class sings, they will play a melodic accompaniment while others provide harmony on keyboard instruments or the Autoharp. The most interesting, vital classroom music program is achieved when musical activities are intelligently combined.

In combining different instruments, one of the chief problems is that of tuning. Both teacher and pupils must constantly be aware of the fact that *sound* is the important consideration. If instruments that are played together are not tuned together, poor musical experiences result. When Tonettes or Song Flutes are played in groups by unskilled players, the total intonation may be very poor. The problem can be met in part by the use of the same brand of instrument. Further, students must learn to adjust breath pressure to correct the pitch. This skill requires maturity in listening and experience in playing.

Facility in playing a recorder-type instrument can lead directly to the study of the clarinet, flute, or other woodwind instruments, because the basic techniques are similar. However, it is of greater concern to the classroom teacher that, through the use of these instruments, pupils learn to play and sing, to listen, to evaluate, and to progress steadily in ability to enjoy their own music-making as their musical judgment matures.

The Orchestral Instruments

In many schools children may have special instruction on band and orchestral instruments if they wish it. Special instrumental teachers usually carry on this important project, but the classroom teacher is concerned in these ways:

1. He promotes interest and assists in discovering students who have special aptitudes, interests, or needs that would make participation in the program valuable to them.
2. He cooperates in the scheduling of such special classes so that they are carried on with greatest effectiveness and yet do not unduly disturb the working of the classroom.
3. He promotes an outlet for the skills and interests developed in the special instrumental classes.

The attitudes of the classroom teacher have a great influence on the opinions and interests of his students. If the special instrumental program is worth having, it deserves the interest and support of the classroom teacher. He must look upon it as an expanded opportunity for his pupils. Some children have innate musical talent that should be developed; others are superior intellectually, and the challenge of learning to play an instrument may enrich their educational experience. However, it is not wise to limit this experience to those who are the better scholars, for occasionally a child who has not found satisfaction in his academic studies may succeed in such a music activity.

The special teacher must work during the school day, taking pupils from their classrooms. Instruction is most effective in small classes of homogeneous instruments (strings, brasswinds, and woodwinds separately). However, since a child's preference in an instrument must be considered, a classroom teacher may have pupils in each group absent from the room at different times. When the special teacher can teach different groups on different days the classroom teacher can set up a study or activity period so that the absent pupils do not miss some vital subject presentation. Very often, however, a specialist must teach all of the instrumental classes in one school on one day of the week. In such schools the classroom teacher is hard pressed to find enough hours in that day, when all students are present, to accomplish the basic studies. However, when the school principal appreciates the value of special music studies, and when the teachers appreciate each other's responsibilities, mutually agreeable solutions can be found.

As students acquire skill in playing their instruments, opportunities should be given them to play in the classroom. The players will not only further acquaint the other children with the standard instruments, but will have an early, sociable use for their skills. Many song books show simple instrumental accompaniments. In classroom singing, the treble instruments can play descants and obbligatos, and the bass instruments can play root tones and chanting parts. (Such accompaniments will be discussed under harmony instruments.)

Those children who are studying piano privately can contribute to classroom activities. Some of the texts show simple left-hand parts for songs with easy melodies, such as "Hop! O'er the Fields" and "Lightly Row" (S&R 144 and 112). Piano students should be encouraged to improvise melodic and rhythmic variations as suggested on page 96. Those students who have a piano in the home will thus find more ways to utilize their developing skills. When they can perform small solos, their classmates may serve as a surprisingly attentive audience.

PLAYING HARMONY PARTS

The playing of simple counterparts along with the singing is a type of harmonic experience suitable for children in the third grade and above. In the intermediate grades, continued musical experiences prepare pupils for more extensive work with harmony. The Autoharp is a stringed instrument that sets up chords when a bar is pressed. Before the invention of the Autoharp it was not a simple task to provide classroom experiences in playing harmony parts on instruments; in order to sound a chord, one had to know what tones comprised the chord and how to make them sound simultaneously. The experiences in harmony came as children sang or played different parts together or listened to harmony produced by others.

When the children can become acquainted with chords through the use of such an automatic chording instrument, they can move on to a successful use of other instruments in which they build the chords them-

DIAGRAM OF CHORD MECHANISM OF THE AUTOHARP*

Press the buttons down with the left hand using the pointer finger on the tonic chord.

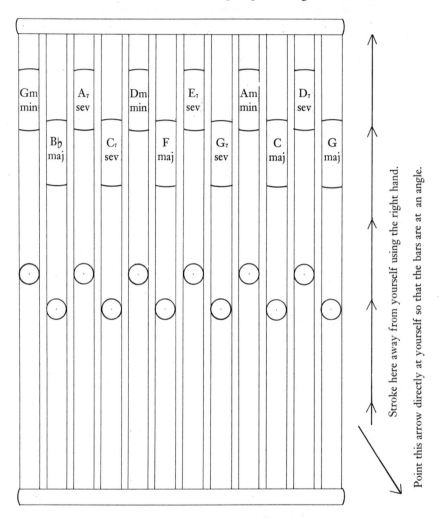

* Autoharp is the registered trade-mark of Oscar Schmidt-International, Inc.

selves. These include the keyboard instruments and the fretted instruments like the ukulele or guitar. Because the Autoharp is the simplest of the automatic chording instruments, a discussion of its use in the intermediate grades will show in what direction a study of harmony might be pursued.

The Autoharp as an Introduction
to Harmony

Five-bar and twelve-bar Autoharps are available; the latter offers so much more variety in keys that it is generally not advisable to buy the smaller instrument. At the first few group lessons with the Autoharp, when only one instrument is available, each student should have a diagram the size of the Autoharp's chord mechanism to familiarize him with the marking and relative position of the chords. Techniques may be presented to the class as a whole, but the development of skills is an individual matter. Arrangements must be made so that students may practice during their free time.

TECHNIQUES IN PLAYING THE AUTOHARP. The primary chords are the tonic (I), subdominant (IV) and dominant seventh (V_7). On the Autoharp, the bars that define the chords are pressed down one at a time by the left hand. When the pointer finger is placed on the tonic chord of a given key, the middle finger falls on the dominant seventh chord and the ring finger on the subdominant chord of that key.

left hand

When the finger pattern is established, the player may use any of the keys on the Autoharp with equal facility and may transpose from one key to another. The pressure of the finger on the bar must be firm so that all unneeded strings are stopped.

The Autoharp is strummed with a pick held in the right hand. A celluloid pick makes a loud, sharp tone, a felt or leather pick a softer tone. The beginner strokes the strings just to the right of the bars. The advanced player may cross the right hand over and stroke nearer the center of the strings, just to the left of the bars, to produce a more resonant tone.

In stroking the strings, the most common method for the beginner is to give equal length strokes on the first beat of each measure, or on the first and third, depending upon the tempo and meter of the song. The experienced player will discover different styles of playing. Some songs suggest a banjo style accompaniment, using a celluloid pick to produce alternating low and high sounding chords. Other songs need a smoother, more sustained stroke.

Before two-hand coordination is established, one player may press the bars to make the necessary chords while another strokes the strings in the appropriate rhythm. It is important that the students understand the two functions of the Autoharp, to provide the key and harmony and to establish the tempo and meter for the song.

To sing with the Autoharp the group must first find the beginning pitch of the song by some variation of the following method:

1. Determine the key and the scale degree on which the song begins.
2. Sound on the Autoharp the tonic chord in that key; or, better, play the chord progression (I–IV–V₇–I) to establish the key in the ear.
3. In the tonic chord, recognize and sing the tonic note, then sing to the scale tone on which the song begins. If the player or singers are unable to sense which of the chord tones is the tonic, the single string may be plucked with finger or celluloid pick.

Next, the player must establish the meter and tempo by stroking a two-measure introduction. If the meter is $\frac{3}{4}$ he may make one long and two short strokes, or he may merely stroke the accent beat and count silently on two and three. If the meter is $\frac{4}{4}$ he may make one, two, or four strokes for the measure, depending upon the tempo and character of the song.

By playing the Autoharp children acquire many important musical concepts. Some teachers, however, fail to pass along an understanding of what is being done, and the process is largely a mechanical, rote acquisition of a skill. Other teachers insist that all technical barriers be hurdled before the students take part in any of the pleasurable activities of playing. A fine balance in these matters is the mark of a good teacher.

When the Autoharp is introduced to an entire intermediate-grade class, it is well to select two or three familiar songs that can be accompanied with only two chords. The approach should be both by ear ("When must we change the chord in order to have it sound right with the melody we are singing?") and by chord indications in the book. In the past, music educators gave so much attention to helping children *read* music that they neglected to train the ear to *hear* it properly. Learning to chord by ear is as important as learning to follow notation.

"Down in the Valley" (ME-26) and the following are good first songs to sing with the Autoharp.

DOWN IN THE VALLEY

Traditional   Kentucky Mountain Song

{ Down in   the   val - ley,   val - ley   so   low, _____
  Hear the wind blow, dear, hear the wind blow, _____

Hang your head   o - ver,   hear   the   wind   blow; _____

From *Music Everywhere* of A SINGING SCHOOL Series, 1943. Copyright Summy-Birchard Publishing Co. Used by permission.

"Deaf Woman's Courtship" (VOA-41) (see page 145)
"Little Bird, Go through My Window" (MAOC-128)
"Little 'Liza Jane" (MN&F-140)
"M'sieu Bainjo" (VOA-52)
"Old Gray Goose" (MOAC-108)

"Paw-paw Patch" (SED-51)
"Polly-Wolly-Doodle" (SED-8)
"Skip to My Lou" (ST-186)
"Shoo Fly" (ST-32)
"Short'nin' Bread" (SIH-89)
"Sandy Land" (MAOC-24)
(see page 66)

LEARNING CHORD NAMES AND CHARACTERISTICS. During early experiences when accompanying is limited to two chords, pupils should be led to hear the distinctive qualities of the tonic and dominant seventh chords. The tonic chord is built on the key note of a scale and has qualities of arrival and stability; it is commonly called the "home" chord. In contrast, the dominant seventh chord has qualities of restlessness and instability so that movement to the tonic chord is desired.

Later, as children play in different keys and make simple transpositions, they will find it important to know that these chords are named in three different ways: in *any* key the tonic chord is built on the first step of the scale and is often labeled with a Roman numeral I. In a *specific* key it has a letter name. Thus in the Key of G, the tonic chord (I) is the G chord. The dominant chord is built on the fifth step of the scale and is labeled V. In a specific key it assumes the letter name of the fifth step of that scale: in the Key of G the dominant chord (V) is D; in the Key of C the dominant chord (V) is G. Pupils should notice that on the Autoharp the form of the dominant chord is the dominant seventh (V_7). This four-tone chord is used because the fourth tone adds a special color and dynamic quality. (See Appendix A for scale and chord charts.)

After mastering two-chord songs, children can readily play three-chord songs and begin exploring the sound of the subdominant chord (IV). The chord progression IV–I has the familiar sound of the "Amen" at the end of hymns. Pupils should compare the sound with that of the V_7–I progression. To follow chord indications in a score, it is essential that the automatic fingering pattern be well established. With the fingers moving by touch, the pupil is able to keep his eyes on the notation. "Gum Tree Canoe" (MAW-58) is a simple three-chord song.

GUM TREE CANOE

American Folk Song

From *Music Around the World.* © 1956, Silver Burdett Company.

Others are:

"Aloha Oe" (VOW-160)
"Four in a Boat" (SED-46)
"Gay Caballero" (SIH-43)
"Little Mohee" (VOW-184)
"Little White Dove" (WS-71)
"Oh! Susanna" (SED-77)
"Old Brass Wagon" (ME-105)

"Sacramento" (OLS-108)
(see page 214)
"Sarasponda" (MAOC-83)
"Swapping Song" (MAOC-136)
"Sweet Betsy from Pike" (ST-91)
"Waltzing with Anya" (SIH-41)
(see page 66)

When good facility and understanding of the primary chords is achieved, some intermediate children will be able to play songs containing other chords. They should learn to hear the distinctive minor quality of the supertonic chord (II) as in "Roll On, Columbia" (VOW-102), "Santa Lucia" (SIH-79), and "Streets of Laredo" (MAW-116).

STREETS OF LAREDO

American Cowboy Song

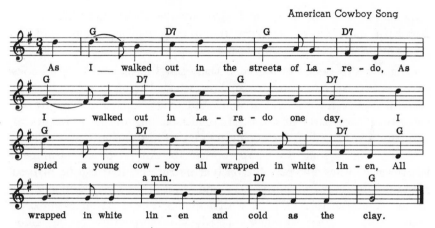

From *Music Around the World.* © 1956, Silver Burdett Company.

Songs such as "Wayfaring Stranger" (AS VI-37), "Frog Went A-Courting" (VOA-42), and "All the Pretty Little Horses" (OLS-122) are chorded for Autoharp and provide opportunities to sing minor songs with this accompaniment.

ALL THE PRETTY LITTLE HORSES

Collected, adapted, and
arranged by John A. & Alan Lomax

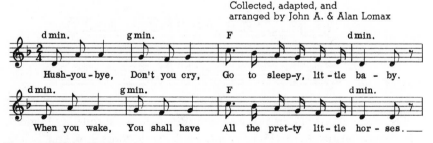

Transposed from E minor

Copyright 1934 by John A. and Alan Lomax in the book *American Ballads and Folk Songs.* Copyright assigned 1958 to Ludlow Music, Inc., New York, N.Y. Used by permission.

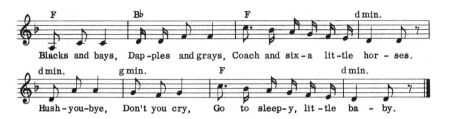

Blacks and bays, Dap-ples and grays, Coach and six-a lit-tle hor - ses.

Hush-you-bye, Don't you cry, Go to sleep-y, lit-tle ba - by.

Experiences in minor keys are limited by the chords available on the Autoharp, but there are sufficient resources to acquaint pupils with the minor mode and its relationship to the major.

CHORDING AND TRANSPOSING SONGS. Many songs in the basic music books have chord letters or numbers to show which bar on the Autoharp to press to change the chord. For unmarked songs, teacher and pupils can make their own harmonizations. An understanding of the principles of harmony gives freedom for exploration on all instruments.

Occasionally a song that is appropriate for Autoharp accompaniment is written in a key not playable on that instrument. If it can be marked with the three primary chords, I, IV and V₇, it may be played in any key on the Autoharp that keeps it within singing range. As an example of both the principles for chording a melody and transposing it on the Auto-harp sixth grade students might study "Go 'Way, Old Man" (OLS-25).

A chord may be built on any step of the scale; the note on which it is built is called the root. Chords built on the first, fourth, and fifth of the scale are the ones often used in American folk songs. To build a chord, three or more notes are piled one above the other in 3rds; a three-tone chord is called a triad.

Key of C:

Key of F:

Key of E♭:

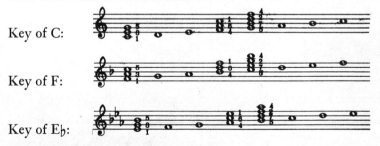

The tonic chord (I), in any key, is made of the scale tones 1, 3, and 5. The subdominant chord (IV) is made of the scale tones 4, 6, and 1. The dominant chord (V) is made of the scale tones 5, 7, and 2. When the dominant chord has another tone added above, step 4 of the scale, it becomes the dominant seventh (V₇) chord, which is used on the Auto-

harp. It is called a seventh chord because the top tone is an interval of a
seventh up from the root of the chord.

In determining the chord accompaniment for a song, the student should
first number the scale steps in the song. Then he should look for groupings of notes in the melody that are represented in a chord:

GO 'WAY, OLD MAN

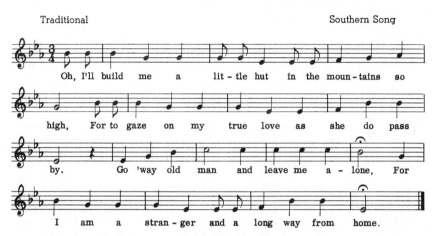

Traditional   Southern Song

Oh, I'll build   me   a   lit - tle hut   in the moun - tains   so

high,   For to gaze   on   my   true   love   as   she   do   pass

by.   Go 'way old   man   and leave me   a - lone,   For

I   am   a   stran - ger   and a   long   way from   home.

From *Our Land of Song*, 1942. Copyright Summy-Birchard Publishing Co. Used by
permission.

In this song the melody to the end of the second full measure is representative of the tonic (1—3—5) chord. The melody in the third measure
consists of scale steps 2—3—4; of these, the 2 and the 4 lie in the dominant
seventh chord. The 3 will be treated as a passing tone and not harmonized.
Next, three measures of tonic chord notes determine the chord used. In
the seventh measure, scale steps 2 and 5 establish the dominant seventh
chord as harmony and lead to the tonic chord in measure eight. In the
refrain, the second and third measures consist entirely of scale step 6,
which must be harmonized by the subdominant chord (IV). In the next
three measures all of the notes are in the tonic chord. As a cadence, in
the next to the last measure, scale steps 2 and 5 indicate a dominant chord
leading to the tonic chord in the last measure.

When the chord numbers have been placed above the song at the points
where the harmony changes, the pupils may decide on the appropriate key
to use on the Autoharp. Consult the chart of keys and chord on the
twelve-bar Autoharp.

KEYS AND CHORDS ON THE TWELVE-BAR AUTOHARP

You have this choice of chords:

		4 2 7		
6 4	1 6	V_7 (5)	5 3	
II (2)	IV (4)	Dominant	I (1)	*You may play*
Supertonic	Subdominant	Seventh	Tonic	*in these keys:*
D minor	F major	G_7	C major	C major
A minor	C major	D_7	G major	G major
G minor	B♭ major	C_7	F major	F major
—	G minor	A_7	D minor	D minor
—	D minor	E_7	A minor	A minor
—	—	D_7	G minor	G minor
—	—	F	B♭ major	B♭ major

1. Determine the range of the song in its present key (in this case, E♭ up to C).
2. Determine the nearest available keys on the Autoharp (in this case move up to F or down to C). Since the range of the song is so limited it can be sung successfully in either the higher or the lower key, although for children the Key of F is preferable.
3. Using the fingering system suggested play the I, IV, and V_7 chords in the key selected, tune up as suggested on page 104, and sing the song.

Harmony with Other Instruments

Following their experiences in making harmony with the Autoharp, children can learn to build chords on other instruments. The Resonator Bells sound well when the tones are struck simultaneously in block chords. Intermediate pupils can play the same chords on the piano, the ukulele, and the xylophone. When they have developed sufficient skill in making and changing chords, they may accompany classroom singing. The value of such activities in building interest is as great as their value in increasing skills and understanding in harmony.

SUPPLYING CHORD ACCOMPANIMENTS. A pupil building chords on Resonator Bells must know the letter names of the notes within each chord. This is called spelling the chord. The key signature must be taken into account; flats and sharps must be used to alter the names of the chord notes as necessary. Thus the activity of accompanying songs with chording instruments provides motivation for learning the names of the staff degrees and the key signatures.

			4 f
	5 g	1 c	2 d
	3 e	6 a	7 b
Key of C:	1 c	4 f	5 g
	I	IV	V₇

$$\text{Key of C:} \quad \begin{array}{ccc} & & \text{4 f} \\ \text{5 g} & \text{1 c} & \text{2 d} \\ \text{3 e} & \text{6 a} & \text{7 b} \\ \text{1 c} & \text{4 f} & \text{5 g} \\ \text{I} & \text{IV} & \text{V}_7 \end{array}$$

$$\text{Key of F:} \quad \begin{array}{ccc} & & \text{4 b}\flat \\ \text{5 c} & \text{1 f} & \text{2 g} \\ \text{3 a} & \text{6 d} & \text{7 e} \\ \text{1 f} & \text{4 b}\flat & \text{5 c} \end{array}$$

Many sixth grade classes learn the essentials of harmonic chording and are able to spell the three primary chords in the easier keys. When a song is suitable for accompaniment with such chords, individuals select single tones of a chord from the set of Resonator Bells, take them to their seats, and sound them in combination at the proper points in the song. Since Resonator Bells are chromatic any key may be used.

Because the piano and the chromatic bells are fixed-scale instruments, the position as well as the names of the tones in the chord must be known. In playing them it is helpful to know that any chord may be inverted without changing its general character. The advantage of inversion is that the notes of all the chords can be made to stay closer together on the staff and also on the keyboard. When playing consecutive chords on the piano, inexperienced players need to move their fingers only one half step or a whole step at a time (see Appendix A).

The principle of the fretted instruments (ukulele, banjo, and guitar) is this: when a string is depressed by a finger, it is brought into contact with the fret just ahead of the finger; the vibrating part of the string then is shortened and produces a higher pitch. Fretted instruments are tuned so that the hand can easily produce the primary chords. However, to change smoothly from one chord position to another requires practice. The ukulele, smallest of the fretted instruments, is useful at the intermediate level for accompanying Hawaiian songs. The tuning and tablature for three chords is shown:

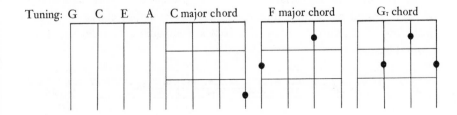

Tuning: G   C   E   A   C major chord   F major chord   G₇ chord

PLAYING ROOT TONES. Intermediate pupils may use the stringed instruments of the orchestra to provide an accompaniment for songs using only two chords. Even a pupil who has not studied the cello or bass viol can pluck the open strings (G and D) to play the tonic and dominant chord root tones in a song such as "Down in the Valley" (see page 105). On the violin the open D string (the fifth of the scale) might be sustained throughout the song, or the open G and D strings might be played following the harmony changes. The instruments are tuned as follows:

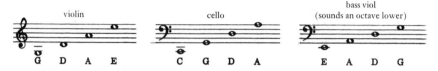

The open strings of these instruments may be used as root tones for tonic and dominant chords in the following keys:

| Key | Chord Roots | | Instrument |
	(I)	(V₇)	
G	G	D	violin, cello, bass
D	D	A	violin, cello, bass
C	C	G	cello
A	A	E	violin, bass

"The Bell Doth Toll" (see page 96) may be harmonized by plucking the open strings of the bass viol or cello repeatedly throughout the song on the pattern of the last four measures.

An easy approach to part singing is provided when some of the children sing that part (an octave above the bass instrument, unless the voices have changed) while others sing the melody. The Metallophone,[2] which is a glockenspiel-type instrument with long tonal duration sounding in the tenor range, is especially valuable for playing root tones and drone bass accompaniments.

One of the favorite variation devices of Johann Sebastian Bach was to take a "ground bass" and improvise different melodies above it. With a little rhythmic interest added, this bass accompaniment could serve as a ground bass:

The original melody goes well with this accompaniment. As the bass viol or cello continues the ground bass, play on the bells or piano the rhythmic and then the melodic variations suggested on page 97. Invent other variations. If the Resonator Bells are set up to form the diatonic scale of G, this will be easier to do. Finally, with the ground bass still going, improvise a melody that fits it but is entirely different from the original. To make this very easy, set up the Resonator Bells or glockenspiel as a pentatonic scale built on G (omit C and F♯); almost any combination of tones will then be acceptable.

For a different harmonic effect, a drone or "bourdon" bass, similar to that produced by bagpipes, may be obtained by playing continuous fifths in the bass:

The bourdon is associated with Scottish folk music and was also used by composers of the early dance, the musette. This is a very useful part to add to songs in the pentatonic mode.

Other rounds and two-chord songs may be harmonized in these ways, and when teacher and pupils are sufficiently inventive, interesting creative sessions can develop. Work with chorded accompaniments should go hand in hand with vocal harmonization, which will be discussed in Chapter Five. It is easy to sing the root tones of chords played on the Autoharp, bells, or piano.

There is enough of interest in instrumental activities to provide vital musical experience every day of the school year. However, the other areas in music are important too, and so the teacher must be selective and use instruments in the ways most suitable to his particular class.

ACTIVITIES FOR COLLEGE CLASSES

A. Written Assignments

1. Find songs with which to show each of the suggested enrichments by melody instruments. Make brief notes for two songs under each heading. Include under handbook Section III-B.

2. Write number notation for two songs to be played on diatonic 8-tone bells.

3. Invent a simple countermelody for a song. Copy the original song on staff paper and write your countermelody on the staff below.

4. Create a melody using the five tones of any pentatonic scale. Set words to it and write it on staff paper.

5. Select and copy a pentatonic song. On a staff above it notate an original ostinato.

6. Chord one of the following songs for Autoharp, using the I, IV, or V₇ chord numbers at appropriate points of change: "Go Tell Aunt Rhodey" (page 31), "Waltzing with Anya" (page 66), "Sandy Land" (page 66), "Spring Gladness" (page 142).

B. Classroom Projects

1. Be prepared to sing and to play instruments for two songs selected in written assignment No. 1.

2. Be prepared to play on the chromatic bells in the Key of C either song for which you made number notation under assignment No. 2 above. Transpose it to the Key of F or G.

3. Arrange a pentatonic scale on tuned glasses or bells using the tones: C, D, E, G, A. Play and sing one song using these tones. Play and sing the same song using the black keys of the piano.

4. Sing and play the melodies created under No. 4 above. Compare and evaluate the results.

5. Select a song that the college class or a small group will sing as you accompany in one of the following ways:
   a. with I, IV, V₇ chords on the Autoharp
   b. with three chords on the piano
   c. with the ukulele or banjo
   d. with the Autoharp or ukulele in combination with the root tones of the appropriate chords played on the bass viol or cello.

CHAPTER NOTES

1. Satis N. Coleman, *Creative Music in the Home* (Valparaiso, Ind.: Lewis E. Myers and Co., 1927), pp. 144-157.
2. Orff-Instruments, made by the Sonor Drum Co., Johs. Link Inc. (Aue/ Westphalia, Western Germany; Educational Music Bureau, Chicago, U.S. distributors).
3. Emma Dickson Sheehy, *There's Music in Children*, Revised and Enlarged Edition (New York: Henry Holt and Co., Inc., 1952), Chapter 3.
4. Carl Orff and Gunild Keetman, *Music for Children, I—Pentatonic*, English adaptation by Doreen Hall and Arnold Walter (Mainz, Germany: B. Schott's Söhne, 1956; Associated Music Publishers, Inc., N.Y.), pp. 66 to 78.
5. Satis N. Coleman, *Creative Music for Children* (New York: G. P. Putnam's Sons, 1922), pp. 108-121.
6. Forrest L. Buchtel, *Melody Fun* (Park Ridge, Ill.: Neil A. Kjos Music Co., 1938).

OTHER REFERENCES

Bishop, Dorothy, *Chords in Action* (New York: Carl Fischer, Inc., 1956).
Fox, Lillian Mohr, *Autoharp Accompaniments to Old Favorite Songs* (Evanston, Ill.; Summy-Birchard Publishing Company, 1947).

Katz, Erich, *Recorder Playing* (New York: Clark and Way, Inc., 1951).

Krone, Beatrice, and Max Krone, *Harmony Fun with the Autoharp* (Park Ridge, Ill.: Neil A. Kjos Music Co., 1952).

McLaughlin, Roberta, and Muriel Dawley, *Sing and Play with the Autoharp* (Los Angeles: Children's Music Center, 1954).

Nye, Robert Evans, and Bjornar Bergethon, *Basic Music for Classroom Teachers* (Englewood Cliffs, N.J.: Prentice-Hall, Inc., 1954). Chapter 5, "Three-Chord Melodies," and Chapter 6, "Singing and Playing in Minor Keys."

Pace, Robert, *Music Essentials for Classroom Teachers* (San Francisco: Wadsworth Publishing Company, Inc., 1961).

Pace, Robert, *Piano for Classroom Music* (Englewood Cliffs, N.J.: Prentice-Hall, Inc., 1956).

Slind, Lloyd H., *Melody, Rhythm and Harmony for the Elementary Grades* (New York: Mills Music, Inc., 1953).

FILMS

The Autoharp, Johnson Hunt Productions, Film Center, La Cañada, Calif.

Keyboard Experiences in Classroom Music No. 8, Bureau of Publications, Teachers College, Columbia University, New York 27.

Music for Children (Carl Orff), Contemporary Films, 267 West 25th Street, New York 1, N.Y.

CHAPTER FIVE

MANAGEMENT OF THE SINGING SITUATION

Singing should be an integral part of the school day in the primary grades. It is at its best when it expresses ideas suggested by a classroom situation or when it meets a need for group activity. In such a setting motivation ceases to be a problem, but the teacher must have a large repertoire of songs and flexible techniques in order to meet the varied needs of the children. A study of the singing situation reveals the need for development from teacher-management in the primary grades to considerable pupil-management in fifth and sixth grade classroom music.

PLANNING AND PREPARATION

Through the years, various methods for dealing with music in the classroom have developed. Rules have been made for scheduling music in the school day, for arranging special seating, and for using the pitch pipe to tune up for singing a song. There are reasons behind the traditional practices, but in some cases other techniques may be more in keeping with current thinking about children and music. The best teaching is based on the teacher's thorough understanding of the situation, and the exercise of good judgment.

Scheduling and Seating

Many teachers include music both at a definite time and at varied points throughout the day as needed for enrichment and for a change of pace. In the kindergarten and first grade a scheduled "music time" may last only ten minutes on some days, more on others. The length of time depends on the type of activity engaged in and the frequency of informal uses of music at other times. Twenty minutes of the school day should be given to music in the primary grades and twenty-five minutes in the intermediate grades. When music has its assigned time in the daily schedule, the teacher is less likely to omit it when pressed by other demands of the curriculum. When unscheduled, the musical experiences become random and less unified. A short period set aside can draw these experiences together, help define them and relate them to one another.

The kindergarten schedule is flexible, and there is no problem in finding a time for music. The grade teacher, however, is pressed to find time for all the subjects in the curriculum, and musical activities are worked into the schedule in various ways. Some teachers use music time as a morning activity break, following reading or number work. Others prefer it as a relief in the middle of the afternoon or as a pleasant activity at the end of the day. However, music itself is important, not only as a refreshing break in the day, but as an activity worthy of the best that children and teacher can bring to it. As often as possible, music should be scheduled for a time when the children are rested and responsive.

To create an informal atmosphere for singing, many teachers have younger children sit in a semicircle on chairs or on a rug much as they do during storytelling time. The intimacy achieved by this arrangement is good, but singing is dependent upon a proper use of the lungs and diaphragm and the posture assumed by children seated on a rug does not permit this. As a daily practice it is preferable that chairs be used. The teacher should sit where he can easily communicate with every child in the group. In such an arrangement, the child with a poor voice should be seated next to a stronger singer so that he will consistently have a favorable model to follow. Seating can be rotated from time to time so that the teacher may be near different voices and thus give more effective vocal assistance.

Many classrooms, however, do not lend themselves to flexibility of this sort and teachers must use the prevailing arrangement of desks in the room. Some teachers prefer that the children remain in their regular seats during the music period. By doing so they avoid the confusion of changing seats and also establish the idea that singing is a part of regular life in the classroom and can take place at any time.

Whatever arrangement is used, the teacher must know how each child sings and must give individuals consistent help and encouragement. To achieve this goal, one practice has been to assign "music seats" on the basis of singing voices. The best singers were seated in the back rows of the room so that their voices came forward to the poor singers seated in the front rows. It was also felt that, by being close to the teacher, the poor singers would receive more help.

This plan of seating has been useful to many teachers and still is recommended by some supervisors. Its strength lies in its provision for a definite method of dealing with problem voices. Because the teacher must classify voices in order to assign seats, he becomes aware of the level of vocal development in each child. Teacher-awareness is the first step in the development of good singing voices. Teachers who do not arrange this formal seating very often neglect to evaluate individual voices.

On the other hand, this formal seating has weaknesses that may be more or less pronounced, depending on the teacher's use of the plan. Children as well as adults are sensitive about their singing voices. When a teacher assigns seats in the front row to poor singers and seats in the rear to good singers, there may be grave psychological reactions that prevent a child from finding whatever singing voice he might develop in a more optimistic environment.

In most situations it is preferable that the ordinary classroom seating be retained for music, but the teacher should be free to move about the room among the children as they sing. In this way he will be aware of each child's vocal development, and will be able to give individual assistance and encouragement when necessary. The teacher should carry a pitch pipe and have facility in its use so that he does not have to go to the piano each time another song is begun.

It is important also that the poor singers not be grouped together. If it is impossible within the regular seating plan to have the poor singers scattered among better singers, it is advisable to make a few seat exchanges whenever any appreciable amount of singing is done.

In the primary classroom, it is neither appropriate nor necessary that formal voice testing be done. The teacher can make a much better evaluation of voices by listening as he moves about the classroom while the children sing. He can also determine abilities as individuals or small groups sing their favorite songs for other children. By the time the teacher is acquainted with the child as a personality he should also be acquainted with his voice. In the fifth and especially the sixth grades, where some part-singing is done and where the tonal range of the songs may be greater, some grouping of higher and lower voices will be necessary. General listening and observation by the teacher and some application of the voice testing procedure suggested for special choral groups will provide a basis for grouping.

The Teacher's Voice

The most desirable singing example that can be provided children is a teacher who sings and who shares a love of singing with his pupils. With training, many more classroom teachers could experience the satisfaction of helping children learn to sing. The teacher needs the flexible, natural voice of the good folk singer rather than the highly developed voice of the concert artist or operatic star. Simplicity in expressing through song the sentiments appropriate and appealing to children is the basic requirement.

Most teachers develop good enunciation and projection of ideas when they tell stories to children, but often they forget that this *same* technique must be employed in singing to children. Flexible, active use of the lips and tongue, and vitality in facial expression will go a long way in putting a song over.

One of the teacher's initial problems is to become aware of the range of the child voice and to relate this to his own vocal range. Many beginning teachers feel that, because the child voice is high, they cannot provide a suitable example. Very often these teachers have no clear conception of the range of the average adult voice, nor do they realize that with use and some directed practice the range of the voice can be extended.

Disuse of the singing voice, lack of understanding of the normal range, and unfamiliarity with the production of tones in the head register are the young teacher's chief problems. Most unused adult voices will produce D with reasonable comfort.

Compare this with the average untrained child's range, C to D and possibly E:

There is no great disparity. True, children should learn to sing higher when they have the vocal capacity, but in classroom singing the range given will permit the development of a large repertoire of songs.

Children can learn songs from hearing the male voice, which sounds an octave lower. However, because the range of the child voice lies within the range of the female voice, the woman teacher is at an advantage in providing a singing example. Some men teachers have developed the falsetto voice so that they can employ it comfortably in the actual child voice range. But falsetto is unnatural and actually unnecessary if a few precautions are taken when the normal male voice is used.

In the early stages of singing for children, the man should present a few songs in the middle register, D up to B, where it is impossible for the children to sing the *actual* pitch they hear.

male range   child range

"Go Tell Aunt Rhodey" (page 31) when sung in the Key of D is a good example. If he uses a higher tenor voice, children may attempt to imitate his actual pitch on the higher tones of a song, and then find the lower notes in the song below their range. After the man has had experience teaching songs in a limited middle range he may select those with a wider range. The following techniques will assure correct placement in the child voice:

1. Play the melody on the piano or bells in the child voice octave as the teacher sings in his octave.
2. Train the children to take the tonic note from the pitch pipe (which sounds in their octave) and to sing to the first note of the song.
3. Employ the voice of an accurate child singer as a sample for others learning a song.
4. Play the melody on the violin, flute, clarinet, recorder, or other instrument. (When the teacher cannot sing as he plays, he will have to be sure the children have previously heard the song enough to know how the words fit the melody.)

Similar difficulties may arise in the use of a recorded male voice, although many of the better singers have eliminated this problem by careful choice of range. In some cases the teacher will find it necessary to help establish the child voice at the proper octave-above level through using the pitch pipe or piano so that the children will be correctly oriented at the beginning of the song, or, if the teacher is a woman, singing the first note or phrase in the proper octave.

Every prospective elementary teacher should have as much singing experience as possible. Some individual coaching is valuable, but the chief need is to sing in a group where good diction, musical phrasing, and accurate intonation are emphasized. The teacher should be able to sing the scale and the tonic chord in tune, for his example will be copied by many children.

The teacher who does not sing well in tune may ask another teacher to teach new songs to the class, or he may find melodic support in an instrument. In addition, he should study recorded materials and learn techniques for using them. Every teacher who has a sincere desire to do so will find some means by which singing can be made a vital part of the classroom activities.

Tuning Up To Sing a Song

When a piano or other chording instrument is used to accompany singing, the player always gives the tonic chord or plays a fragment of the melody to establish the tonality of the song. In classrooms that have no piano, a pitch pipe has been the traditional means of establishing the starting tone. However, if the children are to sing with the Autoharp or bells, the pitch should be taken from the instrument rather than from the pitch pipe. When a record is used, the tonality is set by the recorded introduction, and no other tuning is necessary.

To assure a suitable singing range, songs should be sung in the correct key. Teachers who guess at the first tone of a song not only get the singers off to a false start, but put an obstacle in their path. Some children have excellent tonal memories which, if correctly developed, might lead to the possession of a fine sense of pitch. When a song is sung every day at a somewhat different pitch level, any development in this direction is thwarted. Furthermore, a child with a good pitch sense is bound to be confused because, for him, the song sounds different each time it is sung in a different key.

Any teacher who can learn to sing the tonic chord in tune may successfully use the pitch pipe. It is advisable to buy a chromatic, twelve-tone pitch pipe so that any key note may be sounded. Pitch pipes with tones between middle C and third-space C are more convenient to use than those with tones from F up to high F on the treble staff because the lower tones are more easily matched by the untrained voice.

TUNING UP FROM A KEY NOTE. To sing a song in a major key, the following tuning procedure is recommended when only one tone is sounded on the pitch pipe, piano, or other instrument.
1. Find the key note of the song from its key signature. (See Appendix A for key signature explanation.)
2. Sound the key note on the pitch pipe, sing "do" (1) on that tone, and then sing up or down the tonic chord to the tone on which the song begins, usually "do," "mi," or "so" (1, 3, or 5). (See Appendix A for explanation of sol-fa syllables.) Notice that "so" is an accepted shortening of the traditional "sol."
3. Sing the first word of the song on the correct pitch.
As an example, to tune up for "Three Little Kittens" the key note G is sounded on the pitch pipe and then the following pattern is sung.

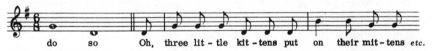

do   so   Oh,   three lit - tle kit - tens put   on   their mit - tens etc.

Often inexperienced teachers sing the syllable pattern correctly but fail to start the first word of the song on the correct pitch; hence rule 3 is important for beginners.

This tuning up process should be accurate and quick. The teacher should train himself to remember pitches so that he is able to maintain the pitch level of a song without undue repetition of the tuning up process.

Prospective teachers often ask: "Wouldn't it be a shorter process to sound the tone on which the song begins?" If the song is very familiar and the melody comes immediately to mind, no problem will arise. However, most songs are key-centered, and the tuning up process not only gives the singer the first tone of the song, but it also accustoms his ear to the key in which he will sing. Notice that in "Three Little Kittens" the tuning up pattern, "do" (1)–"so" (5), is reversed in the first two notes of the song. After hearing this portion of the tonic chord, the ear is prepared not only for the first tone but for the second and succeeding tones in the example, all of which lie in the tonic chord.

As the teacher uses the pitch pipe to tune up, the children may ask about the process. In reply the teacher should say he is tuning up to sing the song. He may have the children "help" occasionally by asking them to sing the syllable pattern after him. During the first grade the children should learn to match a tone on the pitch pipe, singing "do" (1), and then, under the teacher's direction, singing the tune-up for a particular song. Pupils in the third and fourth grades should take an active part in tuning up with the teacher's assistance.

In the fifth and sixth grades pupils can learn to tune up independently. Such training gives them a real need for knowing key signatures and understanding the significance of the key note. A metal and plastic pitch pipe may be *briefly* immersed in a cool sterilizing solution between use by different individuals. Often pupils rotate the responsibility for tuning up, one person being in charge for a two-week period. When a new song is learned it therefore becomes the responsibility of the pupils to understand the tuning up procedure rather than leaving such operations exclusively in the domain of the teacher.

The teacher may provide pupils with a key signature chart such as is shown in Appendix A, or the pupils can learn to find the key note by looking at the key signature. The following rules apply: In the key signature the last sharp to the right is scale step 7 (ti). The last flat to the right is scale step 4 (fa). The key note is 1 (do) or 8 (do).

THE MINOR MODE. It is important that children sing songs in the minor as well as in the major mode. (See Appendix A for examples of minor scales.) With a different organization of tones, a scale has a different sound. The teacher should note that both the minor and the major can

SIMPLE SIMON

Mother Goose   J. W. Elliott

"Simple Simon" from *Music Round the Town* of the New TOGETHER-WE-SING Series, published by Follett Publishing Company, Chicago, Illinois.

convey a variety of moods: whimsical, merry, mysterious, sad. The scale itself does not determine the mood of the song. "Simple Simon" (MRT-118) is an excellent example of a lively song in the minor mode.

In this, as in songs in the major, tone calls (see brackets above song) can be used to bring characteristic melodic fragments to the attention of the children. The system of sol-fa syllables is used to label tones in the minor as well as the major scale. After fifth and sixth grade pupils have had considerable experience with minor songs, they can learn to tune up independently. It is well that they learn to sing and hear the difference between major and minor chords. A good direct example is given when they are instructed to sing the following after sounding the major key tone as determined by the key signature.

To sing a song easily, the tonality of the tonic chord must be established. This process is similar in the major and the minor modes. The first step in tuning up is to determine the position of "do," assuming the song to be in a major key:

In "Simple Simon," "do" remains on the third line regardless of the mode determined. If it is in major mode, the key will be Bb and the tonic chord that establishes this key in the ear will be bb-d-f (do-mi-so). If it is in the minor mode, the ear should be oriented to the minor tonic chord, g-bb-d (la-do-mi), of G minor by singing:

The singing should stop on the tone of the chord on which the song begins (in this case, mi). If one needs to know the name of the key, he must remember that "la" is the minor key note and, therefore, this particular example is in the Key of G minor.

But is it in minor? Any one or all three of these "clues" will help determine the mode:

1. The song ends on "la" ("Simple Simon" does). This is a reliable

clue, because a major song will not end on "la." A song in the minor, however, may end on "do" or "mi."

2. The "core of tonality" in the song as a whole is "la-do-mi" (the minor tonic chord). The tones of the song center around this minor chord more than they do around the major tonic chord, "do-mi-so." (Notice how the melody of "Simple Simon" is woven around these notes.)

3. "So," and sometimes "fa," may be raised by a sharp or a natural sign. The tones are then called "si" (see) and "fi" (fee). This tonal alteration indicates the harmonic or melodic form of the minor mode (see Appendix A for analysis) and is a very good clue on which to base a decision about mode. "Simple Simon" is in the natural minor mode, and so these alterations do not occur.

When one is in doubt about the mode of a song, he should tune up using whichever tonic chord will best prepare him to sing the first phrase.

TRANSPOSING A SONG. Should a teacher change the key of a song to make it more singable for himself or for the children? Certainly, if he has sufficient understanding of the child voice to make a sound judgment and if he knows how to transpose. The comfortable range for the child voice lies between middle C and D or E above, but other factors should be considered.

1. Some children may be able to sing tones higher or lower than those indicated, but the vocal development of the majority should determine the range.

2. The character and topic of the song determine, to some extent, the range of the song. A song about the sky, clouds, or birds might have a higher general range than one concerned with machinery, an elephant, or vigorous activity.

3. The pitch level of sustained or repeated notes needs more consideration than does the pitch of occasional higher or lower notes. A song with a brief high E or F may be much easier to sing than one in which D is the highest tone but is sustained for a longer period. On the other hand, middle C when it is encountered briefly is acceptable, but a song that sustains or repeats this pitch several times should be transposed upward if the upper limits permit.

Raising or lowering a song a half step or a whole step is generally enough to remove range problems. The practice of beginning a song in an undetermined lower key, without reference to a pitch pipe or piano, invariably leads to careless teaching and poor singing.

Although considerable skill and training are needed to transpose a melody on an instrument, there is no great problem when the voice alone is used. This well-known singing game will serve as an example:

THE FARMER IN THE DELL

Traditional

The far-mer in the dell,___ The far-mer in the dell,___

Heigh - o the der - ry - o, The far-mer in the dell.___

1. Determine the key in which the song is written (G) and the scale step on which the song begins (so).
2. Judge whether transposition is really necessary; note the highest and lowest tones in the song (D-E). Might they both be moved upward or downward and still remain within acceptable limits? If so, will one half step or a whole step higher or lower better meet the singing requirements of the class? This is an activity song which may become screeching in quality if sung too high. The song may be moved down a whole step and the lowest tone will still remain within the child range.
3. Having decided what transposition is necessary, the teacher sounds a new key tone on the pitch pipe, as much higher or lower than the original key note as was judged necessary. This tone substitutes to the ear for the home tone, "do." All the notes in the song retain their original number or syllable names. G was the original key and F, a whole step lower, is the new key note. The first tone of the song remains "so" (5).

so do

The teacher may pitch a new song lower or higher if the change seems justifiable. He should then listen to discover whether the range is most suitable for the group. If so, the song should thereafter be sung in that key.

Under older, more authoritarian systems, the music teacher transposed the song and did not discuss with the singers the reason for this action. Intermediate grade pupils can gain understanding about voice range and keys by discussing and experimenting to determine the key most appropriate to their voices. The poorest singer in the group may turn out to have the best understanding of the tuning up process and of the necessity for transposition.

TEACHING THE SONG

In just what setting will a teacher plan the first singing of a song? A dynamic situation may arise into which a new song fits perfectly. One day Billy told, with mixed awe and excitement, about the arrival at home of his new baby sister. Did Billy know a song to sing to his sister? No, he wasn't that well prepared for her arrival. His kindergarten teacher remedied the situation immediately by teaching Billy and the class the delightful "Everybody Loves Baby" (see page 40). No "motivation" was needed; the song was "right" for a situation such as can arise in any classroom. This teacher had been working with small children for three years, and during that time she had collected a useful repertoire of songs. She said that her most successful song teaching occurred when she could meet the need that arose out of such unforeseen events.

In any setting, one prerequisite is this: the teacher must know the song well before he presents it. If the song is taught from a record, the teacher should know the words so that he can sing along with the record when necessary. If he is using only his voice he must be able to tune up quickly and get the song under way without losing the interest and attention of the children.

In his planning, the teacher must examine the possibilities for the use of simple instruments and bodily movement, so that he will be able to guide the children in their exploration of such enrichments. Many young teachers underestimate the need for having a complete command of material and activities.

There is no one formula for presenting a new song. The variable factors are many: the song itself and its appeal, the mood and atmosphere in the class, the teacher's ability to sing a song and to project an idea. A teacher who has a lovely voice and an intimate way of singing can captivate the entire class, and may need little additional aid to make the children enthusiastic about singing. Teachers who are less gifted vocally, who cannot project a mood well, need to give considerable thought to their presentation and should use various methods of motivating the class. In the primary grades, pictures and other objects may be used to capture and hold interest as the teacher sings a song a time or two.

In presenting a song to young children the teacher should hold the interest and attention of the children in much the same manner as he does when he tells a story. He should sing with clarity so that the children can understand the words and can discuss the ideas in the text. As often as possible, the melody and the words should be given together (i.e., sung rather than spoken) so that the process of learning the melody is shortened. If the teacher's enjoyment of the song is shared with the children, they will be eager to make it their own. Obviously such a situation can exist only when the teacher truly likes the music himself. The song that has sufficient appeal will not present formidable teaching problems. Even when the presentation of a song is done by means of a recording, it need not be an impersonal thing. If the teacher is near the record player the substitute voice does not displace the teacher's personal interest and enthusiasm.

Teaching the Song with the Voice

A recording may be a very satisfactory way to present a song; some teachers who sing well use the recorded version to bring variety into the singing program. However, in the actual teaching of the song nothing is as effective as a reasonably good voice. For a simple, repetitious song one presentation may result in the spontaneous singing of it. Many easy songs should be taught because they bring singing success to children with little experience and native ability. A longer song may require three days to a week of study to assure correct singing by the children alone. Even with longer songs the singing should be shared as soon as possible, the children singing along on the easy parts and teacher singing the more difficult spots alone.

SINGING SELECTED PHRASES. The teacher may deal with the new song in a number of ways: He may sing the whole song and then discuss the points of interest with the children. He may then repeat the phrases dealing with the points of interest, with the children singing the phrases in response. "My Airedale Dog" (NMH I-14) is an example.

MY AIREDALE DOG

Marion K. Seavey   Gertrude E. McGunigle

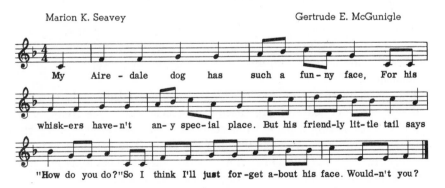

From *Experiences in Music for First Grade Children.* © 1949, Silver Burdett Company.

After the first singing, a conversation about breeds of dogs that the children have as pets might lead into a discussion of their characteristics. A picture of an Airedale would heighten the interest, but the song itself is appealing, and the teacher's first singing of it would undoubtedly capture the interest of the children. Then, if he has sung it clearly, and has put across the ideas in the text he might talk about it: "What is funny about my dog's face?" He then sings:

For his whisk - ers have - n't an - y spec- ial place.

"Can you sing that part?" The teacher re-sings and then the children sing the phrase. "He really isn't very handsome, is he? But he is such a friendly fellow! What shall we do about his face?" The children answer, and the teacher sings:

So I think I'll just for - get a - bout his face. Would - n't you?

"I think you could sing that part too! Try it after I sing it now." Teacher sings and childen sing.

And so the children actually begin to learn the song as they discuss the text. The teacher may then sing the entire song and signal the group to join in on the two phrases they know. The two remaining phrases can be learned separately and then combined as the children sing the entire song.

The technique of combining the learning of phrases with the discussion of the text is practical because it gets the singing going very soon. Talking about the words is necessary for understanding the song and helps the children remember the text, but the words should not be kept separate from the melody. The procedures used for different songs will be as varied as the songs themselves, and there will be little danger of the teacher slipping into a monotonous routine of teaching every song in the same manner.

The "phrasewise method" of teaching a song prevailed for many years and was well defined and organized: the teacher sang the first phrase and the children sang it back; the teacher sang the second phrase and the children echoed it—and so on through the song. The teaching example given with "My Airedale Dog" is a variation of this technique, but it is a more interesting and dynamic way to learn a song.

Although the phrasewise method became a routine, formalized way of teaching, it was useful because it gave the unimaginative teacher a pattern to follow. It is possible that using the varied techniques suggested above could lead to a disorganized approach to singing and could thus be confusing to the children. Flexibility and creativity are highly desirable, but the presentation must have meaning and continuity as well. Creative teaching is based on planning and imagining ahead of time just as formal, patterned teaching involves planning. With the latter, once the pattern is established a daily plan is less imperative. In creative teaching, each new song and each new class of children will suggest new, interesting approaches if the teacher will free his thinking enough to see them.

After the children have heard the song, any pleasing phrase or tone call may be a starting point for them to sing. Often the last phrase serves this purpose, the children chiming in at the end as the teacher re-sings the song. Whatever fragment the teacher selects should be rhythmic and interesting in its melody and words. It should be easy to sing. The harder phrases should be left until the class has heard the song several times.

The phrase endings of the folk ballad "The Little Pig" are suitable fragments for early singing by the children.

THE LITTLE PIG

Traditional   Vermont Folk Song

From *Our Land of Song* of A SINGING SCHOOL Series, 1954. Copyright Summy-Birchard Publishing Co. Used by permission.

The children will listen for the story as the teacher sings the song the first time. Then the teacher may say, "There is a part of this song that sounds as though the old woman is humming to herself. I wonder if you could sing it like this" (teacher sings, then children sing):

The teacher may then say, "As I sing the song all the way through, you be ready to come in with the old woman's hum at just the right time."

The next day the teacher will sing the song with its several verses as the children "help" on the phrase endings. When the children have heard the song several times, the teacher can say, "I think you are ready to sing the whole song now." The group then sings with the teacher helping in a soft voice.

An experienced teacher will know ahead of time that the children may err in specific places because the song fails to follow its own pattern. Sing and compare:

Notice especially that "pig" is sung first on two tones, then on one tone. The best insurance for the correct singing of these fragments will be:

1. The numerous motivated hearings the children had when they sang merely "the old woman's hum."
2. The teacher's consistent correct rendition, which is the result of careful initial study of the song. He should always carefully recheck his singing with the notation because it is easy for small errors to creep in.

If the children's first attempt results in incorrect singing of these fragments, each may be sung separately two or three times as a tone call before the song is sung again.

There was a time when teachers were instructed never to sing with the children. The rule was that the teacher's voice should be used chiefly as an example, and that the children would learn independence in singing if they were not assisted by the teacher. Children need to learn to sing independently, but independence is not the only concern in the early years. It is much more important that children learn to enjoy singing and steadily improve their individual ability to sing. Singing is an activity to share with others. As a member of the child's school society the teacher should expect to share this enjoyment with the pupils. If a teacher sometimes sings along and sometimes listens, independence in singing will develop in a satisfactory manner.

There are other reasons for the old rule that teachers should not sing with their pupils: some teachers do not know how to sing softly! Their voices dominate the singing and they are not able to hear and evaluate the singing of the children. If the teacher is not able to subordinate his voice, he should not sing along at all, or he should whisper the words to give the impression of his occasional participation.

ACTIVITY-HELD INTEREST. Singing is only one means of making music; it should be combined with other activities to assure every child a rich musical experience regardless of his vocal development. Rhythmic movement and the playing of simple instruments are two activities that may build interest in learning a song, and maintain interest until the song has been heard enough times to be sung in its entirety. This technique is a "whole-song" method of teaching. An example is found in the finger-play, "Where Is Thumbkin?" (KBk-51), which, in the third or fourth grade, will be learned as the round, "Are You Sleeping?"

WHERE IS THUMBKIN?

Finger Game   French

From *The Kindergarten Book* of OUR SINGING WORLD Series, Enlarged Edition. Used by permission of Ginn and Company, owner of the copyright.

As soon as the children hear "Busy" (see next page), they are eager to step and tap their feet, clap, turn around, and sit down right along with the rhythmic swing of the song.

As the children have the fun of joining in with the action while the teacher sings, they will spontaneously sing along on some of the easier phrases. What a painless way to learn a song! However, before too many wrong notes creep in, the children should take time to practice without action. As the teacher sings the separate phrases he may use one or two tone calls (see brackets in song). Then everyone sings and moves again to the music before going on to something else. Other songs such as "Old House" (MIOT-83) and "Jingle Johnny" (KBk-140), given on pages 41 and 58, can be learned with the activity as an interest-holding feature.

BUSY

Words and music by Alice E. Workman

From *Experiences in Music for First Grade Children.* © 1949, Silver Burdett Company.

THE PIANO AS AN AID. When teaching a new song, it is preferable to use the voice alone, not only because greater teacher-pupil rapport is possible, but because children can match tones with those of another human voice more readily than with those of an instrument. However, if the teacher feels insecure in singing unaided, he may support his voice by playing the melody line on the piano. Use of the piano is highly preferable to out-of-tune singing. The piano should be at the front of the room so that the teacher may communicate with the children as he plays. Techniques suggested for teaching a song with the voice are applicable, except that the tone is taken from the piano rather than from a pitch pipe.

On occasion the teacher may wish to make the initial presentation of a song with his voice and a piano accompaniment. This may be done if the piano is in such a position that the teacher has eye contact with the pupils and if he knows the song very well. The accompaniment should enhance the song and support but not dominate the voice.

Using Recorded Song Materials

All companies publishing basic song books supply recordings of many of the songs in each book. In addition, many folk singers and artists have made fine records that appeal to children. These records are an invaluable aid to the teacher with limited singing ability, and they enrich the music program in the classroom of a competent singer as well.

QUALITY AND SELECTION OF RECORDS. As with all audio-visual aids, the quality of these recordings varies greatly and each teacher must judge what will be suitable for his room. Some points to be considered are these:

1. The quality of a voice that children are expected to imitate should be pleasant and unaffected. The unnatural "operatic" type voice should be avoided as much as the nasal twang of the "hillbilly" singer.
2. The melody should be within the vocal range of the children who will sing it. One of the chief criticisms made of earlier recordings was that the songs often were too high for the average classroom of children.
3. The interpretation should be expressive, so that the intended mood and feelings are conveyed.
4. The enunciation should be clear, so that the text is understood.
5. The accompaniment should be appropriate and musically performed.
6. The recording should be long enough that the listeners can get a good understanding of the song from one hearing. For very short songs more than one stanza might be used, or an instrumental group might repeat the song.
7. The recorded song should be accurate and should conform to that printed in the text.

The records designed to accompany basic texts and other books are listed with those books in Appendix B. Other records are of value to the teacher. Folkways has recorded songs from Ruth Seeger's *American Folk Songs for Children*.[1] On a record with the same title, Pete Seeger sings with a five-string banjo accompaniment. There is considerable variety among the songs and the activities they are designed to promote. Likewise, *Songs to Grow On*[2] and *More Songs to Grow On*[3] are recorded in very useful arrangements.

Charity Bailey charmed her own class with her songs before her recordings were made by Folkways. In *Music Time* she accompanies herself on the guitar, talks, sings, and invites the children to sing with her. Frank Luther has recorded for Decca Records many song-stories that are appealing to primary children. Tom Glazer, in his recordings for *Young People's Records*, has a pleasant baritone voice in a middle range so that the children have no difficulty singing with the record. He suggests many activities in connection with songs that are related to some central theme.

Young People's Records and the *Children's Record Guild* have issued records that are especially good for individual children to use at home and in nursery school or kindergarten groups. Recordings by well-known choirs and folk singers are useful in the intermediate grades when song literature has an important relationship to the social studies.

TECHNIQUES IN USING RECORDS. Teachers who do not sing well have found that recorded songs enable children to enjoy a great variety of song literature. Techniques for teaching a song with the aid of a record are as varied as those the teacher employs when using his own voice as a model. The chief problem is that difficult parts of the song cannot be isolated and rehearsed as they can be when the teacher sings and has the children sing phrases that need special attention.

In the kindergarten, which is less formal, the chief aid to the learning of a song from a recording is the repeated hearings that children demand. Easy songs present no problems if they are heard several times. In many children's records the artists invite the children to participate in various ways, and so there is little problem for the teacher.

When teaching from other records, the teacher may need to motivate listening by planning appropriate activities so that the children will hear the whole song several times before they attempt to sing it:

1. They may listen two or three times in the process of finding out what the song is about.
2. They may hear it several times as they participate with bodily movement or simple instruments.

Children and teacher should listen for phrases or tone calls where they may briefly join in the singing and then listen again as the artist sings the more difficult parts. This same technique is suggested when the teacher uses his own voice. Early singing is important, for children like to "get in the act" and should do so before their enthusiasm wanes.

Another technique is "whispering" the words as the voice on the record sings. This method is successful after the children are able to follow the text of the song printed in the music book. The practice serves two purposes:

1. It helps to establish the tempo and rhythm in the children's singing response. Often when a group of children first sing with a record, they fall behind because they cannot hear enough to follow the tempo.
2. When the rhythm and the text have been established in their minds, the children are able to connect them with the melody, which they can hear as they whisper.

This mode of participation is not unnatural for anyone who has the words before him and is hearing a recorded song for the first or second time. However, the teacher must use it with good judgment because we want classrooms of singing children, not silent mimics. Young children should not hum with a new recorded song because humming, when attempted with a large group, results in an indefinable sound not at all related to the melody desired.

Other techniques may be employed in the classroom of the teacher who does not sing:

1. A few children who learn songs most quickly and accurately may sing along with the recording before the entire class joins in.
2. After the record has been heard several times and the words have been reasonably well related to the melody, the teacher might play the melody on the piano or other instrument while a small group or the entire class sings. (The instrument would not be played with the record.)

In their first attempts at singing with a record, pupils should sing lightly so that they can hear the recorded voice. The teacher must regulate the volume of the machine so that it gives enough support and yet does not sound unduly loud. On the other hand if the volume is too soft the children, in trying to sing under the record sound, will use such a hushed tone that their singing will be restrained and unnatural.

The teacher may use a recording to teach a new song and to get the singing started, but the class should occasionally sing the song unaided by the recording to develop the ability and the understanding that they can sing independently whenever they wish. The teacher may start the singing by playing the introduction on the record and then lifting the needle, or he may tune up with the pitch pipe or the piano.

Sometimes a teacher may choose to make the first presentation of a song by means of a record, and then use his own voice to assist the children in learning specific portions of the song. This procedure lends further variety to classroom singing and gives the children an opportunity to hear different voice qualities. Even after they have learned to sing a song independently, pupils may enjoy and benefit from a rehearing of the recorded version.

Many times the recorded accompaniment may suggest to children a good way to use their own instruments. Some rhythm instruments may be added to singing with the record, and later the song may be sung and accompanied by the children themselves. These ideas may carry over to songs that are not available on recordings, and thus the entire singing program is enriched.

The Use of Song Books

Most school districts supply a music book for each child from the second grade up. This is a basic requirement for adequate music teaching. The teacher should have single copies of several song books in addition to the basic text, for it is not possible to find in one book the variety of song literature a class should experience in a school term. For those classrooms where books are used effectively, a set of supplementary books gives the children a wider choice in songs.

MUSIC PRIMERS. Although books to aid the song-learning process generally are not used until the second grade, publishers have recognized and responded to child interest in color and pictures related to the songs they sing. The result has been a number of very attractive music primers (see Appendix B). In these small colorful song books the words and melody are included to provide a visual experience for young children. The books may be used to interest the children in learning a new song, or they may serve as an enrichment after the song has been learned.

Children cherish a colorful song book in much the same way that they do their favorite picture-story books. When they know the songs, they delight in following the tune and the words, either individually at the library table or as a group. In some of the books, the songs are arranged in story sequence so that interest is held for several pages. From this visual experience children may develop general concepts about music notation, the left to right flow of melody on the page, the rise and fall of a melody line, the more common rhythmic notation in which groups of notes are associated with movement, the following as "running notes," "walking notes," or "skipping notes" respectively.

However, there should be no attempt to promote music reading per se with these primers. It is vitally important that young children learn to sing and to use singing as an expressive force in their lives before any attempt is made to interpret notation. The experience is equivalent to that of learning a language: the child learns to use the words effectively before he is required to interpret the printed symbols that represent them on the page.

SONG BOOKS IN PRIMARY GRADES. The same use of books carries over into the early second grade. Pupils learn some new songs taken from the music book, which will be used later, and they re-establish singing voices by reviewing many easy, familiar songs. However, there comes a time during the year when the teacher feels that books can be helpful in the learning of new songs and that the pupils will benefit by guidance in observing more in the music score.

Some second grade teachers delay the general use of books until mid-year because using them too early hinders the singing program. The music book is a distraction, for children like to browse, looking at the pictures and the notation. Further, when children have not yet learned to find page numbers efficiently, the pace of the lesson is slower. However, books hold great interest for the children and will aid the music program once their use is established.

When, in his estimation, the children are able to benefit from a general use of the books, the teacher should plan a lesson or two in which the children become acquainted with the books. The pupils will want to look through the book and find the songs they know. They will study the pictures and sing these songs while looking at the words and the notation.

One problem that may arise is that of reading consecutive stanzas in a song if more than one stanza is written under the music line. (In some texts the second stanza is printed in verse form at the bottom of the page.) The first song of this kind encountered should be one in which two or more stanzas have previously been learned without books. Then when the printed song is before them, the children will be able to follow the unaccustomed order of the lines of the text more easily.

One teacher solved the problem by cutting page-width markers of construction paper, which the children held under the words they were singing and moved down the page from line to line on each stanza. The teacher could see by the position of the markers which children did not understand the order of the lines. This device was used for a few weeks, with both familiar and new songs, until the children had established the practice of reading the first line under the music score all the way through the song, and then returning to the top for the second stanza.

Teaching the melody of a new song with books in the hands of the children does not differ markedly from the techniques described earlier. However, the teacher is less concerned with other motivation, because pictures and readable words provide much of the interest. Just how a song is presented depends upon the reading level of the children and the vocabulary in the song.

The teacher may sing the song or play the recorded song and then discuss the topic and the interesting aspects of the music before the books are opened. The children depend on only their ears to tell them about the song. The development of aural perception is basic at all levels of participation in music. The visual perception supports and defines in another way the sounds that the ear hears. When the books are opened, the children see the visual representation of what was heard, and the teacher gradually leads them to understand the accepted notation for specific musical effects.

At other times the books are opened to the new song; the children may notice the pictures, poems, or other items of interest on the page. They may read the text and perhaps talk about it before they hear the music. This approach can be used when the vocabulary is within the reading limits of the children. Specific musical characteristics for which the notation is familiar may be recognized, discussed, and sounded as a preliminary exploration of the way the music goes.

As an example of this visual approach to a new song: a second grade teacher, in introducing "Dundee, Dundee" (see page 86), might ask the children to look at the song to see what it is about. Some of the words would be above their reading level and so he would need to discuss these and clarify the ideas in the text. Next he could ask the pupils whether they can tell anything about the way the song sounds by looking at the notes. "Is the rhythm even or uneven—does it seem to walk, run, or skip? . . . Yes, it is a skipping rhythm. Who can clap a skipping rhythm?" After the rhythm is established, all of the children may clap it and chant the first line of the text in that rhythm.

The teacher may then ask, "Does the rhythm skip all the way through?" The children will see that on the words "Dundee, Dundee" it does not skip. The teacher may play this pattern on the bells and then ask the children to sing it. One child may then play the bell part as others sing it and the teacher, alone, sings to the end of the phrase. The teacher would then sing the song from the beginning with the children chiming in on the part they now know.

Children in the late third grade might be able to go further with their initial visual observations and independent interpretation. If they are experienced in playing bell parts, one child might find the notes for "Dundee, Dundee" unaided by the teacher. With guidance, the children might recognize the basic scale movement in the second line, which then could be sounded out on the bells.

At no time should this process become laborious. The teacher should give enough aid to keep the observations and singing going, but he should also lead the children to feel that musical discoveries of this sort are enjoyable challenges.

Both the aural and the visual approaches to new songs should be used with second and third grade children. Teachers' books for the basic song series give detailed suggestions for such an approach to songs at this level.

INTERMEDIATE GRADE USE OF SONG BOOKS. Children in the intermediate grades learn songs very quickly when they have guidance and the desire to learn. At this level the teacher must not think in terms of teaching "by rote" or "by note," for the only time a song is taught by rote is when it is learned entirely by ear. Children who can read a song text and who have had considerable association with music notation should not be subjected to such song-learning conditions unless it is absolutely essential that they learn a song for which no copies are available. Every song learned with the aid of the printed page offers some opportunity to expand understanding of notation and to apply the skills developed earlier.

In Chapters Three and Four many suggestions were made about the growth of musical concepts through the use of rhythm, melody, and harmony instruments. It is expected that through these experiences, as they are promoted along with singing, pupils will learn a great deal about music and its notation. Pupils should continually be given greater opportunities to interpret notation for themselves. In the following chapter we will consider the sol-fa syllables as another important approach to the understanding of melodic factors in music.

BROADER SINGING EXPERIENCES

Although most of the singing up through the fourth grade is of unison songs, there must be gradual development in awareness of harmony. Experience should be broadened throughout the intermediate grades to the point where sixth grade classes can sing and play music in two or three parts.

The self-contained classroom offers excellent opportunities for intermediate-grade children to develop musical independence. They can learn to tune up and direct their own songs; when student-management is promoted, musical activities are much more important in the out-of-school lives of the pupils. They must be given careful guidance so that skills and musical judgment develop properly, but at the same time musical independence is encouraged.

Learning To Sing Harmony Parts

Traditionally two-part singing has been done in the fifth grade and three-part singing in the sixth grade. We recommend that harmony singing be developed in these grades but that it be done in a manner compatible with the music-making skills of the children. Considerable improvisatory harmony singing should be done, much of it in conjunction with simple harmony instruments. In the self-contained classroom the program can be interesting and vital, but in most cases it does not lead to the impressive three-part unaccompanied singing that has been traditional under the direction of a special teacher. If freedom in two-part singing and some experience in simple three-part harmony can be achieved in the general classroom, a substantial basis is laid for choral singing in special groups under expert leadership.

TECHNIQUES IN THE USE OF ROUNDS. Early experiences in singing harmony are provided by rounds, which can be used in many different ways, depending on the maturity and musical experience of the singers. After the melody has been learned in unison, it may be sung in two equal parts. Later, when skill in hearing and singing two parts is well developed, rounds may be sung in three or four parts. The musical value of the experience lies in the singer's ability to hear the total effect. A group should not try to sing in more parts than the members are able to hear as a whole while they sing.

The following round will serve as an example of musical experiences that may be promoted.

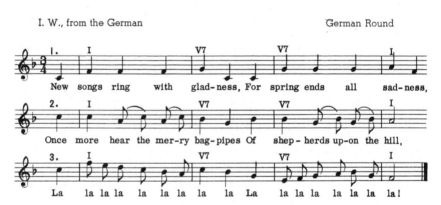

SPRING GLADNESS
(Es tönen die Lieder)

I. W., from the German   German Round

"Spring Gladness," from *Voices of the World* of the New TOGETHER-WE-SING Series, published by Follet Publishing Company, Chicago, Illinois.

Since this is such a fine flowing melody, the pupils should sing and enjoy it alone first. Notice that in spite of the chord figurations in the first two lines, the backbone of the melody in those lines is a scale pattern upward F, G, A, and downward C, B♭, A. The song may be harmonized by the tonic and dominant chords, and voices with a limited lower range may sing the chord roots in this pattern:

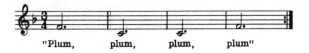

"Plum,   plum,   plum,   plum"

Such a part should be sung rhythmically and with good resonance and sustaining quality, imitating a bass viol.

The round may be sung in three parts with this added accompaniment figure if the students can comfortably sustain that many parts. Bells or flute may play the second phrase of the melody repeatedly as a counterpart if the voices are able to regulate their volume so that a good balance is assured. Thus a four- or five-part composition can be developed from a simple round if the teacher and pupils have sufficient inventiveness and harmonizing skill.

THE DESCANT. A simple melody written above and harmonizing with another melody is known as a descant. One principle of its construction is that it moves *against* the basic melody; hence, when the melody moves slowly the descant may move faster and when the melody moves rapidly the descant may be in sustained tones. Also, as the melody moves upward the descant may be sustained or move downward. An example of a song with descant is "Streets of Laredo" (MAW-116, see page 107). The value of the descant in the intermediate grades is that it provides pleasing harmonic experience, but gives the less familiar part to the higher voices, which frequently sing with more independence at this age. Since it lies in a higher range and is easily heard, the descant often is sung by only three or four voices. It should accompany and not dominate the melody. Bells, Song Flutes, and other melody instruments may play the descant with or without voices. A solo instrumental counterpart is called an obbligato. Varied descants and obbligatos are suggested in the basic song texts.

Early experience in singing harmony may come in songs with simple two-part endings. The children may first hear the teacher sing the harmony part as they sing the melody. When they thoroughly understand and hear the harmony in relation to their own part, a few of the children should join the teacher on the harmony part. Later, they can sing the part without the teacher. "All Through the Night" (see page 169) has an easy two-part ending on three phrases.

SINGING IN THIRDS. Singing simple thirds below the melody line is another early experience in harmony. Sometimes only the refrain is treated in this manner, as in "Gum Tree Canoe" (MAW-58, see page 106). In other songs a harmony part may be sung a third higher or a sixth lower for a pleasing effect, and because the harmony parallels the melody it is not difficult to sing. In "Polly-Wolly-Doodle" (ME-12) we find the harmony part below the melody in part of the stanza and in thirds *above* the melody in the first seven measures of the refrain.

POLLY-WOLLY-DOODLE

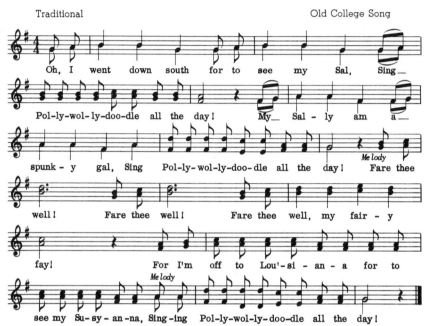

From *Music Everywhere*, 1943. Copyright Summy-Birchard Publishing Co. Used by permission.

ROOT TONES, CHORDS, AND CHANTS. Fifth and sixth grade pupils, partly through the medium of the Autoharp, become acquainted with elementary principles of harmonization and expand their explorations to include simple chants to accompany songs. Singing the root tones is an easily understandable procedure. A song such as "Down in the Valley" (ME-26, see page 105) may be harmonized by the tonic and dominant chords. The singers follow the chord changes as they sing the chord roots: "do" (I) or "so" (V$_7$). A different effect is achieved when "so" is held throughout the song. Harmony is possible because "so" is common to both chords.

If more parts are desired, a solo voice or small group may sing the melody while the class divides into three parts to sound the entire triad on a neutral or sol-fa syllable. This movement of voice parts may be used:

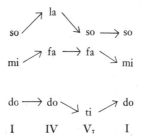

Songs harmonized with three chords–I, IV, V₇–could have added vocal harmony in the form of root tones sung on "do–fa–so–do" or chording using the progression

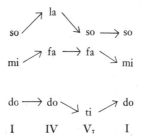

at the appropriate points of change. "Gum Tree Canoe" (see page 106) is easily harmonized in this manner.

Descants above or chants below a given melody are created by selecting tones from the supporting chord structure. The descant suggested for "The Deaf Woman's Courtship" (VOA-41) is a good example.

THE DEAF WOMAN'S COURTSHIP

Southern Folksong

"The Deaf Woman's Courtship," from *Voices of America* of the New TOGETHER-WE-SING Series, published by Follett Publishing Company, Chicago, Illinois.

Passing tones or short scale patterns moving between chord tones also are used in creating descants and chants. The Krones, in *Music Participation in the Elementary School*,[4] have shown how to create such harmony parts. *Our First Songs to Sing with Descants*[5] and other books in the same series give good examples.

Guiding intermediate pupils in singing harmony is difficult for many classroom teachers. In the past the singing of harmony was done chiefly on the basis of formal parts printed in the song books. Teachers were not urged to analyze the harmonic structure with the children in order to see the relationship of the parts. The Autoharp has helped to provide a simple approach to harmony, and its use should be combined with other basic experiences in singing harmony.

After pupils in the intermediate grades have had experience playing chord accompaniments on the Autoharp and bells, it is but one step further to show them the relationship of simple harmonizing parts to the basic chord structure. An understanding of principles of harmonization leads to better singing and an open road for experimentation and improvisation.

Student Management of Singing

From the fourth grade upward pupils can learn to conduct their own songs. Rhythmic conducting movements of a general nature should be an early kind of participation. When rhythmic response is well established, pupils can learn the conductor's patterns for the common meters of $\frac{2}{4}$, $\frac{3}{4}$, $\frac{4}{4}$, and $\frac{6}{8}$. The conductor's pattern can be of great help to a singer in analyzing and singing the rhythm of a song. When the pupils can keep the proper metric beat, they will automatically hold long notes and provide time for rests.

LEARNING TO CONDUCT. When the hand movements are being learned, conducting should be limited to well-known songs that begin on the first beat of the measure. Songs meeting these requirements are:

"Merrily We Roll Along":

Mer - ri - ly we   roll a - long,   roll a - long,   roll a - long, *etc.*

"America":

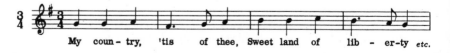

My   coun - try,   'tis   of thee, Sweet land of   lib - er-ty *etc.*

"Lovely Evening":

Oh,   how   love - ly   is   the   eve - ning, etc.

"All Through the Night":

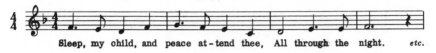

Sleep, my child, and peace at-tend thee, All through the night.   etc.

"Sleep and Rest":

Sleep, oh, my dar-ling and   rest,— Birds are a-sleep in their   nest,— etc.

"Row, Row, Row Your Boat":

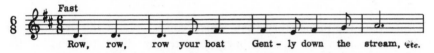

Row,   row,   row your boat   Gent - ly down   the   stream, etc.

In conducting, the hand should be held palm down with a supple rather than a rigid or flabby feeling. The elbow should be slightly away from the body. Only when directing very large groups should the arm be raised high and outstretched. It takes practice to develop an expressive conductor's beat, and with intermediate children the initial objective is to establish the rhythmic movements in the proper direction. The patterns shown are for the right-handed person; when the left hand is used, the opposite left and right directions are taken.

In conducting $\frac{2}{4}$ meter, the movement is essentially down and up with a slight movement to the right preceding the upward stroke. Every conductor must give a preparatory beat to let the singers know when to start; this takes the form of a slight upward movement preceding the downward stroke when the singing begins. For $\frac{3}{4}$ meter the conductor's pattern is in effect a triangle moving to the right. The $\frac{4}{4}$ pattern moves first to the left across the body and then to the right.

$\frac{2}{4}$:

$\frac{3}{4}$:

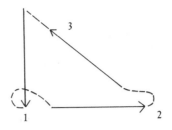

$\frac{4}{4}$:

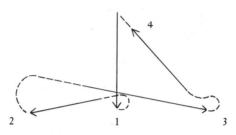

Other than the preparatory beat, which comes only at the beginning of the composition, the dotted lines indicate the slight rebound of the hand between beats which gives the conductor's pattern the necessary fluid rhythmic movement.

$\frac{6}{8}$ meter usually is conducted with the two-beat pattern so that there is a subdivision of three on each beat, in contrast to the "1-and-2-and" two-part subdivision in $\frac{2}{4}$ meter. If a song is sung in slow $\frac{6}{8}$ meter each beat is indicated.

Fast $\frac{6}{8}$

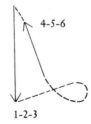

Slow $\frac{6}{8}$

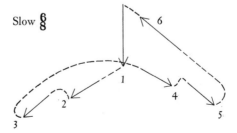

In learning to direct songs the first objective is to establish an automatic rhythmic movement of the hand in the pattern for each meter. Although a conductor does not outline the beat pattern in both hands, in the early stages both hands should be used so that (1) left-handed pupils will not be confused in direction, and (2) the teacher may face the group and not confuse the students by his reverse movement. The ¾ pattern when done with both hands is:

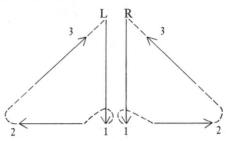

Many songs begin on other than the first beat. Some common examples are:

"America, the Beautiful" in ¼ meter (see page 36)

"The Star-Spangled Banner" in ¾ meter

"Cockles and Mussels" in ¾ meter (see page 169)

"Auld Lang Syne" in ¼ meter

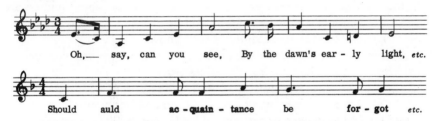

Oh,— say, can you see, By the dawn's ear - ly light, *etc.*

Should auld ac - quain - tance be for - got *etc.*

In such cases the preparatory beat will be that preceding the beat on which the song begins. "The Star-Spangled Banner," in ¾ meter, begins on the third beat; therefore the preparatory beat will take the form of a short movement in the direction of the second beat in ¾ meter:

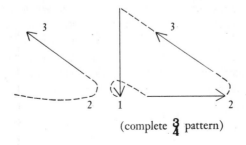

(complete ¾ pattern)

Inexperienced song leaders sometimes count out the entire measure when a song begins on a fragment of a measure. Songs such as "Oh Susanna" pose special problems because they begin on the *last half* of the second beat. In this song the leader can establish the tempo by saying as he conducts:

"Believe Me, If All Those Endearing Young Charms" is in $\frac{6}{8}$ meter but has two beats to the measure. The conductor can conduct the whole measure in duple pattern and say:

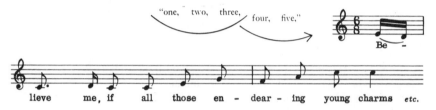

In the early stages the teacher must be selective in the songs children are asked to conduct. However, after skill is developed, more advanced problems may be met successfully in well-known songs.

All intermediate children should be taught the accepted conductor's patterns. Those who develop the necessary skill should be encouraged to serve as song leaders. Fifth and sixth grade groups may elect a song leader for a week or two-week period. Often children who are especially interested and who have richer musical backgrounds become natural musical leaders and are so recognized by the class. Others should also have the opportunity to develop their potential as leaders.

INDEPENDENCE IN LEARNING SONGS. Children learn songs by hearing them sung by their teacher, the music specialist, or a member of the class; they hear songs played on the piano, bells, or other instrument; they hear recordings. If they have books, as they listen, intermediate grade pupils should watch the notation, observe the relationship of what is heard to what is seen, so that they are able to sing successfully at the earliest possible moment, and so that their understanding of the notation will make them better prepared to meet the next new song. The will, interest, and purpose the children have determines how rapidly they develop musical independence.

In one school where the classrooms were self-contained, the music consultant assisted once a week for one-half hour in rooms where the teacher was not a competent musician. One fifth grade class, whose teacher did no singing, was so well organized and motivated that every minute of the consultant's time was used to greatest advantage. The children were eager to learn and prided themselves upon being able to sing a song accurately the week after it was introduced. Rarely were errors made, for the consultant pointed out pitfalls at the first lesson and suggested ways in which the song could be rehearsed to avoid them. The pupils' effective use of these suggestions was based on their growing understanding of musical notation.

Two children served as song leaders who tuned the class with the pitch pipe and rehearsed the songs. At the lesson with the consultant on the week following the introduction of a song the student leaders directed the singing of the song in the manner they had developed during the week. The consultant then made suggestions for phrasing, or assisted the group in establishing a harmonizing part. Often more than one song could be introduced in one lesson because the interest and esprit de corps were high.

The songs were selected jointly by the teacher, the class, and the consultant. When songs were needed for a particular unit study, the class compiled a list of those available, and with the help of the consultant selected the most interesting and musical. Sometimes the consultant suggested songs she thought the class should learn and, because of their enthusiasm for her and for music, the children learned these as readily as any others.

When recordings were used, the pupils managed the song learning process independently. Generally one child operated the record player while another directed the singing. They understood the necessity of listening before singing, of following words and music in the book, of singing alternate phrases or the easy refrain first, and of whispering the words or singing softly in order to keep up with the recorded version. The goal was to learn to sing independently of the record and to learn to use whatever accompanying instruments seemed appropriate.

Although the teacher did not participate musically, he was an important figure in the success of this music program. He was an effective teacher who insisted upon orderly procedure and the thoughtful analysis of problems. The music consultant provided specific musical guidance when necessary and assisted in evaluating the combined efforts. Without such guidance and evaluation the pupils would have made serious errors in music; they would soon have come to the end of their resources and music-making would have stagnated. Musical do-it-yourself programs can be excellent when organization, direction, and rapport are established by the classroom teacher, and expert assistance is given by a respected consultant, who provides guidance from the point of view of the musical needs of the children rather than the demands of an imposed program.

Using the Piano and Other Accompaniments

Traditionally, a piano has been a part of kindergarten equipment, but it has not always been readily available to other grades. If well played, a piano accompaniment adds interest, color, and support to the singing. The teacher who does not play the piano can arrange to have a special music teacher, parent, secretary, or talented upper-grade student serve as accompanist. When a piano is not available in the classroom, one can usually be found in the auditorium or multipurpose room, which can be reserved for occasional singing periods. In many schools a small piano is mounted on large rubber casters so that it can be rolled from one classroom to another as required.

TECHNIQUES IN THE USE OF THE PIANO. The piano should be used as an enrichment rather than as a constant accompaniment to classroom singing. Poor use of the piano often has led to the recommendation that the piano not be used with children's singing. Picture the teacher sitting at the piano with his back to the children, accompanying every song with loud improvised chords. This situation violates at least three important principles in the teaching of singing:

1. Singing should be shared by teacher and pupils; there should be eye contact and rapport, much as there is in storytelling.
2. The teacher should know the vocal development of each pupil and should work in such a flexible manner that children often have an opportunity to sing alone or in small groups and to try their voices on tone calls. The teacher who *always* sits at the piano cannot possibly be aware of each child's vocal development, and cannot give him the personal help he needs almost daily.
3. The rhythmic chording, which is easy to play and "keeps the singing going," is musically unsuitable for many children's songs.

Some songs, such as "Go Tell Aunt Rhodey" and "Yankee Doodle," may appropriately be accompanied by broken chords on the piano. The manner of playing should support rather than cover up the voices. The left hand should play near the middle of the keyboard with a light, crisp touch for lively numbers and a legato touch for smooth flowing songs. Since each song should be expressive in its own way, the accompaniment should help to establish the appropriate mood and feeling. Accompaniment books for some of the music texts show piano parts that are varied and not difficult.

With the achievement of greater independence in singing, children should be challenged to hear more in the music as they sing. For this reason, they should have more experience singing with accompaniments. The piano adds interesting harmonies and rhythmic effects and the teacher must use techniques that train the children to listen as they sing, so that the ensemble is heard. In some accompaniments, the arranger tries to include musical characteristics that express the idea or mood in the song. The piano part for "Silver Moon" (MTY-94) flows along to give the feeling of the moon riding through the sky. The children should listen first without singing; then they should sing and listen at the same time.

SILVER MOON

"Silver Moon," from *Music Through the Year* of the New TOGETHER-WE-SING Series, published by Follet Publishing Company, Chicago, Illinois.

In some accompaniments no separate movement or musical ideas appear. The piano may move along with solid chords that hold up the melody much as pillars support a bridge. The hymn-like accompaniments for "Song of Praise" (MTY-107), "Father, We Thank Thee" (MIOT-42, Teachers' Book) or "Crusaders' Hymn" (S&R-61, Accompaniments) are examples.

CRUSADERS' HYMN

Anonymous   Silesian Folk Song

Fair   are   the   mead - ows,   Fair - er   the   wood - lands,

Robed   in ___   flow'rs   of ___   bloom - ing   spring; *etc.*

From *Singing and Rhyming* of OUR SINGING WORLD Series, Enlarged Edition. Used by permission of Ginn and Company, owner of the copyright.

THE STRUMMING INSTRUMENTS. All over the world people enjoy singing at home and in community gatherings. To accompany this informal singing various instruments are used: the guitar, banjo, ukulele, zither, etc., as well as the piano. A teacher who is able to play one of these should use it often to accompany the singing in his classroom. When musically played, the strumming instruments make the most appropriate accompaniment for folk songs. The teacher may sit facing the students and maintain the desirable rapport for group singing.

Not every song lends itself to this type of accompaniment; song books designed for school use show chord markings that enable the teacher to play the more suitable songs. Different styles of strumming should be used. Those heard on the recordings made by Josef Marais, Burl Ives, Sam Hinton, and Pete Seeger are good examples. If the teacher is not experienced on any of these instruments, he can explore the possibilities of the Autoharp.

A classroom teacher should share in the daily singing activities of his pupils. Although he may not possess a fine voice, the children will readily accept whatever he has. If he has the assistance of a consultant, he should work right along with this person in helping to meet the needs of his pupils. There are many song books and records; a good teacher will find effective ways to use these resources. Singing is truly the music of the people; boys and girls *and* their teacher should make it a part of their lives from the earliest school days.

ACTIVITIES FOR COLLEGE CLASSES

A. Written Assignments

1. Be sure that all songs listed in your handbook have the correct key and starting note in the "tune-up" column. Submit several pages of songs under topical listings so that the correctness of your work may be checked.

2. Find two songs which, if transposed, would be in a better singing range for primary voices. For each, name the new key, the new range, and the syllable of the first note of the song.

3. Find four songs in the minor mode. State the clues that suggest that each is in the minor. For each, list the tone to be sounded on the pitch pipe, the syllable of the first note in the song, and the letter name of the minor key.

4. Hear the recordings of songs from two different books at one grade level. Using the seven points listed under "Using Recorded Song Materials," compare and evaluate them.

5. Go to a record store and hear several singing records designed for children. Evaluate them in terms of their usefulness in the school music program.

6. From any source select six rounds that you believe have musical appeal and are appropriate for intermediate-grade singers. Include different types of rounds. List them in your handbook, with brief teaching notes, under Section II-B.

7. In any basic song books, find one song that is or may be harmonized in each of the following ways. List them in your handbook, with brief teaching notes, under Section II-B.
   a. a descant above the melody
   b. a chant below the melody
   c. a two-part ending
   d. thirds below or above the melody
   e. root tones of the principal chords

B. Classroom Projects

1. Tune up with the pitch pipe and get the class successfully started singing a familiar song.

2. Prepare to conduct one well-known song in a common meter. Tune up from the pitch pipe and direct the class with the correct conductor's pattern.

3. Select an easy but unfamiliar song that can be learned in one or two hearings. Sing it to the class so that the words and spirit of the song are conveyed.

4. Select and teach one song from a basic song book. Have the class use books as an aid in learning the song, and use procedures suitable for the grade level selected. If absolutely necessary, use the piano to support your voice.

5. Select a song that is well recorded. Teach the song, without books, using the recording in combination with effective teaching techniques.

6. In small groups, prepare and sing two songs selected in assignment No. 7 above.

7. Accompany the class in a folk song. Use the piano, Autoharp, or other chording instrument in a manner compatible with the musical qualities of the song.

CHAPTER NOTES

1. Ruth Seeger, *American Folk Songs for Children* (New York: Doubleday and Company, Inc., 1948).
2. Beatrice Landeck, *Songs to Grow On* (New York: Edward B. Marks Music Corporation, Music Publishers, William Sloane Associates, Inc., Publishers, 1950).
3. Beatrice Landeck, *More Songs to Grow On* (New York: Edward B. Marks Music Corporation, Music Publishers, William Sloane Associates, Inc., Publishers, 1954).
4. Beatrice and Max Krone, *Music Participation in the Elementary School* (Park Ridge, Ill.: Neil A. Kjos Music Co., 1952).
5. Beatrice and Max Krone, *Our First Songs to Sing with Descants* (Park Ridge, Ill.: Neil A. Kjos Music Co., 1941).

OTHER REFERENCES

Mathews, Paul Wentworth, *You Can Teach Music* (New York: E. P. Dutton and Co., Inc., 1953). Chapter 4, "Let the Singing Begin."
Mursell, James L., *Music Education Principles and Programs* (Morristown, N.J.: Silver Burdett Co., 1956). Chapter 7, "Singing and Musical Growth."
Myers, Louise Kifer, *Teaching Children Music in the Elementary School*, Second Edition (Englewood Cliffs, N.J.: Prentice-Hall, Inc., 1956). Chapter 3, "Making Music—Singing and Playing."

Nye, Robert Evans, and Vernice Trousdale Nye, *Music in the Elementary School* (Englewood Cliffs, N.J.: Prentice-Hall, Inc., 1957). Chapter 8, "Part Singing."

Snyder, Alice M., *Creating Music with Children* (New York: Mills Music, Inc., 1957). Chapter 4, "Singing."

See Appendix B for listing of song books and records in the basic music series.

CHAPTER SIX

PROMOTING MUSICAL UNDERSTANDING AND CREATIVITY THROUGH SINGING

The most humble of folk songs can help to make children aware of the essential elements of music. Unfortunately many teachers become so engrossed in teaching children to "read notes" that they fail to teach *music*, which is much more than the notes on the page. Until a teacher has analyzed a song from the standpoint of its rhythm, melody, form and harmony, he is not fully prepared to bring these elements to the attention of his pupils. When introduced simply in connection with the singing program, important characteristics of the musical elements can easily be understood by children.

The specific study of melodic patterns and intervals, an important part of any singing program, is furthered by the use of scale numbers and sol-fa syllables. The teacher must have a complete understanding of the teaching processes leading to effective use of these aids. He must also know how children can be guided to work creatively as a group. Personal values as well as a greater understanding of musical elements come to children who are given the opportunity to compose music.

Understanding the Elements of Music

As the children learn to sing, more than anything else they respond to the mood of the music and their own desires to sing. In the beginning, they have no concepts of high and low or fast and slow; they sing the song as they hear it without considering its technical aspects. However, as soon as singing is well established, the teacher may begin directing attention to musical elements as they are heard in songs. Guided aural observations should continue throughout the grades. Gradually the features can be pointed out on the printed page, and specific study of them can be made. A sensitivity to music and an appreciation of the elements that make it expressive are the goals in this work.

ESSENTIALS IN MELODY. Melody may be a single line of fragile beauty or an expression of deep sorrow. When combined with rhythm and dynamics, melody can convey unlimited shades of expression. It is a challenge to search a melody for the factors that contribute to its effectiveness. As a result of their musical studies, elementary pupils should be able to note two or three of the following characteristics of melody.

Range: limited or broad
Interest: repetitious or varied
Climax: one distinct or varied
Mode: major, minor, pentatonic, or other

Phrase: long lines or short fragments
Movement: basically scalewise, chordwise, or large intervals with broken line

160

Often it is not possible to make a clear-cut decision about some of the melodic characteristics, but tendencies can be observed.

Much American folk music is based on the major scale and is of a particular melodic design because the songs grew to the accompaniment of guitars, banjos, mandolins, and other simple chording instruments that were easily carried into the new land. The melody line in songs such as the following fits naturally into the chord patterns easily played on these instruments: "Down in the Valley" (see page 105), "The Deaf Woman's Courtship" (see page 145), "Go 'Way, Old Man" (see page 109), or "Springfield Mountain" (AS V-48).

SPRINGFIELD MOUNTAIN

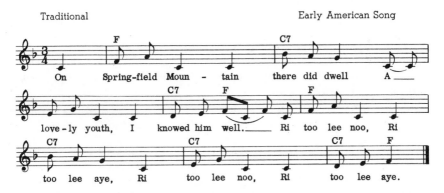

From Beattie, Wolverton, Wilson, and Hinga, THE AMERICAN SINGER, *Book Five.* American Book Company, publishers. Used by permission.

Although it is used in many other settings, to the people of the mountains and the frontier the minor mode suggested melancholy, sadness, or perhaps a lonesome feeling. Minor harmonies were easily made on the accompanying instruments by lowering the 3rd of the chord. "Lonesome" songs, spirituals such as "Wayfaring Stranger" (MAW-154), ballads, and lullabies such as "All the Pretty Little Horses" (see page 107) grew around the minor chords.

The major and minor scales grew out of the European musical tradition. Other scales preceded these and are still heard in the plain song of the church and in the folk melodies of Middle Europe and the Near East. Generally these are seven-tone scales, as are the major and minor scales, but the half steps fall in different places and so the melody has a different musical "color." Often only careful analysis reveals their identity. It is sufficient in the intermediate grades to notice the unusual character of such melodies when they are encountered.

When a song in the pentatonic mode is used, the pupils might play, sing, and write the notes, comparing the scale used with a major scale. "Auld Lang Syne" is a well-known Scottish air based on a pentatonic scale. When compared with F major it will be found that steps 4 and 7 of the scale are omitted.

AULD LANG SYNE

Robert Burns   Old Scottish Air

Should auld ac-quaint-ance be for-got, And nev-er brought to mind? Should auld ac-quaint-ance be for-got, And days of auld lang syne?

Chorus

For auld __ lang __ syne, my dear, For auld __ lang __ syne; We'll take a cup o' kind-ness yet For auld __ lang __ syne.

From *Singing in Harmony* of OUR SINGING WORLD Series, Enlarged Edition. Used by permission of Ginn and Company, owner of the copyright.

Melodic characteristics of three songs mentioned above could be analyzed as follows:

"Springfield Mountain" (page 161)
Range: from middle C up to B (the interval of a 7th), which is short.
Interest: repetitious.
Climax: none outstanding, high tone is touched twice.
Mode: major.
Phrase: short, two-measure phrases with a sequence suggested. Slurred notes in fourth measure give the effect of leading into the following repeated phrase.
Movement: basically chordwise.
This is an early American ballad, sung while traveling or during evening gatherings, often to the accompaniment of a chording instrument. The melodic characteristics reflect this background.

"All the Pretty Little Horses" (page 107)
Range: from low A up to C (an octave and a 3rd, or a 10th), which is average.
Interest: generally repetitious.
Climax: a slight development in first two measures of third phrase due to rising melody in 3rds.

Mode: minor.

Phrase: four-measure phrases; tends toward short fragments.

Movement: scale and stepwise predominating, but some chordwise movement present.

All of these characteristics add to the song's effectiveness as a lullaby, which is essentially quieting.

"Auld Lang Syne" (page 162)

Range: from middle C up to D (interval of a 9th), which is average.

Interest: varied, with directional contrast in melody of first and third phrases.

Climax: evident in fourth measure of chorus due to repetition and prolongation of high D and steady descent to cadence.

Mode: pentatonic, but strongly centered around major scale tonic chord.

Phrase: generally long lines; four-measure antecedent and consequent phrases giving an eight-measure effect.

Movement: consecutive tones of the tonic chord and neighboring tone patterns.

Such a study of the melodic characteristics of the songs they sing is not too difficult for fifth and sixth grade children and can add a great deal to their appreciation of this element of music.

EARLY OBSERVATIONS OF MELODY. Kindergarten and first grade children may be helped to notice some of these characteristics of melody in their songs. Many songs have obvious high and low tones. In "Bye'm Bye" (MIOT-29, AFlk-71) some tone calls can be used to draw attention to high and low (see brackets in song):

BYE 'M BYE

Folk Song from Texas

From *Music in Our Town.* © 1956, Silver Burdett Company.

To associate these tones with high and low the teacher may use hand levels as the song is sung; the children may indicate high and low with their hands and sing a tonal pattern on these tones.

"high   low"

The children's chant, "One Potato, Two Potatoes" (SOOW-41), has high and low tones and an ascending melody for which the children can make their hands climb up just as their voices do. Such songs bring the characteristics of melodic movement clearly to the attention of the singers. One old French folk tune, found in many books (SOOW-22, MIOT-94, MTY-40), moves directly down the scale in the last line. The children can move their hands down step by step.

THE CLOWN

Words by Nellie Poorman   French Folk Song

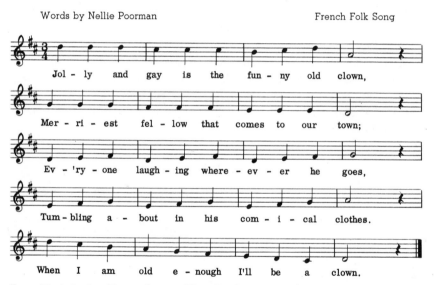

Jol - ly   and   gay   is   the   fun - ny   old   clown,

Mer - ri - est   fel - low   that   comes   to   our   town;

Ev - 'ry - one   laugh - ing   where - ev - er   he   goes,

Tum - bling   a - bout   in   his   com - i - cal   clothes.

When   I   am   old   e - nough   I'll   be   a   clown.

From *Music in Our Town.* © 1956, Silver Burdett Company.

If the song is sung in the Key of C a child may play the Key of C bells along with the descending voices. In the second grade, when the children are accustomed to handling the books, they may see how the notes move down the staff, one step at a time.

Another song, "Rag Man, Bone Man" (AS II-67), shows the scale ascending. "Three Dukes" (AS II-137) has an upward line on the tonic chord, another common melodic movement.

THREE DUKES

Traditional   Southern Singing Game

Here come three dukes a - rid - ing, a - rid - ing, a - rid - ing, Here
come three dukes a - rid - ing, to my hi ho and ran-some tee!

From Beattie, Wolverton, Wilson, and Hinga, from THE AMERICAN SINGER, *Book Two*. American Book Company, publishers. Used by permission.

In addition to hand levels the teacher may give a visual representation on the chalkboard with blank notation and contour lines. The first phrase of "The Clown" is represented in blank notation:

A contour line representing the first phrase of "Three Dukes" would be:

Children may hear the melodic movement better when they sing a short pattern with "la" rather than the words. Later, syllable or scale numbers may be sung for the pattern, so that it becomes more specifically defined. The keyboard instruments aid in establishing concepts about high and low, and large and small intervals between tones.

ESSENTIALS IN RHYTHM. In expanding their understanding of rhythm through singing, intermediate-grade students deal with the following elements:

metric beat	afterbeats
accent	syncopation
typical rhythm patterns	ritardando and accelerando
anacrusis (upbeat)	rubato

In "Springfield Mountain" (page 161) we find a repeated use of the anacrusis or upbeat *leading into* the strong beat of the rhythm. Also, the entire melody is based on one short rhythm pattern:

Afterbeats are characteristic of accompaniments to dancing tunes such as "Turkey in the Straw." Syncopation, the shifting of the accent, is often accomplished by the lengthening of a note on the unaccented beat, as in "Cockles and Mussels" (page 169) or in "Liza Jane" (page 32). *Ritardando* and *accelerando* may be written above the notation and, like rubato, are effected by the performer. "Auld Lang Syne" (page 162) lends itself to such subtle variations in forward movement.

In any study of its component parts rhythm is in danger of being considered a static, dissectible thing rather than the live moving force it really is. Children should experience and understand it in two general ways:

1. In terms of smaller compact patterns, which can be called rhythmic motives.
2. In terms of longer flowing phrases moving forward toward a natural point of release.

No formal study of rhythm can take the place of experience with it. As clear examples of different aspects of rhythm are encountered in singing, the teacher must draw them to the attention of the pupils so that complete comprehension may eventually be achieved.

EARLY OBSERVATIONS OF RHYTHM AND DYNAMICS. As children sing their songs and hear them sung by the teacher or played from a recording, they respond to the mood and expression conveyed by the music. They should be led to understand that music may be loud or soft and later to observe the specific use made of dynamics. They may see contrasts between numbers: a lullaby may be soft, and a song for vigorous activity may be loud. In finer discrimination the children may hear and learn to sing loud and soft sections within one song. Dynamics should always be related to what the music says. In "Silver Stars" (ABC I-17, see next page) the storytelling phrase may be louder than the lullaby itself.

The tempo of a song and the duration of the tones within it may be classified by pupils as "fast" or "slow," "shorter" or "longer." They may move to the music and the teacher may use blank notation to show the relative duration of tones. Both bodily movement and rhythm instruments are excellent means of responding to and understanding elements of rhythm, mood, and dynamics.

SILVER STARS

Paraphrased   Javanese Lullaby

At night, when sil - ver stars are in the sky, My Moth-er

sings to me this lull - a - by: Now go to sleep____ and hush-a -

bye, Now go to sleep____ and hush a - bye.

From Berg, Burns, Hooley, Pace, and Wolverton, MUSIC FOR YOUNG AMERICANS, *Book One*. American Book Company, publishers. Used by permission.

TEXTURE AND HARMONY. Pupils should understand that harmony is the relationship of the tones of music, either within a single melodic line or from the point of view of the melody and its accompaniment. Fifth or sixth grade pupils readily understand the principles of the two basic types of musical texture:

1. Homophonic—that in which one principal melody is present and other tones merely support and enrich this melody.
2. Polyphonic—that achieved when two or more distinct and separate musical lines are sounded simultaneously. The relationship between these melodies is called counterpoint. Rounds and canons are a type of polyphony.

Children who accompany their singing on chording instruments can hear the elemental tonic, subdominant and dominant harmonies of folk music. If the teacher has the development of musical understanding as one of his objectives, he will guide the pupils in an analysis of the chord structures and their relationships (refer to Chapter Four). The minor mode has characteristics that fifth or sixth grade pupils can readily hear. They can learn that a minor chord differs from the major because the third of the chord is lowered a half step. The harmony of some compositions may consist of more complex combinations of chords which the pupils can enjoy for their rich sounds, but which they will not be able to analyze.

When recordings of music of the Chinese, of the American Indian, or of other ethnic groups are heard, the children can notice the *lack* of harmony. In most cases the accompaniment consists of selected rhythm instruments or a melodic line played on a single instrument such as the flute. When pupils perform such music, they should not alter its character by adding an unsuitable harmonic part.

FORM IN MUSIC. The structure of a musical composition can range from the simplicity of a folk song to the complex organization of the first movement of a symphony. Form touches on the more intellectual aspect of music; it is the horizontal design in music as it flows through time. To perceive the form of a composition the intellect must remember, compare, and contrast melodies and rhythms as they are heard. Some teachers make the mistake of waiting until pupils are ready to study the form of a symphony before calling attention to elemental principles of musical form. Even the greatest musical masterpiece is built on basic principles of contrast and balance found in song literature. When a song has a verse and refrain, contrast and balance are present; this is called two-part or binary form. "Short'nin' Bread" (WS-57) illustrates simple binary form.

SHORT'NIN' BREAD

Traditional   Negro Song

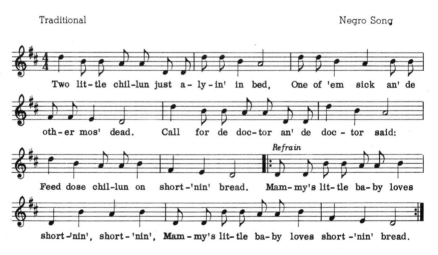

From *We Sing* of A SINGING SCHOOL Series, 1940. Copyright Summy-Birchard Publishing Co. Used by permission.

Repetition after contrast is another principle of musical form. "All Through the Night" (MAOC-115) has four phrases; the second is like the first, the third is different, and the fourth is like the first.

ALL THROUGH THE NIGHT

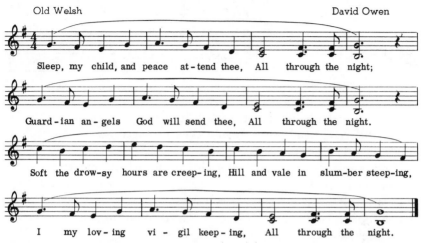

Old Welsh   David Owen

Sleep, my child, and peace at-tend thee, All through the night;

Guard-ian an-gels God will send thee, All through the night.

Soft the drow-sy hours are creep-ing, Hill and vale in slum-ber steep-ing,

I my lov-ing vi-gil keep-ing, All through the night.

This is called a three-part or ternary form and is designated A B A. To take into account the repetition of the first phrase A A B A could be used, but it would still be considered a three-part form. Children in the primary grades can be guided to notice like and unlike phrases in songs.

Some songs have an internal unity and development around one idea so that real contrast is not present. "Cockles and Mussels" (VOW-40) has three eight-measure phrases, all of which flow along in the same pattern.

COCKLES AND MUSSELS

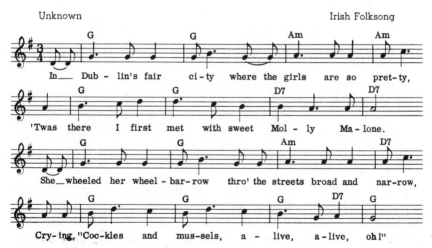

Unknown   Irish Folksong

In__ Dub - lin's fair ci-ty where the girls are so pret-ty,

'Twas there I first met with sweet Mol - ly Ma - lone.

She__wheeled her wheel - bar-row thro' the streets broad and nar-row,

Cry-ing, "Coc-kles and mus-sels, a - live, a-live, oh !"

"Cockles and Mussels," from *Voices of the World* of the New TOGETHER-WE-SING Series, published by Follett Publishing Company, Chicago, Illinois.

The only contrast is between the last half of the first phrase and the last half of the second and third phrases; even that is a matter of embellishment rather than a change in material.

Contrast may be the result of a change in melodic movement or of rhythm, or of both; the song may change from major to minor. Contrasts may be based on differences between phrases or between larger sections. Often contrast and balance are worked out on both smaller and larger levels.

In some compositions, instruments may assist in establishing contrast; a solo group may stand out in one section in contrast to a group in the next. Voices can be used in the same way. Negro spirituals such as "Swing Low, Sweet Chariot" (SIH-118) feature a solo voice with the chorus answering.

There are infinite variations of the basic forms and often it is difficult to decide which is represented. The important consideration is that pupils become aware of the repetition and contrast in the songs they sing. Later, when more complex compositions are heard, they will know better what to listen for, and thus the composer's art will be more understandable to them.

In songs children become aware of patterns created by:
1. the repetition or contrast of phrases
2. the repetition or contrast of larger sections
3. the repetition of smaller rhythmic or melodic motives
4. contrasts in mode, instrumentation, or voices

The pupils will see that to study musical form they must be able to analyze and recognize essentials in rhythm, melody, and harmony.

Syllables and Scale Numbers

There are differences of opinion about the use and value of the sol-fa syllables and scale numbers in the elementary singing program. Some of the controversy about syllables has arisen because of poor methods in using them. Either syllables or numbers, when properly used, can help children establish relationships of the tones of the scale. Scale numbers are favored by teachers who make extensive use of keyboard instruments. The sol-fa syllables are favored by those who have a predominantly vocal approach. Some teachers successfully combine the two, showing the relationship of the syllables and numbers in the major scale with a diagram such as that shown here.

From the third grade such a chart made of tagboard can be helpful as pupils assist in determining syllable or number names for specific melodic fragments. Many songs move both above and below the "home tone," and so fragments of both higher and lower octaves should be shown, but not in a single column, because the completeness of the octave must be evident. A line under a syllable indicates its location *below* the other tones in the pattern when there is a question about the octave intended.

```
                    mi  3

                    re  2

              8  do     1
              7  ti

              6  la

              5  so

              4  fa
              3  mi

              2  re

              1  do     8
                    ti  7

                    la  6

                    so  5
```

When used with singing, the syllables have certain advantages over numbers:

1. They are easier to sing and more euphonious since they use the basic vowel sounds.
2. Once learned, the syllable combinations are more easily remembered in their *sound* relationship to the scale tones.
3. Chromatically altered tones may be sung easily by changing the vowel sound in the syllable (see Appendix A).

BEGINNING USE OF SYLLABLES. To affix the labels to the scale tones, children should sing and hear tonal patterns with syllables. "Tone calls," used for the development of voices, become, in the second and third grades, "tonal patterns" that are identified by means of the syllables.

Each tone call suggested in Chapter Two is a common tonal pattern found in many songs. The two examples from "Are You Sleeping?" are the patterns of do-so-do and mi-fa-so. The "Rig-a-Jig-Jig" tone call is do-ti-la-ti-do. Pupils should sing the patterns with the original words and with the syllables.

In some second and third grade books the syllables are printed over the music at important points in the song. These syllables may identify short tonal patterns, as described above, or outline entire phrases that show important melodic construction. The teacher can use the printed syllables to help children analyze the melody in a simple way, or the children can sing the syllable pattern to accustom their ears to its sound.

Another technique, dating back to the early New England singing schools, is to memorize a syllable stanza for familiar songs. An occasional song in which *each phrase is a basic tonal pattern* (such as "Are You Sleeping?") may be sung with an added stanza in syllables; but it is not a good practice to sing every song with syllables. Other songs composed of common tonal patterns are:

"Three Dukes" (MNLA-25)
"Susy, Little Susy" (MTY-19)
"Skip to My Lou" (S&R-44)
"Hush My Babe" (MTY-129)

"Jingle at the Window" (S&R-13)
"There Was a Man and He Was Mad" (MNLA-51)

The syllables should be introduced in tonal patterns in the second grade, if the patterns were used often as tone calls throughout the first and early second grades. After the syllables have become familiar, the scale as a whole may be presented (late second or early third grade). The teacher must decide when the children can benefit from understanding the relationship of the syllables one to another, and the relationship of the many tonal patterns to the whole scale.

A few songs, such as the French folk tune on page 164, have the entire scale within the melody. The whole scale of syllables may be explained in relation to that song. If the children do not know such a song, the teacher may use the syllable chart to explain the make-up of the scale. The children enjoy singing the scale, especially if one child plays it with the class on the bells.

Singing of tonal patterns should continue and the tones should be related to the syllable chart so that pupils see the relationship to the entire scale. All work with tonal patterns should be done in reference to songs rather than as isolated drill. In a new song a significant pattern may be the first part of the song that the children sing; later, syllables will identify the pattern specifically. A number of techniques may be used to give the children experience with tonal patterns in many songs.

After a familiar song has been sung, the teacher might ask: "What tonal pattern did we find in this song?" "Who can sing it with the words?" "Let's sing it together." Give individuals or small groups an opportunity to sing it as a special help for voices. "Who can sing it with the syllables?" If the syllable chart has been introduced: "Who can point out the syllables as we sing the correct ones for this tonal pattern?" In later stages, if the pattern is simple, the teacher might ask: "Who can play this pattern on the bells?"

To practice aural identification of tonal patterns, the teacher may sing a known tonal pattern with "loo" instead of with the words or syllables. The children identify it by singing it with syllables. In all use of tonal patterns, the tonic note must be sounded and the tonal pattern heard in relation to it. When the work is done in connection with a familiar song that has been correctly tuned for singing it is easy to keep in mind the relationship to the tonic.

Common melodic fragments that comprise tonal patterns are the following:

1. tonic chord: do-so-do; do-mi-so; so-mi; do-do; do-do; etc.
2. scale line: do-re-mi; mi-re-do; so-la-ti-do; so-fa-mi; etc.
3. neighboring tones: so-la-so; do-ti-do; do-re-do; mi-fa-mi; etc.
4. combinations: so-la-so-mi; mi-do-ti-do; mi-re-mi-do; etc.
5. dominant chord: so-ti-re; re-ti-so; etc.

The first four groupings are most common; the dominant chord patterns are introduced later. For most effective use the patterns should be limited to five tones in length.

The minor tonic chord and typical fragments from the minor scale should be used as tonal patterns in the primary grades. This should be done strictly on the basis of providing experience in hearing the different tone color, and no attempt at analysis should be made at this level. Children who have sung syllables in major keys will enjoy these new patterns. Good minor tonal patterns in "Simple Simon" (MRT-118, see page 124) are:

Go-ing to the fair	and	Let me taste your ware.
la - ti -do- re - mi		mi - re - do - ti - la

Halloween songs often are in the minor mode. "On Halloween" (MRT-78) has fine tonal patterns: mi-fa-mi; la-mi-mi-la, and la-ti-do-re-mi. "A Goblin Lives in Our House" (SOOW-100) has tonal patterns mi-la-ti-do-re-mi and la-la-la, both of which are very good to point up minor key characteristics. The patterns are bracketed in the pupil's book.

VISUAL IDENTIFICATION OF SYLLABLES. In the third grade, children can begin to identify tonal patterns visually, if identification by ear has been well established. Tonal patterns such as "so-do-so" occur in many songs. Children may "frame" the tonal pattern in the book by laying one pointer finger on each side of the pattern. The children can construct tonal patterns on a flannel board made by the teacher: Stretch a light-colored flannel tightly over a 10" × 30" plywood board. Make horizontal staff lines with darker shades of yarn stretched tightly about one inch apart. A treble clef and notes made of sandpaper will adhere to the flannel; paint the paper side to harmonize with the flannel and yarn.

In the early primary grades, children should not be concerned about the key in which a song is written. For most people, the syllables have the same sound relationship in all keys. When the children begin to *see* the tonal patterns, it is necessary to explain that "do" changes location on the staff in different songs, and that all the other syllables move in relation to "do." The teacher can mark "do" on the flannel board or chalkboard with an X on the proper line or space. In *Music Through the Year* a colored X indicates the key tone of all the songs in the book.

INTERMEDIATE-GRADE USE OF SYLLABLES. When consistently used, syllables can be an important means of helping pupils learn to hear basic melodic fragments. At the intermediate grade level, when more challenging melodic material is used, such studies should be continued. The syllable chart should include the half steps. Some chromatic alterations are found in major as well as minor songs, and these should be discussed in terms of their relationship to the unaltered tones of the scale. (See Appendix A.) When a song with altered tones is encountered, an analysis of the chromatic scale may be made. "Sleep and Rest" by Mozart contains several alterations. (This song, with some changes, may be found in various basic song books.)

SLEEP AND REST

Mozart

From *The School Song Book*, edited by McConathy, 1919. Copyright Summy-Birchard Publishing Co. Used by permission. (Out of print but available in many libraries.)

bright ____ Shines the moon's sil - ver - y light; ____

Nes - tle your head on my breast; ____ Sleep, oh my dar - ling, and

rest; ____ Oh, sleep, ____ and ___ rest.

In this song the half steps (re-di, la-si, so-fi) should be rehearsed by sing-ing the descending half steps, "do-re-di-re" or "so-la-si-la," etc., to hear and feel the closeness of the half step.

The chromatic syllables become easier to sing if the ascending and de-scending chromatic scale is sung a few times whenever alterations are found in a new song. Chromatic bells and the piano keyboard help es-tablish the *sound* of the chromatic scale. The tones may be played slowly and sung with the letter names: C, C♯, D, D♯, E, F, etc.

The sol-fa syllables were designed for use with key-centered melodies, those built around a scale with the tonic note (do) as the musical "center of gravity." When modulations (changes in key) occur, the location of "do" must be shifted with the key center; this leads to considerations generally beyond the understanding of the intermediate-grade student.

The tones in the tonic chord do-mi-so (1-3-5) have character-istics of stability and repose. Of these, the tonic tone gives the greatest feeling of repose. When a person plays the tonic chord and sings the 3rd or the 5th (mi or so), he will feel a tendency to move to "do." When he sings the root of the chord, "do," there is a sense of arrival. Most songs end on the key tone for this reason. Pupils who learn to use the Auto-harp will have experience with the dominant seventh (V_7) chord and will then develop greater understanding about the characteristics of the scale steps that chord comprises. This, in turn, will assist them in singing melodies centered around this chord.

SINGING INTERVALS. As pupils become more proficient music-makers and deal with more varied song literature, they will need more than this scale-centered and primary-chord-centered understanding of melodic organization. Sixth grade pupils should begin to be aware of the measured distance (the intervals) between tones of scales and chords. Then when the key center changes or eludes definition, as it often does in contempo-rary music, the singer still is able to find his way from one note to the next.

In the primary grades children observed intervals in general terms as steps, skips, or large jumps. Later they named them with syllables or scale numbers. Sixth grade pupils can discuss tonal relationships more specifically; they can learn to hear, recognize, and sing *particular* intervals. There is no definite order in which the intervals should be presented, but when a particular interval in a song arrests attention, it may be identified and sung in isolation a few times so that the children hear its sound and see it in notation. At other times when scales and chords are sung, the intervals may be identified as to their position in the scale or chord and their sound. Pupils can learn that the intervals in the tonic chord are:

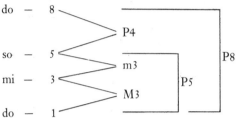

The difference in sound between a major and a minor 3rd is important, for the arrangement of these intervals within the chord determines whether the chord is major or minor. Some people remember the sound of the minor 3rd (m3) by associating it with the first interval in Brahms' "Lullaby":

Lul-la-by   and good-night!   With— ro-ses   be-dight— *etc.*

The perfect 4th (P4) is the interval from "so" (5) up to "do" (1); the first interval of "Taps" helps keep this sound in mind:

etc.

Violin strings are tuned in perfect 5ths (P5), and this idea of sound can strengthen the identification of the interval from "do" (1) up to "so" (5) or the descending 5th from "do" (1) down to "fa" (4), which is more difficult to hear. Intervals are classified in Appendix A.

The study of intervals should grow out of the song repertoire and should be identified in terms of the scale or chord in that particular key. Later a broader study of intervals can be undertaken. What is suggested here is a bridge between the scale-centered approach in the lower grades and the need to read intervals in more advanced choral work.

LEARNING NEW SONGS. Intermediate-grade pupils who understand the sol-fa syllables should use them to analyze the melodic content of new songs. The whole song need not be sung with syllables if the proper *hearing* of typical patterns has been developed. When pupils recognize a group of notes as a scale line, beginning and ending at certain levels, they should be able to tune up in the proper key and hear its sound in the inner ear. However, when they come upon unfamiliar fragments, as in "Sleep and Rest," syllables can help them analyze and sing the troublesome spots.

As they undertake a new song, pupils should consider its rhythmic characteristics, establish the meter, and tap out rhythm patterns that may present a problem. They should consider its melody and form from the general point of view described earlier in this chapter before they try to read the notes. Experienced readers may then be ready to sing the song. Problems may arise, but they can be solved by isolation of difficult phrases.

Less experienced singers may need more assistance; they may hear the song sung by the teacher before they do any of the analysis suggested above. After they have a general idea of the song such students are in a better position to analyze it and to try to sing it. Some songs built around the primary chords (I, IV, V_7) will be read much more easily if the Autoharp is used as a harmonic background. Inexperienced singers might use some of the melody instruments to help them work out a new song.

However the song is studied, the pupils should have a feeling of satisfaction and accomplishment. Unrhythmic, note-by-note spelling out of a melody is not a *musical* experience. On the other hand, rote teaching without any attempt to develop understanding about the music can hardly be considered "education." A varied approach to new songs, with the application of effective techniques in solving melodic and rhythmic problems, is recommended.

Group Creativity in Songs

Creating "our own" anything gives children a real sense of identification and possession. When young children create a song in the classroom, the teacher may write the music with the words on a chart so all may see it. A child may draw an illustration to be mounted at the top of the chart. Older children can write out the song themselves and by doing so can learn more about music notation. Such a project may have particular importance to an individual; it may bring music closer to him and help him to identify it as something special in his life. He may begin to explore music as a personal interest when he discovers that he and his friends can create their own melodies.

LEARNING MUSIC THROUGH CREATING MUSIC. As children create melodies for selected verses, they become more acutely aware of line in the melody and form in a composition. They begin to note, with purposeful interest, how melodies in the songs they sing rise and fall; how most songs have one high point; how melodies in a two- or three-tone range tend to be uninteresting. They may look with renewed interest at the repetition and contrast in sections of the songs they sing and think of ways to improve the form of the song they are creating.

When children write additional stanzas for an existing melody, they are made aware of the rhythm of the words and the necessary relationship between word syllables and the rhythm patterns in the melody. They should be led to hear the accents of important words and to discover that these accents correspond to the metric scheme of the music. Many other details become meaningful to pupils as they create verses and melodies. Younger children notice fewer details; the creative act itself is the most important part of the experience. The teacher must assist the children with certain technical considerations they are not yet ready to comprehend fully.

Song-writing must grow out of activities that establish a readiness to create. Children who feel at home with singing find music a natural means of expression. When a topic is of concern and interest to them, children may feel the urge to express it in some new way, associating words and melody. Any classroom teacher can establish conditions favorable to the creation of melodies. He is in a better position to do so than is the special teacher who sees the children infrequently and is not acquainted with their intimate interests. However, unless the classroom teacher is skilled in identifying melodic patterns, he may need the help of a music specialist to notate the melody. The teacher may record the melody on tape as it is sung by the children. Later a musician can notate it correctly. Or the teacher may make a simple notation so that he or the children can remember the melody and sing it to a person able to write it.

Sometimes a classroom teacher may develop the idea of creating a song up to the point where the children are ready to sing their melodic ideas. Then the music specialist, if he is well known to the children so that they feel free to create in his presence, may come to the classroom to help develop the song.

CREATING WORDS FOR A MELODY. Children sometimes want to add another stanza to a song they know. This relatively simple first step in creativity is important because it shows children that they can successfully make up words for a song; it lends dignity and importance to an activity they carry on spontaneously in their play. The project in the classroom, however, should not be done in a way that makes this simple creative impulse a self-conscious one. The teacher should work with the natural aptitudes and habits in creativity that already exist.

Among the folk and activity songs, we find a natural setting for the creating of added stanzas. "What Shall We Do When We All Go Out?" (AFlk-59) and "Toodala" (AFlk-54) are two of the many songs Ruth Seeger points out as natural improvising songs in *American Folk Songs for Children*.

TOODALA

From *American Folk Songs for Children*. Doubleday & Co., New York, 1948. Copyright by the Texas Folklore Society, 1941. Used by permission.

"The Green Dress" (MTD-27) and "What Shall I Do?" (MRC-42) invite the child to make up new words to please his fancy or match his activity. More thought is required to add a stanza to other songs. "Trip a Trop a Tronjes" (FGB-61) is a lively, rhythmic melody in a foot-riding song.

TRIP A TROP A TRONJES

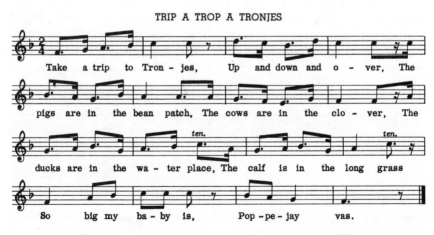

From *Americans and Their Songs* (Harper and Brothers). Reprinted by permission of the author, Frank Luther.

Instead of "Take a Trip to Tronjes" second grade children might wish to take a trip "to the country," "to the playground," or "to Disneyland."

If Disneyland were the subject, they might sing the first phrase and find that these words can be used:

After this beginning, facts and fancy about Disneyland would be put into words that fit the rhythmic pattern of the melody. Questions to individuals would bring out ideas that the teacher might list on the chalkboard:

"When did you go to Disneyland?" "On our vacation"
"For the holiday"
"For a little trip"
"In the summertime"

"What did you do there?" "We rode on the river boat"
"We had a ride on the mule's pack"
"We saw Frontierland and real Indians"

"When you were away again what did you think about it? Did you really like it?" "I had lots of fun." "I want to go back again next year." Answers will furnish ample material for a new stanza.

The next step is to adapt the words to the melody. Ask the children to sing the new words for the first phrase and then to continue with "loo" on the second phrase as they try to find words to fit the melody. Slight rhythmic changes are often unavoidable, but not a serious deviation from the original as long as the metric beat and general rhythmic swing are maintained. Sometimes several syllables will need to be sung on one beat. Compare the following alterations:

It is not necessary that the verses created by young children form a rhyming scheme. This is a refinement that can be learned later.

The chief things a teacher should do are:

1. Be sure that the children know the melody well.
2. Keep ideas flowing so that when a phrase does not fit the music another may easily be found.
3. Have the children *sing* their ideas, either as a group or individually, to hear whether they can be adjusted to the musical phrase.
4. When an idea is especially good, suggest small word changes that will help it conform to the rhythmic scheme.

Notice that the important words in a song occur on the accent beat and that articles and prepositions are usually on the upbeat as in "The pigs are in . . ."

The words adapted should be in the mood and spirit of the melody. Decide whether the melody is lively and rollicking (as in "Trip a Trop a Tronjes") or contemplative (as in "Sleep and Rest") and more appropriate for descriptive word pictures.

CREATING A MELODY. Children take unusual pride and interest in a melody they create for a poem. It may be a poem written in response to some topic of interest, or one enjoyed in choral reading or some other setting. Activities preliminary to the creation of such a melody in the classroom are those that the children use in vocal play. Simple song-chants are natural and easy for children. As Satis Coleman has suggested (Chapter Two), musical conversations on one or two tones help free the singing voice. The teacher may ask questions in a singing voice to which the children may reply:

When pupils are able to respond freely in this simple way, they will be more successful in singing melodies for verses they may choose to set to music.

Instrumental melody-making, suggested in Chapter Four, is a good background for more extensive creation of songs. However, when the teacher works with the children as a group, catching, developing, and recording the melodies they sing, the melodies may be longer and much more varied than those created with a limited number of tones on an instrument.

It is best to select, for the first such creative experience, a poem with considerable rhythmic movement. The first stanza of "A Swing Song"[1] by William Allingham would be a good choice:

> Swing, swing,
> Sing, sing,
> Here! my throne and I am a king!
> Swing, swing,
> Sing, sing,
> Farewell, earth, for I'm on the wing!

The teacher may write the poem on the chalkboard, with some space between the lines for notation. The children are asked to read the lines aloud several times until they find its natural rhythmic swing. The teacher may observe which words are accented and underline these. Since the accented word will fall on the accent in the music, a measure bar may be drawn before each:

| Swing, swing, | Sing, sing,

| Here! my throne and | I am a king!

Notice that this verse swings in two beats to the measure. Third grade classes who have worked with the metric beat and accent, as suggested in Chapter Three, may understand the placement of measure bars. They can help to identify the accents as they chant the lines.

Once the natural rhythmic swing of the verse is determined and the pupils are well acquainted with the words, the development of a melody can begin. Discuss the poem with the children. What kind of a melody is required? Do the words suggest the movement of the melodic line at different points? Since it is "A Swing Song," the smooth movement of the swing should be present. Further, there should be definite high and low points in the melody. Because the last line ends with "I'm on the wing!", probably the melody should rise rather than fall at the end.

Ask the children to chant "Swing, swing, Sing, sing" to themselves as they try to find a melody for it. One child may sing softly a snatch of melody that might be a good beginning. Ask this child to sing his melody louder. Assume this to be the melody:

Immediately the teacher and/or the class should sing what was heard in order to capture it in memory. Re-sing once or twice. Does it seem like a good beginning? If so, the teacher or pupils must find suitable notation so that it is not forgotten. Perhaps blank notation, scale numbers, or syllables will help:

Swing,	swing,	Sing,	sing
1 2 3	5	1 2 3	6
do re mi	so	do re mi	la

Syllables or numbers can be used if the teacher or pupils are able to tell which tone has the position of "do" or "1" in relation to the other tones. The ability to identify tonal patterns by ear is valuable. A piano or bells may be used to pick out the melody, but often, in the search for the tones sung, other tones are played that interfere with the original melody.

Once the melody for the first phrase is captured on paper or tape recorder or is secure in the memory, the next phrase must be related to it. Ask all of the children to sing the first phrase aloud and then to continue chanting or singing the next. There may be considerable sound but when someone raises his hand, the teacher should ask him to sing his melody. The teacher and/or the class immediately re-sings it as close to the original as possible. Then they go back and sing both first and second phrases consecutively. If it sounds convincing, this added phrase is put down in notation or recorded on tape. If it is not appealing to the group, other children may sing melodies for the line until something suitable is found.

It is important in this work to sing the preceding phrase as a lead into the creation of a new phrase. In this way, the two will be related to each other. If each phrase were created separately, the result might be quite disconnected.

Some teachers establish a key by playing a tonic chord and having the children sing the chord before they begin to create their melody. These teachers impose limitations on the young composers by assuming that the major is the scale suitable for a composition. Perhaps a child will hear a minor scale fragment for the first melody:

Swing, ____ swing, Sing, ____ sing

He may not know that he is singing in the minor. His chief concern is that he has a melody that appeals to him! The major scale, although it may be more common in our civilization, has no claim to being "better" than other scales. If a child sings an unusual melody and the class finds it satisfactory, it certainly should be used. It is sometimes interesting to play an arbitrary chord progression over which a melody is improvised but, for the greatest freedom in creating a melody, no key or chord should be imposed.

The meter signature is not of concern to young children, but it may be a problem for the teacher or older pupils. It was found that "A Swing Song" moves in two beats to a measure. Common metric schemes in two beats per measure occur in $\frac{2}{4}$ and $\frac{6}{8}$ meter. The following difference exists:

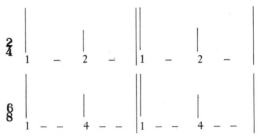

"A Swing Song" fits the metric scheme for $\frac{6}{8}$. This is especially evident when three separate syllables demand three divisions of the beat:

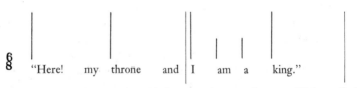

Usually verses that are smooth and flowing in two beats will best fit into $\frac{6}{8}$ meter. More square-cut rhymes will be in $\frac{2}{4}$.

If a verse has a longer line, uninterrupted by accents, it will be better notated in $\frac{4}{4}$ meter. The first stanza of "The Idle Shepherd Boys"[2] by William Wordsworth is an example:

$\frac{4}{4}$ The |valley rings with mirth and joy;
A - |mong the hills the echoes play
A |never, never ending song,
To |welcome in the May.

If read in $\frac{2}{4}$ meter, the effect is jarring and broken by unnecessary accents:

$\frac{2}{4}$ The |valley rings with | mirth and joy;
A - |mong the hills the | echoes play, *etc.*

After pupils have had some experience in such melody writing, they will find that a melody that is too closely tied to the metric scheme of the poem may be pedantic and unimaginative. The subject of the poem may suggest the meter. A lyrical imaginative text might suggest a more free-flowing, florid melody. "The Idle Shepherd Boys" might be set in a waltz rhythm with a greater variety of note lengths and some slurred passages. Children who croon to themselves might produce such a melody, while those who use music in relation to rhythm activities will create songs with a more chant-like character. Both types of creative singing should be encouraged. Listening critically to their compositions will help pupils appreciate songs in both types.

When a melody has been established for the entire stanza, the children should sing it several times. If they are not pleased with all parts of it, changes can be made. A good song always gives a sense of completeness at the end, unless there is some special reason for an unfinished effect. If the new song does not sound complete, the pupils should make some adjustments in the ending. If the tonal range of the new song is too high or too low it may be transposed. When children who have made creative attempts sing other songs, they will have greater interest in noticing endings, the repetition of phrases, and other characteristics of the melody.

In this creative activity, the chief problems are:

1. To capture the melodic ideas of the children. Sometimes the melody is sung with uncertainty. The teacher and pupils must listen carefully to sing and notate it as it was given.
2. To develop an integrated melody, not a composite of unrelated melodic ideas from several sources.
3. To use melodic ideas of the children, not unduly influenced by the teacher's notion of what the melody should be like.
4. To record the song so that it may be correctly sung later.

Composing a melody can be very important to some individuals and a fine experience for the group of children as a whole. Here the pupils are able to use all of their understanding of the elements of music and its notation. Although it may take several music periods to complete one song, it is well worth the time spent. More than one opportunity of this kind should be arranged during the year.

ACTIVITIES FOR COLLEGE CLASSES

A. Written Assignments

1. Select two contrasting songs and analyze their musical characteristics: rhythm, melody, harmony, and form. In what ways are these characteristics in conformity with the subject and purpose of each song?

2. In a second or third grade song book, find examples of the tonal patterns listed on page 173. Write these out, putting the correct syllables under the words. Be sure that each pattern has a sense of unity and completeness.

3. In three minor songs find significant tonal patterns that may be isolated and sung with syllables. Write out these tonal patterns with the text fragment; put the syllables below.

4. Select a song in which a chromatic alteration of tones occurs. Write out the phrase in which the alterations occur and put the syllables below the notes. What pattern of syllables could children rehearse to assure the correct sound for the chromatic notes? (See page 175.)

5. Create and notate a short song, either for an original verse or for a poem you select.

6. See No. 1 under Classroom Projects.

B. Classroom Projects

1. Select a second or third grade song. Prepare to teach the song to the college class, assuming that books are available to each member. First, make a complete study and written report of the song:
   a. List ways in which the song may be enriched with instruments, movement, etc.
   b. Analyze the melody, rhythm, harmony, and form of the song. How will these factors determine the way in which you will teach the song?
   c. Assume a certain musical experience level for your "class." Let this level and your own abilities determine what teaching techniques you will use.
   d. What musical details will you attempt to bring to the attention of the children? Make specific plans for teaching whatever rhythmic or melodic concepts seem appropriate.
   Present your complete analysis and lesson plan to the instructor for evaluation. Since the class time for teaching is limited, select only that part of the total lesson plan that will demonstrate your mastery of important teaching techniques.

2. Play on the bells and sing your song (see No. 5 above) to the class. Discuss its melody, form, and rhythm. In what ways would you say that the melody conveys the meaning and feeling of the text?

3. Make a flannel board for use in an elementary music·class. Bring it to class and demonstrate its use.

CHAPTER NOTES

1. William Allingham, "A Swing Song," found in *The Moon Is Shining Bright as Day* by Ogden Nash (Philadelphia: J. B. Lippincott Company, 1953).

2. William Wordsworth, "The Idle Shepherd Boys."

OTHER REFERENCES

Boyden, David D., *An Introduction to Music* (New York: Alfred A. Knopf, Inc., 1956). Part One, "The Fundamentals."

Fox, Lillian Mohr, and Thomas L. Hopkins, *Creative School Music* (Morristown, N.J.: Silver Burdett Company, 1936). Chapter 4, "Creating Songs," Chapter 5, "Developing Original Poetry," and Chapter 6, "Developing Original Melody."

Mursell, James L., *Music and the Classroom Teacher* (Morristown, N.J.: Silver Burdett Company, 1951). Chapter 8, "Creative Activities," and Chapter 9, "Musicianship."

———, *Music Education Principles and Programs* (Morristown, N.J.: Silver Burdett Company, 1956). Chapters 5 and 6, "Music Reading and Musical Growth," and Chapter 12, "Creation."

Myers, Louise Kifer, *Teaching Children Music in the Elementary School*, Second Edition (Englewood Cliffs, N.J.: Prentice-Hall, Inc., 1956). Chapter 5, "Creating Music."

Nye, Robert Evans, and Bjornar Bergethon, *Basic Music for Classroom Teachers* (Englewood Cliffs, N.J.: Prentice-Hall, Inc., 1954). Chapter 8, "Creating Your Own Songs."

Perham, Beatrice, *Music in the New School* (Park Ridge, Ill.: Neil A. Kjos Music Co., 1941). Chapter 5, "Creative Learning."

CHAPTER SEVEN

THE USE OF
BODILY MOVEMENT

Rhythmic movement is one of the most satisfying ways in which children may respond to music. It is used extensively in the music program of the kindergarten and first grade, but, in general, fails to move ahead in the other grades. Only in rare instances does it go beyond the initial steps and develop its potential as a creative, expressive outlet for children. Music has movement and dynamics that suggest mood and ideas to the individual; children need to develop the freedom to respond to music and to express what they feel. At the same time, they can arrive at broader understandings about music, its rhythm and form.

Expressive movement, as an activity in music, is related to the programs in physical education and creative dramatics; skills in movement and freedom for expression are necessary in all. The objectives in the use of music differ among these areas. In physical education, the objectives of expressive movement are physical development, health, and poise; music assists by helping to make the movement rhythmic. In creative dramatics, movement expresses what the individual himself feels; music is selected or composed to support ideas already present. In both of these areas music is an assistant.

The objective for movement in the music program is to learn to listen to music, to explore it with natural movements and imagination, and to hear and feel the expressive ideas in it. Whether the immediate activity is creative movement, folk dancing, or a study of rhythmic patterns and phrases, this objective for the music program remains the same. However, work in the other fields is valuable and contributes toward a richer musical experience, for the more flexible one is physically, the greater are his possibilities for expressing what he feels in the music. The imaginative approach to movement that is developed in creative dramatics gives the individual the necessary feeling of freedom to express confidently what he hears in the music.

BASIC EXPERIENCES AT THE PRIMARY LEVEL

The development of rhythmic response may be initiated in any grade, preferably in the kindergarten and first grade. If it is not begun there, teachers at other levels will find it necessary to establish attitudes and skills that will permit bodily movement to be included in the music activities.

*Approaches to Rhythmic and
Creative Movement*

The teacher must approach rhythmic movement at the point of understanding for the child, develop the physical ability and freedom to move in expressive ways, and then relate this movement to music. The early steps can be taken in several classroom situations.

CHILD-CREATED MOVEMENT. During "sharing time," when children tell of their experiences, the teacher may say in response to a child's narration, "Yes, Jeanie, show us how you walked to the store. Did you feel happy? Were you in a hurry?" And perhaps Jeanie will be able to reconstruct her mood and movement so that the whole class may know how she felt. This is creative dramatics; it is not related to music at this point; yet it is the type of experience on which the interpretation of music is based. The teacher may guide the rhythmic experience a step further by suggesting that other children "go with Jeanie to the store just as she went." The experience becomes an impersonation when the other children follow the pattern set by Jeanie.

Stephen may one day give his physical interpretation of the way the bear moved in a story. The teacher may support his movement by playing a deep-sounding drum or sandblocks in the rhythm Stephen establishes. If the teacher is able, he may improvise a piano accompaniment for Stephen's "bear"; other children may join in or take turns being the bear. In these early stages of rhythmic training, rhythm instruments or piano provides the best accompaniment for movement because the teacher can adjust the tempo to that of the child so that he will have the optimum freedom in movement.

Tired children, happy children, "bears," and "elephants" will walk in their distinct ways. "Ponies" will trot and gallop in the pasture; children will run and skip to school and they will begin to listen for rhythms and sounds that suggest particular ways of moving. To assist in the gradual development of movement responses to music, the teacher must:

1. Work from the child's fundamental movements, such as walking and running,
2. Help the child find freedom of movement within limits of the classroom,
3. Show him in what respect his movement is rhythmic,
4. Relate his movement to rhythmic sound,
5. Provide opportunities for him to move with other children in their rhythm,
6. Help him learn to move in any of the fundamental rhythmic patterns at will,

7. Help him arrive at the point when he is able to adjust his movement to music in a predetermined tempo.

The individual children, the group, the situations that arise, and the teacher's own way of working, all help to determine how the steps are accomplished.

Activities in physical education develop coordination and skill in movement, and a program in creative dramatics encourages freedom of expression. The teacher will find Chapters 5 and 6 of *Creative Rhythmic Movement for Children*[1] by Andrews particularly helpful in establishing freedom in movement.

᾽ MOVEMENT WITH SINGING. Many songs provide opportunities for children to respond with the fundamental movements. A song may be so strongly rhythmic that, regardless of the text, it will suggest skipping, running, galloping, or marching. "What Shall We Do When We All Go Out?" (AFlk-59) and other similar chanting songs lend themsélves to improvisation on endless activities during the school play periods or with friends at home.

"Yankee Doodle" (see page 59) is representative of many songs that children sing while strutting or marching. In contrast, the French nursery tune suggested as "A Work Chant" (MTD-24) may serve the individual as a vocal accompaniment to his private activities.

Dancing tunes may inspire movement in basic patterns. "Come, Let's Be Merry" (S&R-18), the English country dance tune that Percy Grainger used in his "Country Gardens," is fine for either skipping or marching.

COME, LET'S BE MERRY

Lilla Belle Pitts   English Country Dance

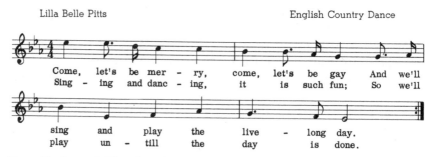

From *Singing and Rhyming* of OUR SINGING WORLD Series, Enlarged Edition. Used by permission of Ginn and Company, owner of the copyright.

SINGING GAMES AND DANCES. In their most informal setting, singing games are played by small groups of children on the playground, clapping, walking, skipping or using other suitable movements. Younger children often learn the games from older children. Most kindergarten and first grade song books contain a variety of singing games. "Ring Around a Rosy" is an example. (See page 88.) Other traditional titles are:

"The Farmer in the Dell"	"Did You Ever See a Lassie?"
"Looby Loo"	"London Bridge"
"Mulberry Bush"	"A-Hunting We Will Go"

Less familiar examples, some from foreign countries, have been given a place in the more recent primary song books:

"Bounce Around" (AS I-95)	"Round and Round a Circle" (KBk-39)
"Cat and Mouse" (KBk-40)	
"Ha, Ha, This-a-way" (MTD-6)	"Willowbee" (ECh-65)
	"Kagome" (MRC-36)

Although singing games are the first group dances used in the classroom, very soon the children will enjoy simple folk dances that have words to tell what to do. The words may be incidental, and singing is not expected to be the only accompaniment, as it may in the singing game. It is not until the children are able to enjoy a rhythmic, patterned movement that they use the folk dance rather than the singing game. A few are used in the first grade, but more extensive participation in folk dances begins in the latter second and third grades.

Some of the earliest dances used, with and without words, are:

"Bow, Belinda" (FGB-52, ECh-64)	"Klappdans" (Swedish) (RCA Victor LPM-162)
"Paw-Paw Patch" (MTY-15)	
"The Old Brass Wagon" (ECh-64)	"Shoemaker's Dance" (RCA Victor LPM-1624)
"Sandy Maloney" (FGB-47)	
"Pop Goes the Weasel" (MNLA-122)	"Chimes of Dunkirk" (RCA Victor LPM-1624)
	"Seven Steps" (AS I-100)

There are two essential parts to a folk dance. The foot pattern is the response to the basic recurring rhythm of the music. Primary children need not learn such definite steps as the schottische, polka, two-step, and waltz. The easiest foot patterns are skipping, marching, a bouncey walk, or a step-slide to the side. For many dances more than one type of foot pattern is suitable; the selection of a particular one is determined by the tempo of the music and the children's skill in dancing.

Phrasing and sectional form in the music determine the floor pattern, the directional movement that the dancers take. The words may tell them in what direction to move. American square dancers follow the directions of a "caller"; in other dances the participants learn the sequence of movement and follow the phrasing and sectional changes in the music. The most beautiful folk dancing is that in which the dancers keep precise rhythm and execute the various directional patterns in perfect coordination with the changing phrases and sections of the music.

Folk dancing contributes to the social and physical development of the child. The musical values are not so easy to realize. If the activity is to be a part of the music program, the teacher should keep these musical objectives well in mind:

1. To give the pupils another opportunity to respond rhythmically to music.
2. To help them hear and respond to phrasing and form in music through an enjoyable physical activity.

As they dance, the children must learn to listen, feel the rhythm, and finally experience the synchronization of movement with music. The activity must be a joyous one, and at the same time the teacher must call attention to rhythm, phrase structure, and musical form. To point up the rhythm, he may have some children sing and clap while others use the basic foot pattern in a simple line or circle formation. A few rhythm instruments may be played to underline the metric beat.

The most simple sectional construction children notice may be the difference between rhythmic movements required for the verse and for the refrain. In "Rig-a-Jig-Jig" (see page 40), which is often used as a simple dance, the verse suggests walking while the chorus suggests galloping or skipping.

In most folk dances the foot pattern remains the same throughout, but the floor pattern follows the phrase changes in the music. To help the children notice the phrase construction, the teacher may omit the regular floor pattern and ask the children to use the foot pattern as they move in a line formation and then go in the opposite direction on each new phrase. "Paw-Paw Patch" may be danced with one of several foot patterns, and the short phrases may be worked into varied floor patterns.

PAW-PAW PATCH

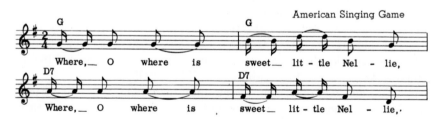

"Paw-Paw Patch," from *Music Through the Year* of the New TOGETHER-WE-SING Series, published by Follett Publishing Company, Chicago, Illinois.

Where,_ O   where   is   sweet_ lit - tle Nel - lie?
'Way   down   yon - der in   the   paw - paw   patch.

The following dances are suitable for third grade pupils using the techniques described:

"Rig-a-Jig-Jig" (MIOT-38, S&R-16)   "Old Brass Wagon" (MNLA-121)
"Pop Goes the Weasel" (MNLA-   "Paw-Paw Patch" (MTY-15, AS III-
122)   54)
"Shoo Fly" (MNLA-118, AS III-52)   "Skip to My Lou" (S&R-44, MIOT-
    59, AS II-24)

Many good recorded folk dances are now available. Some of the easier ones are found in these collections:

RCA VICTOR series: *The World of Folk Dances*, "First Folk Dances" (LP record) or single records such as "Kinderpolka," "Klappdans," "Shoemaker's Dance," "Dance of Greeting"
BOWMAR RECORDS: *Singing Games*, Album 2; *Singing Games and Folk Dances*, Album 3
WHEELER-EVANS: *Folk Dance*, Album 3

Folk dancing is musically valuable when the dancers can listen to and follow the music rather than simply count the steps. Many teachers make the mistake of selecting a dance in which the foot pattern is too intricate or the floor pattern too varied for an inexperienced group. To promote the desired *musical* objectives, the traditional dance may be simplified or a new one invented that will be more appropriate.

Early Interpretive Movement

In changing from child-created movement, discussed earlier, to the interpretation of music, children are asked to adjust their movements to what they hear, rather than having the accompaniment pick up their rhythm. It will be a gradual transition in which the teacher must patiently accommodate a wide variety of individual aptitudes for movement. The teacher who can play the piano may select short musical sketches to which the children respond.

THE FUNDAMENTAL MOVEMENTS. One day the teacher may say: "Yesterday after school I saw two boys from Mrs. Edwards' room going down the sidewalk, not side-by-side but one after the other. Perhaps this rhythm will tell you how they were moving." Then the teacher plays a running rhythm on the piano or establishes a brisk running pattern by playing coconut shells or a high-toned drum. Perhaps some of the boys can run just as the rhythm says the other boys ran. The same day, or another day, the teacher plays a walking rhythm, and the children interpret it through movement, noticing that different moods in walks can be heard, such as those described in "Variations on a Walk" (ECh-56, 57). Children should think and move imaginatively in response to "Who is walking?" "How does he feel?" "Where is he going?"

Since running and walking are the rhythmic movements of all children, they should be used first. Gradually skips and gallops may be added for variety and challenge to those who are ready. However, several levels of participation should be planned; do not abandon the use of child-created movement (page 191). Some children are physically less well coordinated and need continued experience on that level.

The teacher should plan for variety in the music used during one lesson. When the children hear obvious differences in rhythm, tempo, and mood, they understand the necessity of moving in different ways. Every kindergarten and first grade book provides music for the fundamental movements such as walking, running, marching, skipping, and galloping. The following compositions are suggested for different types of movement:

For walking:

"Der Kleine Wanderer," Gurlitt (KBk-23)
"Promenade" from String Quartet, Opus 100, Schubert (MIOT-109)
Sonata, Opus 14, No. 2, Beethoven (AS I-111)

For running:

"The Fair," Gurlitt (AS I-117)
"Round Dance," *Piano Pieces for Children*, Vol. I, No. 10, Bartók (MTD-135)
"Run, Run, Run," Concone (KBk-11)

For marching:

"March in F," Anderson (FGB-36)
"March in D," J. S. Bach (MTD-140)
"Soldiers' March," Schumann (AS I-115, KBk-130, OFM-97)

For swaying:

"Waltz," Opus 39, No. 2, Brahms (MTD-137, KBk-31)
"Waltz Serenade," Poldini (KBk-100)

For skipping or galloping:

"The Reaper's Song," Schumann (AS I-149, FGB-122, OFM-171)
"Tarantelle," Prokofieff, Opus 65 (MTD-132)
"Gigue" from Suite No. 3, Corelli (MTD-132, KBk-13)

The folk tunes and other selections in *Music for Active Children*[2] are suitable for young children. The music is arranged in classified rhythmic groupings for easy location of appropriate compositions for the fundamental movements. In his own piano repertoire a teacher may find portions of compositions that move at a steady pace suitable for rhythmic activities. Or he may improvise simple accompaniments using the basic I, IV, and V chords as suggested in the *Kindergarten Book* of the MUSIC FOR YOUNG AMERICANS Series.

If the teacher cannot use the piano, he should explore the possibilities of the simple percussion instruments. The rhythm sticks or two halves of a coconut shell struck together may suggest running.

The same pattern played more slowly may suggest walking. The drum, alternately sounded in the middle and tapped on the rim in a ⅜ pattern makes a convincing skipping rhythm.

The rhythm patterns for skipping and galloping are interchangeable. However, the ⅜ pattern gives a feeling of flow and roundness to skipping. Galloping is a more sharply defined movement, for which the following ²⁄₄ pattern is more suitable.

Any of the rhythm instruments used for song-enrichment may be used for accompaniments to bodily movement. When marching, pupils may choose to add a drum on the metric beat or the accent. When they know a melody well, they may use the small rhythm sticks playing the melody rhythm as an accompaniment. Special effects may be produced by cymbals, gong, or triangle on climaxes or selected accents. Children may accompany galloping and skipping by a simple playing of the metric beat; the teacher and older children may make a more exciting accompaniment by playing the characteristic recurring rhythm pattern on the drum or coconut shells (see examples above). When recorded music is used, these instruments may be added in similar ways. They should serve as an enrichment and therefore should not be used in large numbers.

USING RECORDED MUSIC. Having learned to follow the rhythm of the drum and the piano, primary children will be ready to interpret recorded music. In its early use it is important that this music be:

1. In a tempo to which children are able to adjust their movements easily. Music suitable for the free rhythmic activities of young children is somewhat faster than that appropriate for adults.

2. Steady in rhythm without breaks or retards to interrupt the basic movement.
3. Musically good in all respects: rhythmic, rich in tone color, and conveying mood and feeling as well as rhythm. Quality is important because a musical experience is only as valuable as the music used. In the early stages of rhythmic movement, the music must be simple; but there is a difference between simple, uncomplicated music and music that is poor in quality and unappealing.

City and county music consultants as well as teachers of music education in the colleges are usually informed of the available records. The teacher may keep in touch with new releases through these persons or he may obtain one of the annual catalogs published for school use (see Appendix B for names and addresses of record companies).

The first three albums in *Rhythmic Activities* (RCA Victor RECORD LIBRARY FOR ELEMENTARY SCHOOLS) have been especially useful for rhythmic activities in the primary grades. They are available in most schools and are used as examples in the following discussion. ADVENTURES IN MUSIC, a new record library for elementary schools, is issued by the RCA Victor Record Division. A number of compositions in this group will be valuable.

Some recordings are accompanied by narration or a song and others are merely piano or small instrument ensembles. The Greystone Record Corporation has "A Visit to My Little Friend," "My Playful Scarf," and others under the *Children's Record Guild* label. Among their *Young People's Records* are "When the Sun Shines," "A Rainy Day," and others. *Bowmar Records*, *Ruth Evans*, and *Phoebe James* are among those who have created series of records for this use.

In addition to these special educational recordings, the teacher is advised to look for suitable compositions in his own record collection or in that available at his school. Excerpts from many compositions, especially dance forms and incidental music from the Classic Period, are usable.

PHYSICAL ARRANGEMENTS AND TECHNIQUES IN GUIDANCE. Children need space in order to feel free to respond in the desired movement. Skipping, galloping, and twirling require more space than walking and marching, and when the space is limited fewer children are able to respond simultaneously. Those who do not participate in the full body motion may use movements of the arms and the trunk as they sit in their chairs. This permits them to respond in a limited way and orients them to the rhythm so that they will be more successful when it is their turn to move with the full pattern. The teacher uses some music for large free movements and other music for more limited movements such as swaying, stepping, or rocking so that the entire class may respond occasionally as a group.

A fruitful program in rhythmic movement in the classroom often requires some readjustment of furniture so that there are two or three wide aisles or space at the front of the room. The classroom has the advantage of being available at any hour and many teachers feel that a finer response to music is obtained in the friendly atmosphere of the home room.

A multipurpose room or a gymnasium has more space for movement. However, in a very large room, there may be so much space that movement seems to have no limitations. When free creative movement is the goal, this is ideal, but when the objective is the interpretation of music, the intimacy of the project may be lost and the teacher's directions and the music may be difficult to hear.

Children should experiment with movement, going in different directions to develop freedom and originality. Some children are very creative and imaginative; a few prefer to follow the lead of other children. To get the timid child started, the teacher may suggest, "Tommy, go with Joe," or "Sue, follow Mary." Children who feel insecure in this activity generally will be happier moving in a group than individually.

One or two children may be very well coordinated, imaginative, bursting with ideas and eager to "perform." If the child is sincere and creative rather than a "show-off," the teacher sometimes may use this child to initiate ideas, but he must be careful not to promote a "star." Such a child can discourage other children from participating.

Classification of compositions by rhythmic movement can be a convenience for the teacher, but it tells little about the kind of movement and mood the music might elicit from a child who is responsive to music and who has a sense of freedom in movement that will permit him to express what he feels. One composition may suggest several movements. Children should be encouraged to try out these possibilities in order to judge which seems the most appropriate. "Gigue" from *Suite Number 3* by Corelli (Rhy I, MTD-132, KBk-13, see next page) is suitable for skipping, galloping, walking, bending, swaying, or "rowing boats."

There is nothing boisterous or heavy about this composition. Whatever movements are adopted should be carried out in a gay dancing spirit with a sense of freedom and flow. Movement in response to music must be conceived in terms of its mood as well as its rhythm, and therefore the ideas expressed will go beyond thinking merely that "this is music for skipping" or "this music sounds like running."

GIGUE

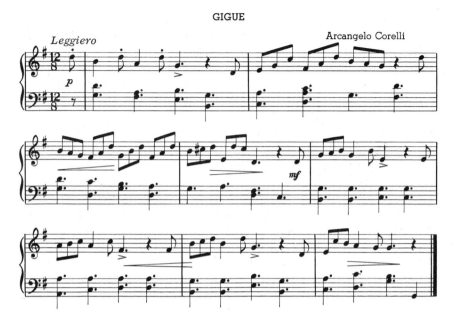

From *The Kindergarten Book* of OUR SINGING WORLD Series, Enlarged Edition. Used by permission of Ginn and Company, owner of the copyright.

A teacher may relate the music to a poem or a story that will influence the movement of the children. The RCA Victor RECORD LIBRARY FOR ELEMENTARY SCHOOLS and the ADVENTURES IN MUSIC series have "Notes for Teachers" that suggest poems, stories, and pictures that might be used with the compositions. Each teacher may have other material that is appropriate to certain pieces of music. Too many stories and pictures deprive a child of the opportunity to make his own interpretation of the music. A balance must be achieved between guidance and freedom, if the children are to learn to respond directly to music itself.

Sometimes the teacher may tell the children the title of a composition before they listen or attempt to move to the music. Most often, it is best to let the music itself suggest the movement because the title may limit the imagination, and the idea it suggests may not be as appropriate as the interpretation of the children. For example, "High Stepping Horses" (Rhy I) may be interpreted as trained circus horses parading around in a ring, tossing their manes with haughty air, if the children have seen such horses. When not given the name of the composition, most children interpret this music as a lithe animal moving through the woods, stopping to look around in a curious but cautious manner. For the children, their own interpretation is most valid if it portrays the rhythm and character of the music.

In response to music through bodily movement, a continuous awareness of the music is fully as important as the physical response, and certainly the emotional response must be an integral part of the total activity. The different parts of the music program cannot be isolated, for whatever happens in the listening activities, to be discussed in Chapter Eight, is surely akin to this.

Characterizations and Drama

It is impossible to draw a line between fundamental movements in a child's normal activities and his movements in impersonation. One moment he may be creeping on tiptoe as himself; the next moment his imagination may have added dramatic locale and characters. There is no reason to be concerned about the presence or absence of the dramatic situation, but the child who throws himself into a characterization may lose some of his self-consciousness and move with more freedom.

The imagination cannot be forced, but the teacher can encourage its use for the sake of the freedom and vitality it brings to rhythmic movement. Just a suggestion of a costume, ears for a rabbit, a simple mask for a bear, helps a child achieve a sense of realism. Scarves help to create the flowing line that is needed in the interpretation of some compositions. A scarf should be about 2½ times the height of the child so that he can hold it extended between both outstretched arms or let it flow freely behind him to give a feeling of elongation and grace to his movement.

INTERPRETATION OF SONGS AND SHORT PIECES. In many songs, both the text and the rhythm of the music suggest the activity. In some of these, rhythmic movement may be combined with pantomime. For "Old Mister Elephant" (see page 63) children may clasp both hands, bend from the waist, and let the continuous arc of the back, head, and arms suggest the head and trunk of the elephant. Since "Mister Elephant" is a heavy fellow, all movements are heavy and slow. The class may need to sing the song several times, readjusting the tempo of music and physical movement until both synchronize in a swaying rhythm that is just right for the elephant the children have in mind. Different groups of three or four children may move as "elephants" along "the jungle trail" as the other children sing.

Pantomiming the rhythmic movements of a heavy piece of machinery such as the wrecking machine in "Old House" (see page 41) will please the boys. "What kinds of movements does a wrecking machine make?" "How heavy is it? Show us." "How fast does it move?" "Yes, we have several good ideas now. Let's sing our song again, thinking about the movement, and see if we can get the music going at a good speed for these wrecking machines to operate." Thus, through leading questions and encouragement, the teacher helps the children develop rhythmic movement to accompany their song.

A more ambitious type of dramatization may involve two or more characters in related action. Here the possibilities are limited only by the imagination of the pupils and the time available for working out the details. "The Old Gray Cat" (MTD-37) is an excellent song for creative dramatic play.

THE OLD GRAY CAT

Alabama Folk Song

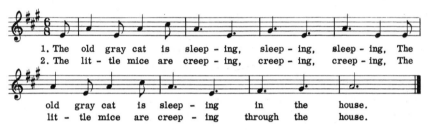

1. The old gray cat is sleep - ing, sleep - ing, sleep - ing, The
2. The lit - tle mice are creep - ing, creep - ing, creep - ing, The

old gray cat is sleep - ing in the house.
lit - tle mice are creep - ing through the house.

3. The little mice are nibbling in the house.
4. The little mice are sleeping in the house.
5. The old gray cat comes creeping through the house.
6. The little mice all scamper through the house.

From *Music Through the Day.* © 1956, Silver Burdett Co. Used by permission of Dr. Byron Arnold from whose collection of Alabama folk songs it is taken.

Some of the children are mice who creep and nibble around the house, always slightly fearful and watching as the old gray cat sleeps; but watch how they scamper when the cat wakes up!

Ideally the teacher is a guide, helping the pupils develop, evaluate, and refine their responses rather than imposing his own ideas. Rhythmic activity related to songs can provide one of the best early means for promoting expressive movement in the classroom. In the words of the song are the ideas upon which to build an impersonation. In the music, if the music and text are well mated, are the rhythmic characteristics for the movement. In some songs, although the text may describe an animal or other character, the musical rhythm may not be appropriate for movement. Teacher and children should evaluate the rhythmic possibilities of their songs, using movement only when it is convincing.

Some music may be equally appropriate for boys and for girls. However, in the early stages of interpretive movement, when the subject is of greater importance to the children than the movement itself, the boys may prefer to characterize animals and bolder subjects while girls may be fascinated with fairies or butterflies. The teacher must be sensitive in his selection so that in every lesson there is something of appeal to each group.

Many composers have tried to bring characters to life through music. Among the animal sketches available for piano are these:

"The Wild Horseman," Schumann (AS I-128, FGB-24, OFM-232)
"The Elephant," Still (MIOT-80)
"Postillion," Godard (FGB-22)
"Bear Dance," Bartók (KBk-122)

"Butterflies," Opus 37, No. 2, Concone (OFM-268)
"Papillons," Opus 2, No. 8, Schumann (KBk-108)

Suggestions and suitable music for "Animal Antics" are given in *Come and Caper*.[3] "Animal Sketches" by the contemporary American composer, William Grant Still, have been included in *Music for Early Childhood*, pages 49 to 53.

Like the painter, the composer may use a combination of techniques to create a small composition depicting one character. When such compositions are interpreted through bodily movement, more varied techniques must be used. "Fairies and Giants" by Elgar (A in M, III-1), "Fairies" by Schubert, and "Clowns" by Mendelssohn (Rhy I) are delightful musical characterizations. Both boys and girls will find some part of MacDowell's "Marionettes" (Lis III) that will appeal to them, for here in one group are sketches of "Witch," "Clown," and "Villain." Tchaikovsky's version of "The Witch" is available in *Rhythmic Activities* Volume III.

It is highly important that, over a period of time, boys and girls have experience interpreting many short sketches. Part of this work should be teacher-directed so that the children expand their understanding of what may be heard in music and the varied ways of expressing these ideas through movement. Balancing this directed work there should be ample opportunity for the pupils to listen carefully to other short compositions and develop their own interpretations.

LONGER DRAMATIC PROJECTS. Generally, short, separate musical sketches provide the greatest experience with different musical rhythms and characterizations. On occasion, several of these sketches, developed individually, may be combined in a story sequence. Or, after the children have had considerable experience, a larger piece of music may be interpreted. *The Nutcracker Suite* by Tchaikovsky, a group of eight short compositions based on a fairy tale, is a considerable challenge. The story and the music are delightful, the sections are short and varied and lend themselves to expressive movement.

Peter and the Wolf by Prokofieff has the narration of the story integrated with the music and offers older children interesting opportunities for character portrayal. The music makes the listener feel that Peter is an active, happy, outgoing boy with lots of friends. Grandfather is a gruff, stern old man, who walks stiffly and heavily. The cat, of course, is an agile, stealthy creature. Whether or not the complete story is dramatized, it is a fine experience for the children to portray some of these characters through movement. Such activity will help them direct their attention to details in the music, which suggest the character even more than does the narrator.

The Comedians by Kabalevsky is taken from incidental music that the composer originally wrote for the children's play, *Inventor and Comedian*. This suite has ten short sections, all evocative of characterizations and dramatic action in expressive movement.

"Prologue," which is lively and jocular, has some suggestion of stiff mechanical movement.

"Gallop" is vigorous and rapid, suggestive of rodeo activities or other good-natured, vigorous sporting play.

"March" suggests tiptoeing and stealth with some grotesque qualities.

"Waltz" has graceful running or soaring lines. It suggests birds, butterflies, and bees.

"Pantomime" certainly should be music for bears. Several big, gruff bears!

"Intermezzo" is lively, witty, and dancing.

"Little Lyric Scene" is a short restful interlude, perhaps a night scene.

"Gavotte" is an early morning dance of sunbeams and fairies in a meadow.

"Scherzo" may suggest a chase.

"Epilogue" brings back some of the vigorous activity and jocular character of the first two sections.

Many of these sections can be used separately, but the suite as a whole is well balanced and may be tied together in a story sequence if the pupils are imaginative enough to create one.

In order to interpret such varied music a child must use a combination of rhythmic movements, following important melody lines and retards as well as sectional changes. In doing so he may become so immersed in his impersonation that he is unaware of the movements he uses. This is not a problem, for of prime importance is the fact that he is developing a sensitivity to music, to its rhythm, tone color, and mood.

Children should be encouraged to "live" the character they portray; facial expression, body weight, and posture as well as rhythm should be representative. To do this the class must bring to the work a seriousness of purpose. The teacher must give constructive evaluation, ample encouragement, and praise.

Noticing Detail in Musical Composition

Primary children may successfully move in response to the metric beat, general rhythmic swing, and mood in music. The musical purposes for this early experience are to give the children a meaningful reason for listening to music, to direct their imaginations to it as an expressive medium, and to give them experience with its rhythmic elements. However, bodily movement can be used with both songs and recorded music to analyze and to develop a more precise understanding of details in melody and rhythm.

PORTRAYING MELODIC MOVEMENT. The melodic line is an important element to which the children may direct their attention. As the melody rises and falls, circles, or moves on one plane, the children move their arms and bodies in these ways. The basic rhythm in "Ballet" by Gluck (Rhy I) is a light running pattern, but the melody moves in long flowing lines, sometimes circling and swaying and at other times climbing steadily. While the feet of the children move in the running pattern, their arms and bodies can reflect this melodic flow.

Sometimes rapid rises and falls in a melody line suggest turns and whirls. "Tarantelle" by Mendelssohn (Rhy II) seems to do this within a lively running or skipping pattern. The turns come at the end of each of the first four phrases; then a whole series of descending turning patterns leads to a semicadence followed by a repetition of the first section. This is a jolly tune that might suggest the busy playfulness of any small creatures.

FOLLOWING BREAKS AND RETARDS. Breaks, holds, and retards in music capture the attention and make a composition interesting. When these additional techniques are encountered, several hearings are necessary before the children know the music well enough to follow it accurately. A familiar composition, such as "The Wild Horseman" by Schumann (OFM-232), may be played on the piano with a break at the end of the first phrase to show the children how unpredictable the galloping horses might be. Or, instead of galloping full speed throughout the composition, by the use of a retard they can be made to slow up as the composition ends. See next page for music of "The Wild Horseman."

A waltz can be used to illustrate the retard or hold. At a break all movement stops, but at a hold there is a continuity that may be shown by the slow rising of the arms or turn of the body.

THE WILD HORSEMAN

Robert Schumann

WALTZ

Opus 39, No. 2
Johannes Brahms

From *Music Through the Day*. © 1956, Silver Burdett Company.

"March Militaire" by Schubert (Rhy III) will surprise the children if they march to it on the first hearing, for there is a retard just before the main theme returns at the end of the piece. The retard gives the last statement of the melody a feeling of new vigor. "Valse Gracieuse" by Dvořák (Rhy III) has a legato melody with a hold near the middle and a break just before the ending. If the children are "trees" swaying in the summer breeze, the pause in the middle may represent one of those moments when the leaves and branches seem suspended in stillness only to move again when the breeze returns in the next moment.

INTERPRETING CONTRASTING SECTIONS. To give variety and dramatic interest to longer compositions, the composer uses contrasting sections. He achieves balance as well as variety by repeating the original section after the contrasting one. To interpret the music, the pupils must listen as they move and change their movements with the music. Contrasts are present in all music from the simple dance suite to the symphony. When children learn to understand and listen for them in conjunction with their work in expressive movement, they develop their potential powers as music listeners and performers as well.

Preliminary experience in following changing rhythms may be had with rhythm instruments or the piano. The teacher might play eight measures for walking, then, without a break, change to a running or skipping rhythm. Any of the piano compositions suggested for fundamental movements may be used if they are in the same key and sound well played consecutively. Hood and Schultz, in *Learning Music Through Rhythm*,[4] give a detailed study and several piano compositions suitable for preliminary work in changing rhythms.

Contrasting sections are a challenge as the children try to interpret music in terms of imaginative characters and situations. "Boating on the Lake" by Kallak (Rhy II) is a clear example of this sectional form in music. In the first and last sections the rhythm is gently swaying or rocking and might suggest calm waters for canoeing. In the middle section small ripples and waves seem to interrupt this smooth rhythm. If this section is interpreted with bodily movement, tiny rapid steps combined with turns and vertical movements might be appropriate.

"Praeludium" by Järnefelt (Rhy III) has five sections, which may be labeled A, B, A, C, A. The main theme (A) is a tripping dance tune. It is followed by a smooth swaying section (B) and then by the slower, more languid section (C). An entire story in movement can be created around this one composition.

When working with the smaller unit of musical form, the phrase, children can express contrast through bodily movement by (1) changing the direction of movement at the end of a phrase, as suggested with folk dances, (2) moving the arms in broad arcs, or (3) raising and lowering the body and arms to indicate the rise and fall of a phrase. Phrases may be represented on the chalkboard as broad arcs. If phrases are the same length, the arcs should be the same length.

Physical response to rhythmic, structural, and descriptive elements in music is an important and interesting activity for all classes. It is often a part of singing and listening and should be used more extensively as a basic experience in the music program.

PROMOTING MOVEMENT IN THE
INTERMEDIATE GRADES

Music with strong rhythm has a natural appeal for children of all ages. Pupils who have not had experience in moving to music in the primary grades may be reluctant to begin at the intermediate level. Three approaches are suggested:

1. Use well-defined forms such as marches and lead gradually to more expressive interpretive movement.
2. Build freedom for, and an appreciation of, expressive movement through direct response to highly rhythmic dance music of several types.
3. Use movement with singing.

Pupils should be given freedom and encouragement to improvise their own rhythm patterns in playing and dancing. When rhythm becomes an expressive medium for them, they will be more responsive to rhythm in the music of others.

Rhythmic Participation in the Study of Marches

The march is a historically important musical form. Its rhythmic appeal makes it a natural musical study for intermediate grades. If the boys and girls have not had previous experience in moving to music, the march might open the way to expressive movement in the interpretation of music. Marching may first be done in the multipurpose room or gymnasium where the pupils can work out interesting two- or four-abreast formations. When one of the rousing Sousa marches is used, the pupils participate eagerly because they can identify with a marching band or a regiment of soldiers. Such marching, however, is only a beginning, a means to an end and not the musical objective.

When marching has produced an enthusiasm for participation and the pupils have developed an appreciation of moving in rhythm with the music, the teacher should begin to look for variety in marches. Good sources are the *Rhythmic Activities* Volumes IV, V, and VI of the RCA Victor RECORD LIBRARY FOR ELEMENTARY SCHOOLS. To begin, pupils and teacher may discuss the different uses for marches: military or school-band marches, wedding and other ceremonial marches may be suggested. "How do these differ and why?" Excerpts from two marches might be played and discussed. "March" from *Aida* by Verdi (Rhy IV) may be compared with "March of the Three Kings" from *L'Arlesienne Suite* by Bizet (Rhy IV). The former is triumphant and military, the latter is solemn and dignified.

"Notes for Teachers" provides themes and rhythm patterns to play and sing, and gives historical and story backgrounds for the compositions. These are helpful in preliminary discussions. After hearing the compositions, part of the class may march in a manner appropriate to the music. Encourage the children to experiment with body carriage and steps of different lengths in their attempts to portray the spirit of the march. This is the beginning of *expressive* movement. Costumes and props may aid in establishing the mood.

In addition to the rhythmic experience, it is important that pupils determine what use of musical elements produces the characteristic sounds in each march. Listen to and sing the melodies. How do they differ? How does the rhythm differ? Does the instrumentation contribute to the general character of the music in a significant way?

Other marches may be used in the same manner with these objectives: (1) rhythmic movement, (2) expressive movement, (3) continuing growth in understanding of the elements of music, and (4) familiarity with a basic repertoire of musical compositions. In addition to the two numbers suggested, Volume IV has excerpts of two marches from the opera *Carmen* by Bizet: "Toreador Song" and "Street Boys' Parade." Of the six marches included in Volume V, four might be used in a similar study:

"March" from *Carnaval* by Schumann   "War Song" from *Miniatures* by
"March" from *Iphigénie in Aulis* by   Reinhold
   Gluck   "March Grotesque" by Sinding

The following group from Volume VI makes especially interesting studies in rhythm, form and instrumentation:

"March" from the *Love for Three*   "Procession of the Sardar" from
   Oranges by Prokofieff   *Caucasian Sketches* by Ippolitov-
"March of the Pilgrims" from *Harold*   Ivanov
   in Italy by Berlioz

The above titles are available in most schools. Other marches may be presented in similar groupings. In *Tales of Olden Days*[5] Kinscella devotes four sections to marches; Stringham, in *Listening to Music Creatively*,[6] Chapter Two, "Music and Ceremony," suggests the following marches for a study in contrasts.

"Triumphal March" from *Aida* by   "Marche Militaire" by Schubert
   Verdi   "Pomp and Circumstance" by Elgar
"Wedding March" from *Lohengrin*   "Stars and Stripes Forever" by Sousa
   by Wagner   "Polonaise Militaire" by Chopin
"Funeral March" by Chopin

Varied Approaches to Dancing

Intermediate grade children can learn to respond to music through rhythmic, expressive movement; and, as they respond to the music, they learn to hear it more sensitively. Some teachers approach expressive movement gradually through marches. Others prefer to develop an appreciation for expressive movement and freedom for its use through direct, unpatterned response to very rhythmic music.

The spirit and techniques for developing expressive movement are evident in the work of Gertrude Knight with the children in the film "Building Children's Personalities with Creative Dancing."[7] Encouragement, a sense of freedom for movement, discovery and yet supporting guidance, are evident in her work. When this teacher wants the children to feel the rhythm within themselves, she suggests, "Find the ball way down inside of you and make it bounce"... "bounce inside so the bounce comes outside," etc. Musicians know that a feel for rhythm is not limited to the fingers or toes, but is deep inside the body. As early as possible, children should find this deep feeling for rhythm.

The use of descriptive, "feeling" words helps children loosen up and move expressively with all parts of the body. Mrs. Knight says, "My fingers are the end of me."... "How far can you grow out of your fingers?"... "How tall can you get?"... "Grow from inside like a tree." ... "Put your fingers in the sky and pull it right down."

The music used in this film ranges from the classic compositions:

Brandenburg Concerto No. 1 (Menuetto and Trios) by Bach
Rondo *Alla Turca* by Mozart

to primitive dances with direct rhythmic and sensuous appeal:

Hopi "Butterfly Dance" (Ind Alb)
Sicilian "Tarantelle" (Victor LPM 1621)
Suite Primeval by Skilton: Cheyenne Indian "War Dance" (Ind Alb) and
    Rogue River Indian "Deer Dance" (Lis IV)

Other recorded music can be useful in the early stages of expressive movement:

"Carillon" from *L'Arlesienne Suite No. 1* by Bizet
"Farandole" from *L'Arlesienne Suite No. 2* by Bizet (A in M, VI-1)
"Golliwog's Cakewalk" from *The Children's Corner Suite* by Debussy
"Dance of the Automatons" from *Coppélia Ballet Suite* by Delibes

This music has rhythmic strength and general continuity. It is colorful, expressive, and it appeals to the imagination.

DEVELOPING LISTENING THROUGH MOVEMENT. After some freedom is established in moving to music, children will benefit from combining movement with the music listening program. The classical dance types are a good source of music for the study of rhythm as well as form in music. Such compositions are found in each of the RCA albums for *Rhythmic Activities*. The following is an example of how a composition can be studied to point up rhythm and form through expressive movement.

Using "Shepherd's Dance" by Edward German (Rhy V), the pupils listen to the music to determine what movement is basic to the rhythm of the composition. They explore the possibilities and feel the flow of the rhythm in its patterns and phrases. A foot pattern such as the following is appropriate:

$$\begin{array}{c} \frac{6}{8} \quad \quad \quad \quad \quad \quad \quad \quad \quad \quad \quad \quad | \\ \text{step - close - step} \quad \quad \text{step - close - step} \\ \text{L} \quad \quad \text{R} \quad \quad \text{L} \quad \quad \quad \text{R} \quad \quad \text{L} \quad \quad \text{R} \end{array}$$

Pupils can move all around the room with this or another suitable foot pattern until they feel in balance and the whole of them is responding with the gentle rocking rhythm. Then they begin to notice the accents in the music. Some of these accents come only at the beginnings of long phrases. A heavy step or a leap may be incorporated into the foot pattern whenever the accent is heard.

The attention may then be directed to the melody with its long flowing lines climbing or falling in sequential patterns. When the melody climbs continuously with tension toward a high point, the movement can be shown by the body, arms, and hands. A middle section of "Shepherd's Dance" is smoother, with the skipping pattern absent from the accompaniment; this may suggest a rocking movement rather than the step-close-step foot pattern suggested above. Following this general exploratory experience in feeling the rhythmic pulse and flow, the pupils should be ready to sit, listen to, and discuss the music, trying to discover what the composer has put into it. Information such as the following should grow out of such a discussion.

"Shepherd's Dance" has a light-hearted, bouncey rhythm that could be associated with a pleasant pastoral scene where the shepherd boys have time to skip and dance and entertain themselves. The composer uses a swinging two-beat grouping of three tones in which the outstanding rhythm pattern is:

There is some contrast between short and long tones suggesting crispness and smoothness respectively.

Melodically, there is some chordwise and much scalewise movement. Exact rhythmic-melodic sequences, both rising and falling, are important musical characteristics (compare phrases in brackets).

SHEPHERD'S DANCE

Edward German

"Shepherd's Dance"—first eight measures of the melody only. From Incidental Music to *Henry VII* by Edward German. By permission of Novello & Co., Ltd. (From "Notes for Teachers" of *Rhythmic Activities*, Volume V, RCA Victor RECORD LIBRARY FOR ELEMENTARY SCHOOLS.)

The composition is in the major mode with simple harmonies and a delicate use of strings and woodwinds, all of which is appropriate for a "Shepherd's Dance."

An important aspect is the strong tension and flow that the rhythm and melody create; the melody climbs relentlessly to a high point and then floats downward in gentle circling patterns. Children who, to some degree, can experience through movement the beauty of this music will have a most worthwhile aesthetic experience. If movement is not a natural expressive medium, color and design may be used. Finger-painting in delicate colors, upward arcs and downward spirals would express the mood and feeling as well. Should there be a child with a talent for poetic writing, let him be carried away by the music so that it comes out in some descriptive lines.

AN ASSOCIATION WITH THE SOCIAL STUDIES. When movement is an accepted part of the study of music, it takes its place as an aid rather than as a dominating activity. Most children in the fifth grade study American history, and the fact that the culture and social customs of this country are indebted to the European peoples who came here should be a consideration of the social studies. The pupils can study and dance "Shepherd's Dance" as representative of English country dances in the Old World. "Gavotte in D Minor" by Grétry and "Minuet" from *Don Giovanni* by Mozart will give the pupils an idea of the restraint and elegance of the court dances that were enjoyed by the more aristocratic settlers in this country. "Turkey in the Straw" by Guoin is a concert arrangement of one of the most famous reel dances of the vigorous people on the American frontier. Some research on social customs and manner of dance, as well as experimentation with traditional dance steps, can make this a rewarding study.

Sixth grade pupils study the music of other lands and peoples. The following compositions, based on the dance rhythms and melodies of three countries, provide much opportunity for the teacher to guide his pupils in understanding the use composers make of folk melodies and rhythms. It may be observed how an original melody is varied, through changes in orchestration, rhythm, and harmony, to make the composition interesting as a concert piece.

"Country Gardens" arranged by Grainger (Rhy VI)

"La Czarine," Mazurka, by Ganne (Rhy VI)

"Spanish Serenade" by Bizet (Rhy VI)

"Spanish Dance" No. 1 from *La Vida Breve* by Falla (A in M, VI-1)

Background material and descriptive notes for a number of Classic dances are given in Baldwin's *Music for Young Listeners*,[8] and in Chapter One of Stringham's *Listening to Music Creatively*.[6] The teacher can adapt this information to the level of the class.

Song Interpretation Through Movement

With the rich repertoire of songs available in the basic music books, there is no problem in finding material for use in expressive movement. Three types are especially suitable: (1) ballads and dialogue songs that tell a story or suggest dramatization, (2) dance songs, and (3) songs that may be interpreted by unison movement.

BALLADS AND DIALOGUE SONGS. The values derived from the dramatization of songs are great. Children learn to express feeling and ideas, and those children who have less success in singing find a way to participate. Success in simple dramatizations prepares children for more significant expressive movement with other music. Actual rhythmic movement may be of less importance than the sincere portrayal of an idea that in turn can lead to more expressive singing. The following songs lend themselves to dramatization:

"Barnacle Bill, the Sailor" (ME-31)   "M'sieu Bainjo" (VOA-52)
"Deaf Woman's Courtship" (VOA-   "O No, John" (SIH-50)
41)   "O, Soldier, Soldier" (SIH-51)
"Fish Peddler" (MN&F-134)   "Robin Hood and the Tanner"
"Ida Marina" (VOA-121)   (VOW-26)
"Long John" (MAW-136)   "Sis Joe" (MIOC-98)

SACRAMENTO

American Sailor's Chantey

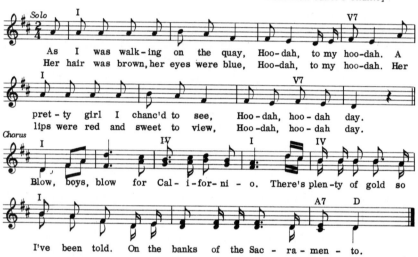

3. I raised my hat and said "How do?"   6. "I have a sweetheart young and true,
   She bowed and said, "Quite well, thank you."   And cannot give my love to you."

4. I asked her then to come with me,   7. I said "Goodbye" and strode away,
   Down to the docks my ship to see.   Although with her I longed to stay.

5. She quickly answered "Oh dear no."   8. And as I bade this girl adieu,
   "I thank you, but I cannot go."   I said that girls like her were few.

From *Our Land of Song* of A SINGING SCHOOL Series, 1956. Copyright Summy-Birchard Publishing Co. Used by permission.

In this sailor's version of Stephen Foster's "Camptown Races" a boy and a girl may act out the story told in the solo parts. The entire class or a smaller group might pantomime sailor movements such as hoisting sails, winding the capstan, and swabbing decks rhythmically as they sing the refrain after each stanza. For young actors the greatest problem is filling in suitable movement when there are no directions in the song text. Considerable experimentation and some guidance is necessary before they can find movement patterns that are satisfying to them.

SONGS FOR DANCING. Dancing should be an integral part of music in the intermediate grades. The chief concern is to help pupils learn to listen and to follow the basic rhythm of the music, using, when possible, a foot pattern that is typical of that dance rhythm. It is not necessary to work out all the intricacies and variations the native dancers put into their art, although pupils should, if possible, learn to appreciate and understand those dances. The general procedures in developing dancing are these:

1. Promote a feeling for the basic rhythm of the song and learn to move with the characteristic foot pattern of the dance. Some of the pupils should play rhythm instruments and sing as others do the pattern moving individually or in a line around the room.
2. Determine how the appropriate foot pattern is related to the metric beat and accent of the music.
3. When partners are needed, learn to do the foot pattern with another person in the manner suggested.
4. Develop floor patterns that follow the phrase structure of the music. Using a circle or a line formation, some basic floor patterns are these: reverse direction on alternating long phrases; move into and back out from the center of the circle on shorter phrases; turn around a partner on shorter phrases, etc.

Songs and dances used in a program correlated with social studies include the polka, which is a couple dance of Bohemian origin in lively $\frac{2}{4}$ meter. The schottische is similar to, but slower than, the polka and is often used with songs in $\frac{4}{4}$ meter. Adaptations of both can be used in the intermediate grades. The foot pattern for the schottische is smooth and even:

$$\frac{4}{4} \quad \text{♩} \quad \text{♩} \quad \text{♩} \quad \text{♩}$$
step - step - step - hop

The polka is a combination of slide, step, and hop; its pattern varies, depending on the beat on which the music begins. Children can learn to do these patterns for the polka:

$$\frac{2}{4} \quad \text{♪} \quad \text{♪} \quad \text{♪} \quad \text{♪}$$
step - slide - step - turn
L   R(up) L   L
or
step - slide - step - hop

"The Weggis Dance" (WS-102) is a good song with which to practice any of these patterns.

THE WEGGIS DANCE

Translated by David Stevens   Swiss Song Dance

When we walk in__ Weg-gis fair,__ Hol-di-ri-di-a,
Hol-di-ri-a, Shoes nor stock-ings__ need we wear,__
Hol-di-ri-a-do, Hol-di-a! Hol-di-
ri-di-a, Hol-di-ri-a-do, Hol-di-ri-a! Hol-di-
ri-di-a, Hol-di-ri-a-do, Hol-di-a!

From *We Sing* of A SINGING SCHOOL Series, 1940. Copyright Summy-Birchard Publishing Co. Used by permission.

When this song is danced as a schottische or polka, a step is taken on each eighth-note value. On the other hand, in a song such as "Dancing and Whirling," listed below, a step is taken on each quarter-note value. Boys and girls in these grades should study out such problems and be aware of the relationship between dance steps and metric beat. The following are dancing melodies:

"Ach Ja!" (MN&F-40)
"My Homeland" (AS VI-135)
"Dance Song" (VOW-108)
"Flicka, Will You Dance with Me?" (ST-40)

"At Break of Day" (VOW-104)
"Dancing and Whirling" (SIH-40)
"Song of the Gypsy King" (MIOC-198)
(The three above are all the same melody.)

Many songs are suitable for waltzing. Because the chief concern is that the pupils be free to respond to the rhythm of the dance rather than that they learn complicated steps, it is recommended that the simplified "waltz-walk" be used first. A large step is followed by two smaller steps as the dancers progress around in a single circle. As soon as they are able the children may try leading first with the left and then with the right shoulder so that a swaying effect is achieved. "Waltzing with Anya" (SIH-41, see page 66) and the following are suitable for waltzing:

"Dutch Dance" (AS IV-175)
"Fiesta" (ME-146)
"Katrina's Wedding" (VOA-112)

"Little White Dove" (MAOC-42)
"Skaters' Waltz" (MN&F-67)
"The Skaters" (ST-154)

Dance songs of America can be studied along with other aspects of the culture. Many of them are also suitable for physical education activities. The basic foot patterns are a skip, a bouncey walk, and a step-slide to the side. Pupils should experiment to see what movement is best adapted to the rhythm of the music. The following songs can be used for dancing:

"Sourwood Mountain" (ST-50)
"Turkey in the Straw" (MIOC-93)
"Sandy Land" (MAOC-24) (see page 66)

"Brown-eyed Mary" (OLS-138)
"Buffalo Gals" (AS V-64)
"Captain Jinks" (VOA-98)

Waltzes and tangos of the Latin-American tradition are varied and colorful. Boys and girls should hear the music and move rhythmically in appropriate patterns. The tango is associated with Argentina and has African origins, as have the habanera of Cuba and the samba of Brazil. The basic step of the tango embraces two measures of $\frac{2}{4}$ meter:

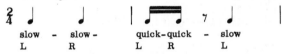

slow - slow -   quick-quick - slow
 L   R   L   R   L

"San Severino" (ME-158) lends itself to this foot pattern as do:

"Angelique-O" (MAW-60)
"Rosario" (OLS-79)
"San Sereni" (MAOC-39)

"Sambalele" (MIOC-156)
"The Count of Cabra" (VOW-167)

SAN SEVERINO

Song-Dance from Chile

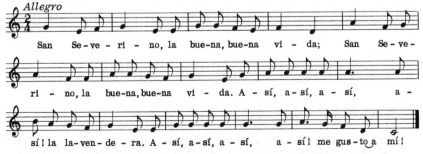

From *Music Everywhere* of A SINGING SCHOOL Series, 1955. Copyright Summy-Birchard Publishing Co. Used by permission.

UNISON EXPRESSIVE MOVEMENT. Some songs suggest a type of movement that pupils may work out as a group. Movement in this setting is more free and creative; the musical elements may be of more importance than the text itself. "Down the Stream" (see page 60) may be dramatized with simple movements.

In such a song we may express the ideas of the text as well as the musical elements of the song. In this there are two ideas: (1) "Down the stream all the leaves go." Smooth-flowing movements of the body accompanied by rippling hand motions may be used here. (2) "Who can say, who can know where the leaves go?" This may suggest uplifted, outreaching arms as though asking the question. In addition, there is a gradual rising line in the melody at the beginning and a falling line leading to the ending. This might suggest body elevation from a low crouch at the beginning to an upright position on the climax of the third phrase and back to a position of rest at the end.

Other songs that might be interpreted in a similar fashion are:

"Above the Plain" (MAW-126)   "Little Man in the Woods" (SED-
"For the Beauty of the Earth" (SIH-   146)
  133)   "In Hawaii" (WS-164)
"Glides Our Canoe" (SIH-173)   "Singing Up the Corn" (MAOC-35)
"Roll On, Columbia" (MAOC-10)   "The Sunrise Call" (ST-138)

If the children have had previous opportunities to interpret music through movement, they may be encouraged to create their own patterns of movement for songs such as these. Although the teacher will find it necessary to provide some initial examples, his goal must be to arrive at the point where the pupils are eager to work out original expressive movement for such songs. Songs that are suitable for this use have characteristics distinct from the dialogue song and those suggesting dancing. They have a sincerity of thought that evokes dramatic movement. The phrases are often majestic and flowing in contrast to the more sharply patterned rhythm of a dance. As a result, the movements are broad and sweeping, using hands and arms as well as body pose and elevation to suggest meaning.

ACTIVITIES FOR COLLEGE COURSES

A. Written Assignments

1. Hear and move to one group of the short recorded selections from a source suggested on page 198. Write your evaluation of them in terms of their suitability for movement and their musical qualities suggesting mood and imagery.

2. Find portions of two other recorded compositions that you believe to be suitable for fundamental movements. State exactly how much of the recording would be used and what movement might be appropriate.

3. Visit a record store and listen to children's musical-activity recordings not listed in this chapter. Select four and evaluate musical quality, rhythm, subject, and approach. For what grades might they be used?

4. From a basic song book select a good example of a ballad or dialogue song that could be dramatized. Write a short paragraph stating the possibilities for movement and drama that you see in the song.

5. Choose a song suitable for unison expressive movement. Write a paragraph describing its possibilities for movement.

6. List with brief notes in your handbook, Section IV-B, any of the above material that seems particularly useful for the grade you have selected.

B. Classroom Projects

1. As others move, accompany at least two contrasting fundamental rhythmic movements in one of the following ways:
   a. improvisation on the piano as suggested in references
   b. suitable piano compositions
   c. rhythm instrument

2. Make a simple costume that creates a sense of realism for a particular character. With a piano or recorded accompaniment, create movement that effectively characterizes the subject.

3. Use a scarf as an aid to expressive movement. Select an accompaniment (piano or record) that provides a suitable mood and rhythm.

4. Listen to "Praeludium" (Rhy III) several times. Invent a story to reflect its moods and sectional form. In a small group work out appropriate rhythmic movement to be shown to the class.

5. In a small group study carefully and interpret, through movement, MacDowell's character sketches, "Witch," "Clown," and "Villain."

6. Select individuals to portray the characters while the first part of "Peter and the Wolf" is played on a recording.

7. In small groups, work out movement that is expressive of selected numbers from the suite "The Comedians."

8. In a small group, select and create an appropriate dance for a song in one of the following groupings:
   a. schottische or polka
   b. American reel or circle dance
   c. Latin-American waltz or tango
   Arrange a suitable accompaniment for the singing.

9. In a group of six or eight, learn two folk dances mentioned in this chapter. Use a line formation to show the foot patterns possible with any dance selected. Show how a dance could be simplified or varied to accommodate the children who might dance.

CHAPTER NOTES

1. Gladys Andrews, *Creative Rhythmic Movement for Children* (Englewood Cliffs, N.J.: Prentice-Hall, Inc., 1954).
2. Elsie Braun, *Music for Active Children* (New York: Stephen Daye Press, Inc., 1957).
3. Virginia B. Whitlock, *Come and Caper* (New York: G. Schirmer, Inc., 1932), Part II, pp. 40-60.
4. Marguerite V. Hood and E. J. Schultz, *Learning Music Through Rhythm* (Boston: Ginn and Company, 1949), Chapter 3.
5. Hazel Gertrude Kinscella, *Tales of Olden Days* (Lincoln, Nebr.: University Publishing Company, 1951), pp. 132-143.
6. Edwin John Stringham, *Listening to Music Creatively* (Englewood Cliffs, N.J.: Prentice-Hall, Inc., 1943, 1946).
7. "Building Children's Personalities with Creative Dancing," University of California, Extension Division, Film No. 5844.
8. Lillian Baldwin, *Music for Young Listeners: The Green Book, The Crimson Book, The Blue Book* (Morristown, N.J.: Silver Burdett Company, 1951).

OTHER REFERENCES

Cole, Natalie Robinson, *The Arts in the Classroom* (New York: John Day Co., Inc., 1940). Chapter 4, "Free Rhythmic Dancing."

Mursell, James L., *Music and the Classroom Teacher* (Morristown, N.J.: Silver Burdett Company, 1951). Chapter 4, "Expressive Bodily Movement."

Perham, Beatrice, *Music in the New School* (Park Ridge, Ill.: Neil A. Kjos Music Co., 1941). Chapter 6, "Music and Rhythms."

Sheehy, Emma Dickson, *Children Discover Music and Dance* (New York: Henry Holt and Co., Inc., 1959). Chapter 7, "Dance," and Chapter 8, "Guiding Movement and Accompaniment."

See Appendix B for listing of record companies.

CHAPTER EIGHT

EXPERIENCES IN
LISTENING TO MUSIC

Sculpture, a visual art, is enjoyed as one sees it and perhaps feels it with his hands. Painting, likewise, is a visual art in color and design, but music must be heard. A person responds to it in proportion to his sensitivity to its tone colors, melody, rhythm, form, and harmony. Listening to music is an experience everyone may have, but it is also an art which, when cultivated, will yield richer rewards to the individual.

What does the individual cultivate? First, he can develop his sensitivity to the mood and message in the music and his freedom to respond imaginatively to what he hears. Second, he can increase his capacity to hear and understand the elements of music: the development of the melody line, its harmonic basis, the interplay of varied rhythms, the interrelationship of themes and sections, and the instrumentation. Understanding comes through guided listening and experience with music. It is the intellectual response to music whereas the other is the emotional response. Both are important and interactive, but the emotional response is more basic and, with children, should be developed in advance of the intellectual response.

Because listening to music should create a response, be it emotional or intellectual, the teacher may wish to provide avenues through which this response may manifest itself. Some children express themselves most naturally by talking, others by moving, and still others by painting. It is helpful but not always necessary for children to define and interpret their feelings in these ways. The important thing is that in some way, through one of the many opportunities in which the teacher makes music available to them, the children begin to listen and to respond with their imaginations.

In addition to the studies outlined in this chapter, children should have other contacts with music—experiences of a more random nature which nevertheless have value. Each teacher has his own favorite reference books and recordings, and he can adapt the appropriate material for use in his classroom. A teacher with a special musical interest can enrich the experiences of his children in his own unique way by sharing this interest with them.

If a teacher is to judge competently what might be of benefit to children, he must understand the limits of their ability to hear and comprehend music. Generally speaking, the child before puberty understands that which is simple, direct, and objective. The music, literature, and art to which he will respond must have these characteristics. A teacher who uses these criteria in his selection of music will reject for use with children certain otherwise excellent pieces of music. Melodies which are well defined and expressive are good as long as they are not sophisticated or sensuous in a manner not understandable to children. Rhythm has a natural appeal, but preadolescent children do not understand rhythms that are too complicated. Teachers need not be concerned about jazz before the seventh or eighth grade; even at that level only those students who have a good understanding of simple rhythms and those who have had experiences in rhythmic and melodic improvisations are ready to benefit musically from a study of jazz and other such improvisatory forms. Jazz and contemporary dance music are not taboo in the classroom, but they must be considered incidental rather than integral to the program in music education at this level.

The hearing of harmony, as more than a mere pleasant sound, begins to develop only in the intermediate grades. Certain subtle harmonies are not noticed by children at all, and they find some of the lush harmony and rich orchestrations of the Romantic period overpowering. In all styles of music there is that which, for well-founded reasons, is less suitable for children.

In this chapter reference is made to materials that are generally available in teacher-training institutions and may serve as examples to be explored by future teachers. Appendix B contains a code for the identification of important groups of recorded examples designed especially for elementary schools. Other recordings are referred to by company name or abbreviation and number. Sources of information on music and composers referred to in this chapter are listed in the chapter bibliography.

Learning To Listen

Children listen to music in many ways and learn to accept it as a part of their environment. The great concern of music educators is the quality of music children hear. Referring to the initial discussion, "What is the value of music?" we must reaffirm the belief that the music which best serves the individual is that which is expressive of the wide range of human feeling and experience. Young children have their own levels of emotional response, and music to satisfy their needs must be supplied in various ways.

MUSIC AS A BACKGROUND. Music, like lights and color, can do much to enrich the environment. It has been a tradition of better hotels and restaurants to provide a more enjoyable atmosphere for dining through the use of pleasant music. Likewise, in business houses and factories music is used to provide a more favorable environment. Children are much more impressionable and responsive than adults. Well-selected music can help them relax during rest periods. When they are listless and tired, music in a happy mood, played as they go about their quieter activities, makes them feel cheerful and more alive.

Background music is valuable not only because it supplies a suitable atmosphere for different occasions, but because it provides another opportunity for children to hear music. Most people experience pleasure upon hearing a favorite melody. The adult rarely stops to think where he made the acquaintance of the many lovely musical compositions he knows. We have a precious heritage of music, but it is only precious to those to whom it is familiar. Many children do not hear a fine variety of music at home; it is the responsibility of the teacher to make it a part of classroom experience.

There are two general uses for background music in the classroom; the type of music varies with the situation. Music for resting should be melodious and soothing. It should not be rhythmically lively and should have no loud climaxes or contrasting sections. Lullabies were written for this purpose.

"Lullaby" and "Little Sandman,"   "Rock-a-bye Baby"
  Brahms   "Cradle Song," Schubert
"Hush My Babe," Rousseau   "Berceuse," Järnefelt
"Sweet and Low," Barnby

These are among the most familiar. Other melodies such as "Minuet" by Paderewski, "Melody in F" by Rubinstein, "Humoresque" by Dvořák, and "Minuet in G" by Beethoven are "classics" that everyone should know. Those listed are in the RCA Victor Record Library, *Listening Activities*, Volumes I and II (Lis I, Lis II). This is a convenient source, but not the only one the teacher should draw upon.

Excerpts from longer compositions may be used if they are soothing and uninterrupted with loud climaxes.

"The Swan" from *The Carnival of the Animals*, Saint-Saëns
"Air" from *Suite No. 3 in D*, Bach
"Arabian Dance" from *The Nutcracker Suite*, Tchaikovsky
"Clair de Lune," "Afternoon of a Faun," and "Nuages," Debussy
"Nocturne" from *A Midsummer Night's Dream*, Mendelssohn
"On Hearing the First Cuckoo in Spring," Delius
"Liebestraum," Liszt
Second Movement (Largo), first section only, of the *New World Symphony*, Dvořák
Third Movement (Adagio Cantabile) of *Quartet in D* ("The Lark"), Haydn
"Nocturne" of *Quartet No. 2 in D*, Borodin.
Second Movement of *Trio No. 1 in B♭*, Opus 99, Schubert
Second Movement (Molto Adagio) of *Quartet No. 8 in E Minor*, Beethoven

Some slower-moving compositions have qualities of suspense or intense passion, which make them unrestful. The popular love song should not be used because the sentiment is not suitable for young children. There is "good" music of every type: if the music of a love song is "good," it must convey the sentiment of the text. If it succeeds, it will probably be inappropriate for children.

Music used as a background should be loud enough to be heard by everyone and to obscure room noises, but not loud enough to excite the listeners. When children particularly like a musical selection, they will want to hear it often. They should know its title so that they can ask the teacher to play it. Records should not be played so often that they become tiresome.

As a background to classroom activities, music should be a change rather than a constant accompaniment. Fifteen or twenty minutes of lively music can accompany routine seat work or craft projects. Carefully timed, well-selected music can counteract fatigue and eliminate a general undercurrent of noise. Each teacher should determine what is the best "work music" for his pupils; and in doing so he can acquaint them with worthy music that will enrich their lives for many years. Some of the Strauss waltzes, Schubert waltzes, classical dance suites, and serenades such as "Romanze" from Mozart's *Eine Kleine Nachtmusik* are suitable.

THE FOUNDATIONS FOR LISTENING. In the highest type of analytical listening, the ability to follow a melody line within the texture of the musical composition is of basic importance. Thus, as the child learns to listen to and sing a melody, first in short fragments and later in longer phrases, he is developing his ability to follow and remember the melody line. When he tries to make his own singing express the meaning of the words of a song he begins to understand that a melody itself can convey feeling. Later he notices specific characteristics of melodic phrases—temporary points of repose and contrasting moments of pushing forward. He then has a clue to the subtleties of phrasing that make each artist's performance unique.

The principle of balancing repeated phrases or sections with contrasting material is basic in musical design. The teacher helps the child understand such musical organization by directing attention, in songs and in music used for movement, to phrases that are the same and those that contrast.

The understanding of rhythm is as important to perceptive listening as following the melody. The listener who fully comprehends Grieg's "In the Hall of the Mountain King" recognizes the accelerando in the repetitious rhythmic motive as the outstanding feature of this music. Both Ravel's "Bolero" and Stravinsky's "Rite of Spring" are characterized by an insatiable rhythm that the listener should not only feel, but comprehend as the important element in these compositions.

Movement is an almost universal response to rhythm. Some listeners at concerts move their heads or fingers in time to very rhythmic music. Other listeners feel a physical response without actually moving. In the classroom, movement to music helps pupils become more aware of rhythm; they must listen to it in order to follow the music and interpret it effectively.

Sharp lines cannot be drawn between the classroom music activities. A lesson in "listening" or in "rhythmic activities" may motivate pupils to express with movement what they hear. Later, when they have had considerable experience in moving to music, pupils may be quite satisfied with responding through feeling, without much physical motion. The teacher must keep in mind the fact that experiences gained in the program of rhythmic activities provide a significant basis for listening.

MATERIALS AND EQUIPMENT. Several media are useful for bringing music into the classroom. In many areas, radio and television programs are planned for use on a particular grade level. Many of these are valuable, but they do not always provide the flexible type of music program that is recommended. A few teachers are able to play the piano or another instrument with artistry and can provide some of the music in the classroom. Valuable as these skills are, they do not meet the listening needs as completely as does a good quality record player and well-selected records.

If a full, rich musical program is to be carried on, each classroom should have its own three-speed record player, ready for use at any time. Good recordings are likewise essential. A well-planned school record library has multiple copies of basic records that many teachers use regularly, as well as a wide variety of other records.

However, a new teacher does not, generally, walk into his classroom and find this equipment waiting for him. Although parents and school administrators want music for children, many of them are not yet convinced of the need for a record player in every room. The limitations of a shared phonograph can be overcome only in part by careful planning. The school budget should allow for necessary equipment. If this is not the case, an interested group such as the PTA or a music club can assist in raising funds. This is a good way for these people to show their interest in music for children.

The condition of the records and the record player is important, for the value of the musical experience is determined in considerable degree by the quality in the sound heard. With high-fidelity sound experienced by so many through radio, in the motion picture theater, and through home record equipment, children cannot be expected to listen with interest to antiquated recordings that are scratched and worn from numerous playings. For maximum service from records, teachers should protect them from heat, dust, and scratches, which are their chief destroyers; keep them stored vertically in folders; use a good needle of the proper size; handle the tone arm carefully; touch records only on the sides or center label; and, if dust accumulates, remove it with a clean, damp sponge.

Many songs and other short compositions are recorded at 78 RPM and are more convenient to use. However, it is not advisable to purchase a single-speed record player because many compositions are available only at 33⅓ RPM. Schools should avoid purchases of cheaply made record players because they are so often in need of repair. Those with very small speakers and poor amplifying equipment have inferior tone quality. Because selected portions of recordings are played in shorter periods of time, an automatic record changer is neither necessary nor advised for school use.

Another useful piece of equipment is the phonograph to which headsets are attached for individual listening in literature as well as in music. With this equipment, children who are especially interested in music have an opportunity to select private listening fare from a collection of recorded stories or music, without distracting the remainder of the class. This is another means of meeting individual needs and enriching the school program.

Descriptive Elements in Program Music

Music often is categorized as either "program music" or "absolute" music. In program music the composer has established a descriptive title or notes concerning his intent in the music. Short descriptive compositions are excellent studies for both primary and intermediate grades. Many of these are portions of larger musical works that later may be studied in their entirety. The categories are not mutually exclusive. Program music may have a well-defined form or absolute music may have strong descriptive elements.

SHORT STORIES IN MUSIC. Some compositions are based on traditional stories. A classic example among pieces for children is MacDowell's "Of a Tailor and a Bear" (Lis II), based on one of Grimm's fairy tales. The story can be found in "Notes for Teachers,"[1] A Listener's Anthology,[2] or Folk Tales from Many Lands.[3] The chief musical themes, which may serve as clues to the action, are on page 108 of Music Now and Long Ago.[4] (Page 81 of the Teachers' Book gives brief teaching suggestions.) If the classroom has a piano, the themes may be played along with the first telling of the story.

The children may discuss the story briefly and then listen to the recorded music. After the first hearing the children should be ready to tell how the music suggests a part of the story. If they do not include important details in their comments, the teacher may ask: "How did you know when the bear was taken away?" "How did the tailor feel at the very beginning of the music?" "You didn't notice?—Let's play a little of the music again to find out." After the discussion, the children can listen to the record again for more of the story details. On another day one of the children can tell the story as he remembers it; the record can then be played while the pupils listen for items that were not mentioned. Again, the music and its relationship to the story can be discussed, and, if desired, all or parts of it may be dramatized.

The brief composition "Sleepy Time," by Pinto, (Lis I) is based on a short poem (see "Notes for Teachers"). The obvious programmatic details include:

A cuckoo clock sounding six times as the composition begins
A cradle-rocking movement and melody
A break in the music suggesting something disturbing, perhaps the owl in the tree
Frightened "ma-ma" cries of the dollies
A return of the comforting lullaby

This composition is so short that it is best not to describe it for there is then no opportunity for the listeners to use their own imaginations. Before playing the record the teacher may say, "What do you do to make the baby sleep?" "Yes, we very often rock him. Listen and remember where you hear rocking music in this piece. You will hear some other things too, and since you have such good imaginations we will play the music first and then you can tell what you heard."

After hearing the music the children should be encouraged to discuss what they noticed. Then the recording may be played again once or twice so that everyone can hear and evaluate the interpretations given by individuals. There is no single "right" interpretation for any of the different parts of the music, but there are those that might be less appropriate. Several playings of these compositions are necessary if the children are to notice and include the musical details in their interpretations.

"March of the Gnomes" (Lis III) is from the *Christmas Tree Suite* by Rebikoff. The contrasting sections in the composition may be interpreted as a story, such as that suggested in the "Notes for Teachers."

"Danse Macabre" by Saint-Saëns is a longer descriptive composition. There are a few specific program notes on the music, but the major portion of the interpretation is left to the listener's imagination. This is the dance of "Death" and all his ghostly followers in the graveyard on Halloween night. The harp strikes twelve tones indicating the arrival of the magic hour of midnight, and then "Death" tunes his fiddle in preparation for the revelry that goes on until the cock crows, announcing the arrival of dawn. Throughout the composition the spirits dance, sometimes in a frenzy of movement and sometimes sadly; the wind blows and the skeleton bones rattle. A translation of the poem by Henri Cazalis, on which the musical composition was based, may be found in *A Listener's Anthology*, Volume II.[2] The musical themes and the imaginative interpretation given in the book may provide a helpful background for the teacher. Themes may also be found in *Music Through the Year*.[3] A composition on a similar idea, "Night on Bald Mountain" by Moussorgsky, will be enjoyed by students in the fifth and sixth grades.

LONGER TALES IN MUSIC. Among the longer works is Prokofieff's *Peter and the Wolf*, which has narration incorporated with the music. The important thing to notice here is that the music as well as the narration tells the story: Peter is a happy boy and so the stringed instruments play a happy melody to represent him in the musical story; when the duck and the bird have an argument one hears the argument in the music between the oboe and the flute, which take the parts of these characters.

The Nutcracker Suite by Tchaikovsky, suggested for use with rhythmic movement, may first be heard in relation to the story. With younger children at the first hearing, the music can be played as a background for the story, which is told in *The Music Box Book*[7] by Skolsky. The "Miniature Overture" can describe the children's party and the "March" can suggest the midnight magic when the toy soldiers parade around the Christmas tree and the great battle ensues between the mice and Prince Nutcracker's army of toys. The remaining sections are a part of the entertainment provided Marie during her dream-visit to the land of the "Sugar Plum Fairy."

The teacher must practice in advance, reading the story aloud, making vocabulary adjustments necessary for his own effective narration, and timing the recording to see how long he should wait during each break in the story. The objective is to direct the children's attention to the music as much as possible so that it may suggest the mood and events. The total program will take about 45 minutes, but, with younger children, it is advisable to present it in two lessons. A stop after "Arabian Dance" makes a good break; at the second session the children can assist in a review of the first part of the story in preparation for hearing the remainder. After the pupils have heard the music integrated with the story, they should be able, at later hearings, to listen to sections of the music alone and remember the story that goes with it. Any complete orchestral recording of Tchaikovsky's *Nutcracker Suite* may be used. It is preferable that children *first* learn to know the music in the form in which Tchaikovsky wrote it rather than in a modern "pops" version, entertaining though it may be.

CHARACTER AND ANIMAL SKETCHES. Musical literature abounds in sketches that are impressions of characters or animals and their activities. Among the musical pictures that delight children as well as adults are "Golliwog's Cakewalk" (Lis II) from the *Children's Corner Suite* by Debussy; *The Wand of Youth Suite* by Elgar with "Fairies and Giants" (A in M, III-1), or "Fairy Pipers," "Tame Bears," and "Moths and Butterflies" (Lis II); and *The Mother Goose Suite* by Ravel.

Classroom topics, special days, pictures, and songs may suggest musical sketches that pupils would enjoy hearing: "Clowns" by Mendelssohn (Rhy II) or "Clown" from MacDowell's *Marionettes* (Lis III). Selected "portraits" from Saint-Saëns' *Carnival of the Animals* are useful to the primary teacher: "The Royal March of the Lion," "Hens and Cocks," "The Elephant," or "The Swan," which was suggested also as music for quiet resting. Some compositions by contemporary composers may be meaningful to children: Aaron Copland's "Scherzo Humoristique: The Cat and the Mouse," Villa-Lobos' *The Doll's Family*. These sketches can be used in the classroom in many ways and at different times if the teacher has a flexible program.

When one goes to an art gallery and sees a picture he looks at it from various angles. He makes himself receptive to the feeling the artist was trying to convey and perhaps agrees that the painter did successfully give the subject life and feeling on the canvas. A similar thing takes place when one hears a musical sketch at a concert; he listens, and if he is in a receptive frame of mind the characterization in the music has meaning for him. This type of an experience can come to children if a receptive frame of mind can be established.

Very often this mental and emotional readiness may be produced by an event in the classroom or on the playground.

A teacher observed his pupils chasing and "flying with" the butterflies at recess time on a warm spring day. When they returned to the room they were filled with impressions about butterflies, tired, but content to listen and evaluate in terms of their experience two compositions the teacher played for them: "Moths and Butterflies" by Elgar (Lis II) and "The Bee" by François Schubert (Lis III).

Everyone agreed that the first represented butterflies better than the second. Someone said that he thought the second number was something about a bee, and that he had heard it before. Then the children listened to both sketches again and decided that the first was better music for butterflies because it seemed lighter and changed its speed. They felt that sometimes the butterflies were soaring and gliding and at other times they darted quickly between or lighted momentarily on the flowers.

The second composition characterized a bee because it moved faster, and the violin's fast playing sounded like the humming of a bee. This interpretation and evaluation of the music was based on the children's own personal experience and observation of the creatures represented in the sketches. Fortunately, the teacher was able to take advantage of a playground event that prepared the children to listen.

Sometimes a teacher may give the pupils a descriptive background before playing a particular number. The atmosphere created is much like that of storytelling. Baldwin's books, *Music for Young Listeners*, which were designed for intermediate grade readers, are an excellent source of ideas for the primary teacher. *The Green Book*⁵ contains notes about the composer, Edward MacDowell, and his love for the tales of Uncle Remus. Br'er Rabbit, Br'er Fox, and the Tar Baby (MTY-95) are related characters. In both books are musical themes to help the children hear MacDowell's characterization in "Of Br'er Rabbit" (Lis III). Having separate musical themes played on the piano helps pupils identify musical ideas within the fabric of the total composition. This technique is used more often with older children, who also benefit from seeing the musical themes written out on the chalkboard.

Some parts of the music heard for storytelling or as musical portraits may later be interpreted in color and design with finger paint, colored chalk on wet paper, or water colors. Individual pupils may hear a piece of music and then draw pictures of their impressions of it. Sometimes the teacher may use art expression to motivate the class for listening to music. When this is done, the art supplies should be prepared ahead of time and each child should have them ready for use as the music is heard.

Before they begin to paint, the group may wish to discuss briefly what they hear, and the title of the music may be used as a guide for the picture content. "Little White Donkey" by Ibert is a sketch in which the music suggests the spirit of the donkey and his unpredictable inclination to trot along or shy, balk, and sit back on his haunches. The music should be played several times so that the children may reflect its spirit as much as possible in their pictures.

Another whimsical musical portrait is "The Little Train of the Caipira" by Villa-Lobos. It was written as the "Toccata" in *Bachianas Brasileiras No. 2* (A in M, III-1). Listening to the music one can see and feel this little back-country train as it starts out from the station, runs merrily across the countryside, stops to take on produce, and finally arrives at its destination. In the resultant art expression, the spirit and whimsical characterization of the train are more important than the form which it takes in the picture.

More experienced listeners should give progressively more consideration to the means by which the composer creates specific effects. Toward this end the teacher might ask: "What events do you hear in the journey of the little train?" "Do you find a melody that might characterize the train itself?" "Can you sing part of it?" "How does the music show that it is a little train rather than a big one?" In reply to all of these questions pupils should consider the composer's means of creating the effect heard —the instruments used for specific effects and the use of rhythm to assist in portraying the feeling.

MUSIC CONVEYING IDEAS AND MOOD. Composers do not limit themselves to picture painting. Some of the most delightful musical sketches are those in which the composer tries to convey an idea or a mood to the listener. Debussy wrote an impression of "Snow is Dancing" in his *Children's Corner Suite* (A in M, III-1). Robert Schumann's *Scenes from Childhood* includes "Strange Lands and People," "Curious Story," "Catch Me If You Can!" and "The Pleading Child." Children will enjoy these quiet sketches if the teacher can present them in the right setting. Baldwin's notes in *The Green Book*[5] are helpful.

Mendelssohn composed many short reflective pieces. "Spring Song" (Lis III), more than suggesting a picture, tells how the composer felt on a lovely spring day. Compositions of this type may be used as background for resting or they may engage the attention of the pupils for a short time. Some of the children may have a word or two to say about the feeling the music arouses in them. A good vocabulary of descriptive adjectives is very helpful when children begin discussing what they hear in music. Descriptive words on the chalkboard help children in their discussions and at the same time build vocabulary. Description is useful, but the teacher should remember that music can convey feelings and impressions that go beyond words. If words could speak as well, there would be no need for music.

Some composers who use landscape titles are really mood painters. Grieg's "Morning" from *Peer Gynt Suite No. 1* reflects his strong feeling for the forested mountains and the fiords of his native Norway. *The Grand Canyon Suite* by Grofé follows his day at the Grand Canyon from "Morning" to "Sunset." Some of it is very impressionistic of scenes and events as "On the Trail" and "Cloudburst"; other sections are more reflective of feelings. Intermediate-grade children find these descriptive compositions easy to understand.

There are many sources for information on program music. The two RCA Victor series, RECORD LIBRARY FOR ELEMENTARY SCHOOLS and AD-

VENTURES IN MUSIC, are designed especially for teachers. Much material is included in Baldwin's books, *Music for Young Listeners*,[5] for which the musical compositions are recorded in the MUSICAL SOUND BOOKS.[6] Notes from concert programs and record jackets are good sources. The teacher who is continually expanding his own musical horizons can add books on music appreciation to his personal library. Bernstein's *An Introduction to Music*,[21] Stringham's *Listening to Music Creatively*,[22] and Copland's *What to Listen for in Music*[23] are good choices. There is interesting material in several paperbound books now available. As the teacher's musical experience is broadened, he will enjoy sharing some of his reading and listening with his class.

Color, Design, and Form in Music

Children should learn that musical compositions are an expression of musical ideas within a design. They should also have experience in directing their attention to musical line, design, and color without the necessity of projecting specific meaning into it.

EXPERIENCES WITH ART AND MUSIC. The association of color and design in visual arts with these characteristics in music is meaningful to children and gives them a new and challenging reason for listening to music.

Just as in the visual arts we have colors that are "cool," "warm," "restful," or "active," so in music the composer has a whole palette of tone color with which to work. The various orchestral instruments have distinctive tone colors and although these in themselves do not produce a mood or a scene, they are contributing factors. Music's rhythm and flow of melody easily find their parallels in the rhythm and dynamics of line and design in art.

Simple contrasts help pupils discover how music's tone color, rhythm, and melodic movement can be interpreted in terms of color and design. As an introduction to this idea two short, contrasting musical compositions may be used. There should be no contrasting sections *within* the two numbers. "Waltz in A♭" by Brahms (Lis II) and "March" from *The Love for Three Oranges* by Prokofieff (Rhy VI) are good contrasts.

The teacher should tell the class the plan of action and then play both numbers consecutively so that the contrast is quite evident. The titles should not be given, for children are more free in their interpretations when they work from the impressions they receive directly from the music. After the initial hearing, each composition should be played several times as the children make their color design for it.

Pupils who have had much experience interpreting music through bodily movement and considerable art work might be asked to make, without preliminary discussion, designs on two papers, one to represent each musical composition. Some children may need guidance, which could be given by asking them to interpret the music first through bodily movement. Discussion may follow: "How would the graceful movements be shown on paper?" Color qualities can be brought in—cool colors, warm colors, and feelings associated with each.

Many times adults as well as children, in their initial experience relating design to music, immediately respond to the rhythm by making the crayon, brush, or fingers move in time to the music. This is a natural reaction because people are accustomed to keeping time to the music, but it does not lead to the most expressive design. The essential process is to hear the music, notice the characteristics of the melody and rhythm, and recreate the design as line and color on the paper. The procedure cannot be explained directly to young children; they must discover it through experience and by evaluating the work of others as expressions of the music heard.

When the two designs are finished, the children can hold them up in pairs to see the difference in design and color. "Can everyone tell which design represents each piece of music? What tells us?" The comparison of color in the two designs should be an important item. "Waltz in A♭" is restful and graceful in rhythm and melody. Repose may suggest pastel colors and light application of the medium. When crayons are used, the flat side of a broken piece produces a broad, restful line. In contrast, "March" is very active, and has dissonant tonal combinations. Red and orange may be considered active colors; intense application of blues and greens gives more feeling of activity than do light strokes of the same colors. Combinations of certain colors promote a greater feeling of activity.

The arrangement of lines may provide the contrast between pictures. "Waltz in A♭" has a smooth, flowing melody line; it rises in an interesting design of three short patterns. Curved lines may express this type of melodic movement. On the other hand, "March" is erratic and angular; visual design related to it may have sharp corners bumping into other lines.

How the space in a design is used may suggest the relationship of the elements in the music. If the music sounds "busy," the busy-ness might be conveyed by small intricate shapes. A piece of music that is not broken up by an interplay of parts may be interpreted on paper with no clear-cut divisions of the space.

Very often teachers are satisfied with one successful "experiment" with color and design in music. This is unfortunate for it is not until the third or fourth experience that the children feel at ease making designs to music; it is only then that they begin to interpret sensitively what they hear.

The following are suggested as contrasting numbers which may be used. Pastel and smooth flowing rhythms:

Boccherini, "Minuet"   Mendelssohn, "On Wings of Song" *120*
Offenbach, "Barcarolle" (A in M,   MacDowell, "To a Wild Rose"
  III-1)   Dvořák, "Valse Gracieuse" (Rhy III)

Lively color contrast and angular design:

Tchaikovsky, "Chinese Dance" from *179* Shostakovich, "Polka" from *The
  The Nutcracker Suite* *126*   Golden Age*
Dett, "Juba Dance" (Rhy VI)   Khachaturian, "Fire" from *The
Herbert, "Dagger Dance" from   Gayne Ballet Suite No. 2* *124*
  Natoma (A in M, III-1)

For further discussion of design as used in music and art, see Chapters 11 and 12 of *Preparation for Art* by June King McFee.[24]

DISCOVERING PRINCIPLES OF DESIGN AND FORM. The basic principles of form employed in musical composition were discussed in connection with song literature. Contrast that is evident in *two-part* (binary) form was shown in the verse and refrain of a song. Three-part (ternary) form was shown to employ the principles of contrast and balance. Such forms are basic to musical composition in general. Many of the short sketches mentioned in the previous section are based on the simple three-part form. "Cradle Song" by Houser (Rhy III) is another example. Children of the intermediate grades can understand even more of the composer's art of design in music.

When the principle of repetition after contrast is extended (A B A C A D A etc.), a rondo is the result. "Praeludium" by Järnefelt (Rhy II) is a simple rondo, A B A C A. "Amaryllis" by Ghys (Rhy B) is a modified rondo. It is quite easy for children to hear the design of this composition:

A A' B A A' C C B C A A'

Each section is eight measures long; some sections are repeated as indicated by the double letters. In addition, the precise patterning of the composition makes it possible to break the form down into identifiable four-measure phrases within the larger sections. Well-known rondos by Mozart are "Romanze" from *Eine Kleine Nachtmusik* and "Alla Turca" from *Sonata in A Major*.

Variation on a single musical idea is an old technique in musical composition; composers of the Baroque era used it extensively. Of the many types of variation, the ornamental treatment of a melody is an easy one for children to understand. Johann Sebastian Bach often used a hymn tune, known as a chorale, around which he composed an elaborate composition. "Jesu, Joy of Man's Desiring" (ST-98) is a chorale that the children may sing, both before and after they hear the florid accompaniment Bach gave it (Victor LM-1877).

In the Classic era, Mozart arranged many sets of variations on well-known musical themes. One such theme, which boys and girls know as "Twinkle, Twinkle Little Star," he arranged into a set of twelve variations. This work (Köchel No. 265, in C major) may be found in collections of his piano works and on records (Angel 35069). The original title was *Twelve Variations on "Ah vous dirais-je, Maman."* When children know a theme as well as they do this one, they have no problem hearing and understanding the techniques in variation the composer used. Of the twelve variations, the fifth, eighth, ninth, and tenth are the most simple and show clearly four different treatments of the theme. The first eight measures of the theme in the simple statement as Mozart presented it are shown here:

Variation V is a change in rhythm:

Variation VIII is set in minor mode; it employs passing tones filling in the melodic line, imitation in the lower line, and rhythmic syncopation that heightens the tension of the melodic line:

Variation IX is again in major, similar to Variation VIII in the use of syncopation and imitation but without the embellishment of passing tones:

Variation X employs a rhythmic embellishment and an important addition of chromatic passing tones that give the melody line new strength:

It is preferable that the pupils hear and analyze the variations by ear first. Later the teacher may put the notation on the chalkboard.

Dohnanyi used the same theme in "Variations on a Nursery Tune" for orchestra and piano, Opus 25. If the art of variation is interesting to sixth grade pupils, they may hear a portion of this work. It is interesting to compare this more recent composer's treatment of the theme with that of Mozart. Excerpts of the Dohnanyi musical variations and some discussion of them are given in Baldwin II.[2] Recordings are available (Cap. SP-8373).

Another set of variations that may be used after the theme has been made familiar is the fourth movement of Schubert's *Quintet in A Major* ("The Trout") for piano and strings. The first three variations and the last maintain the original theme with clarity. This theme will be found in *At Home and Abroad*.[9] The American dance tune "Pop Goes the Weasel" was set by Cailliet in the form of a theme with variations. Other musical styles are used as the basis for the variations. To appreciate them the children should have some understanding of the characteristics of the gigue and the minuet of the Classic dance suite.

Haydn wrote the third movement of his *Surprise Symphony* as a theme with four variations. This is a well-known work and the theme, which is 32 measures long, is often used in elementary classes because it has the loud "surprise" chords. However, the variations are considerably more involved than those in the compositions suggested above.

Composers use their thematic material in varied ways in other compositions as well. They employ rhythmic changes, the use of different instruments, fragments and different combinations of the original melodies as well as extensions and embellishments of these melodies. A group of children, captured by the idea of analysis, discovered the design in Brahms' "Hungarian Dance No. 5" (Lis VI). They observed characteristic uses of instruments, repetition, contrast, embellishment, and extension in the handling of the themes. Brahms used three themes with a sectional pattern of A A B B C A B B.

Having analyzed the form the pupils noticed that A is composed of one musical idea played twice but embellished and extended in its repetition. The teacher helped the pupils understand the composer's varied treatment of a musical theme by suggesting the analogy of making two *different* dresses from one basic pattern. Lace and bows might be "embellishment," sashes and ruffles might be "extension" and a change of color might be the use of different instruments, etc.

Each B section has three parts based on one idea, played in sequence, retarded, and supplied with a fast ending. Section C is interesting in that the rapid moving phrases are interrupted twice by curious accordion-like effects. Since the composition is based on folk dance themes, such effects, suggesting the traditional use of violin and accordion by the Hungarian folk dance musicians, are quite understandable. This concert piece vividly portrays the spirit of these people and is not far removed from the folk music that inspired it.

LARGER MUSICAL FORMS. A larger musical form with which older children should become acquainted is the suite. They will readily understand that a suite is a group of related items, whether it be a suite of furniture, rooms, or musical compositions. There are three prominent types of suite in music. The oldest is the *Classic dance suite*, a group of contrasting dances. In their earlier listening, pupils have heard some of these singly, especially the gavotte, gigue, and minuet (see Rhy IV and Rhy V). When such suites are heard as a unit, the contrast among the dances adds interest. Suggested for study in intermediate grades are:

Mozart, *The Little Nothings* (Gr Bk)[5]

Bach, *Suite No. 3 in D Major* (Bl Bk)[5]

Corelli, *Suite for Strings* (Mus to Rem)[10]

Purcell, *Suite* (Prelude)[9]

Some of the suites for solo instruments are also appropriate if the teacher is well acquainted with the music and can select three or four shorter contrasting movements. The use of bodily movement is an important aid in realizing the distinct rhythmic differences in these dances.

The *ballet suite* is a later form in which the music of a ballet has been rearranged for concert performance. If *The Nutcracker Suite* has not been studied in its entirety earlier, fourth grade pupils will find it very rewarding listening, for it is a story as well as a suite of contrasting dances. Single compositions from ballet music that may be used at this level are "Waltz" from *The Sleeping Beauty* and selections from *Coppelia* by Delibes (*Olden Days*[3]).

Orchestral suites of a programmatic nature also are introduced in the intermediate grades. Descriptive notes are available and should be used to give the class an understanding of the composer's intention. Those most often used are:

Mother Goose Suite by Ravel (Gr Bk)
Children's Corner Suite by Debussy (Cr Bk, A in M, III-1)
Peer Gynt Suite by Grieg (M&R)[11] (Baldwin II)[2]
Grand Canyon Suite by Grofé (Baldwin II)
Carnival of the Animals by Saint-Saëns (Gr Bk)
Pictures at an Exhibition by Moussorgsky-Ravel (Baldwin II)

Other suites of special interest may be included. Classes that study American music may like to hear Aaron Copland's suite, *Billy the Kid* (A in M, VI-1), in which the composer uses frontier melodies. *Suite Symphonique* by Ibert is delightful in its descriptive qualities. The six short movements express musically six aspects of Parisian life.

The *tone poem* is a larger descriptive work of a narrative or a contemplative type that has the unity of a single composition. Intermediate grade pupils enjoy tone poems that are sufficiently vivid and not too long. Descriptive notes and musical themes help the children hear the sequence of events and are of assistance in studying the way the composer has used his musical materials. The previous listening experience of the children will determine how much verbal description and explanation must be given in order that they may find the music understandable. Active listening demands that minds be engaged by the music. The following numbers are listed in a general order of difficulty. Sources for information about each are also given.

"Danse Macabre" by Saint-Saëns (Baldwin II; M&R)
"Invitation to the Dance" by Weber (Mus to Rem; M&R)
"Sorcerer's Apprentice" by Dukas (Baldwin II; M&R)
"Night on Bald Mountain" by Moussorgsky (Baldwin II)
"The Moldau" by Smetana (Baldwin II)
"On the Steppes of Central Asia" by Borodin (A in M, VI-I)

Such longer compositions usually comprise a unit of study in themselves. Two or three lessons should be devoted to each suite or tone poem so that the music can be heard several times; the composer's more obvious techniques in the use of rhythm, melody, harmony, form, and instruments should be studied. In any of this experience with descriptive music the teacher may encourage boys and girls to express the musical pictures and designs in art work or in creative writing. Occasionally the entire class may undertake such a project, but more often the individual should be encouraged to pursue these activities in his free time. If a record player with headsets is available the pupils may play the music whenever they want fresh inspiration for their creative work.

An introduction to opera is possible in the intermediate grades. The songs and recorded music from *Hänsel and Gretel* by Humperdinck can be combined with a study of the story. *We Sing* and *Singing Together* both contain a simple version of the play with the important songs. A child's story of the opera will be found in *Haensel and Gretel*[13] by Robert Lawrence. RCA Victor *Listening Activities* Volume IV provides one record of the more important musical compositions. Excerpts from other recordings should be used when possible, but it is not advisable to present the complete recorded version unless the children have had a chance to see it on the stage. When the story of the opera and its chief musical themes are known to the class, a study of the Prelude to the opera may be undertaken (Bl Bk, Prelude).

Amahl and the Night Visitors is a short opera by the contemporary composer, Menotti. Both a book[12] and recordings are available.

The music of *Carmen* by Bizet is captivating and often is combined with the story in a listening unit for sixth grade. Portions of arias may be used, but at this age children tend to prefer orchestral versions unless the teacher is able to develop in them an appreciation for the operatic voice. The opera singer spends years developing his voice to its greatest capacity. Since he is a dramatic actor as well, and sings from a stage in a large auditorium, he must be able to express and project to his audience all shades of feeling in his singing. On the other hand, the folk singer performs to a small audience; his is a more intimate type of singing, much closer to that natural to young people.

Children who have an opportunity to hear and see an operatic singer on stage will more readily understand his dramatic production; they will have an appreciation for operatic singing as an expressive art that has a place in the world of music. If such direct experience is not possible, the teacher will need to develop an appreciation for the voice in other ways and he must be selective in his choice of recordings.

The story *Carmen*,[13] by Robert Lawrence, may be read aloud by the children or the teacher. Two or three arias and one of the following orchestral arrangements of other important melodies may be played at appropriate points in the story:

Music from "Carmen" (Victor)
Carmen, Opera for Orchestra (Columbia)

The color and vitality of the music is appealing and such a presentation can prepare the children to fully enjoy an actual operatic performance.

Other opera overtures and excerpts often used include:

"William Tell Overture" by Rossini (Bl Bk; M&R; A in M, III-I)
"Overture" and "Dance of the Comedians" from *The Bartered Bride* by Smetana (Baldwin II; M&R)
"Ride of the Valkyries" and "Magic Fire Music" from *Die Walküre* by Wagner (Bl Bk; M&R)
"Prelude" to Act III of *Lohengrin* by Wagner (A in M, VI-I)

Musical events in the community and particular interests of the class or the teacher may provide the incentive for other studies in opera at the intermediate level.

Composers, Instruments, and Concerts

Other important purposes of the listening program are (1) an acquaintance with the sound and the characteristic use of the various orchestral instruments, (2) some opportunity to hear them played in actual concerts, and (3) a beginning appreciation of famous composers. Mozart, Haydn, MacDowell, Stephen Foster, and others will be of interest to children. Resources for the teacher will enable him to select information and music for the compilation of a unit that he can present in a convincing manner. Each basic song series for the intermediate grades contains special information on two or three selected composers. Pictures of the composers are often given, and songs and recorded compositions are usually suggested.

RESOURCES ON COMPOSERS. *Children's Record Book* by Barbour and

and Freeman contains brief biographical material and suggested recorded music for different ages. *Music for Young Listeners*[5] by Baldwin contains biographical material and selected compositions with teaching notes. *Stories in Music Appreciation*[3] by Hazel Kinscella is a set of graded readers for children containing biographical facts and anecdotes about the composers and their music. Opal Wheeler and associates have written children's books on the composers and their music. Among these are *Joseph Haydn, The Merry Little Peasant*,[14] *Franz Schubert and His Merry Friends*, and *Stephen Foster and His Little Dog Tray*. The recordings in the VOX MUSIC MASTER Series combine the story and the music of the most famous composers under titles such as "Johann Sebastian Bach, His Story and His Music."

Any study of a composer should be combined with a study of his music. Biographical facts are not as important as are human incidents that make the composer a real person to the children. Many people have the erroneous impression that the music of the "masters" is predominantly serious and pompous. Actually, Bach, Mozart, Haydn, and the rest wrote much of their music for the people and events in everyday life. That which is suitable for children is delightful in its gaiety and humor, delicacy, or wholehearted aggressive spirit. To listeners who are receptive, the best revealer of the composer is the music he has written.

KNOWING ORCHESTRAL INSTRUMENTS. Children have a great interest in musical instruments. An acquaintance with those in the orchestra is a natural extension of the exploration of sound in simple instruments. This acquaintance should not be technical; in the primary grades it need include only the more common instruments.

An important way to learn to know the instruments is through hearing them in the background music for resting and quiet activities. Violin, cello, and piano solos can be used in these ways and, as they are played, the teacher may show the picture of the instrument. In this way the sound of the instrument becomes familiar. Flute, trumpet, and clarinet might occasionally be heard in solo. Until the boys and girls have become well acquainted with the individual sounds of the instruments, it is not possible for them to identify one particular instrument in a group.

Many very effective recorded stories about the instruments are available for children. The first or second grade teacher will find "Tubby the Tuba" (Cl-671), "Pee Wee the Piccolo" and "Rusty in Orchestraville" an excellent means of making these instruments and their sounds known to the class. In the third grade more information may be given the children; "The Wonderful Violin" (YPR-3111), "The King's Trumpet" (CRG-5040), and "Sparky's Magic Baton" are good choices. These recordings are quite informative and yet they keep the study on the story level appropriate in these grades.

In addition to hearing the recorded stories and voices of the instruments, it is important that children have an opportunity to see the instruments first hand. Older children in the school may bring violins, clarinets, or trumpets into the classroom and show the primary children the essentials of the instruments. Demonstrations help not only the children who see the instrument close at hand but also the older child who explains his instrument.

Pictures are useful, and children as well as teachers may collect them. Those showing the player holding the instrument are preferable, for then the relative size and the manner of playing are evident.

Children in the intermediate grades should make a systematic study of the four "families" of instruments in a symphony orchestra. An outline such as this may be followed:

The Strings	*The Woodwinds*	*The Brass Winds*	*Percussion*
violin	piccolo	trumpet	snare drum
viola	flute	French horn	bass drum
cello	clarinet	trombone	tympani
bass viol	oboe	tuba	cymbals and gong
	English horn		assorted small
	bassoon		rhythm instruments
			xylophone, orchestra
			bells, celeste

These books, records and pictures are valuable in organizing such a study:

Books:
Tune Up[15] by Huntington contains excellent photographs and brief descriptions.
Picture Book of Musical Instruments[16] by Lacey contains pen sketches of the instruments with historical résumé on each.
The Wonderful World of Music[20] tells of the development of instruments in an interesting, beautifully illustrated historical study for young readers.
Alice in Orchestralia[19] by La Prade is an entertaining and informative story.

Recordings:
Pan the Piper by Kleisinger-Wing (Columbia). This is a fanciful narration of the beginnings of the instruments with musical examples.
The Wonderful Violin (YPR-311)
The Hunter's Horn (YPR-421)
The King's Trumpet (YPR-420)
Licorice Stick, Story of the Clarinet (YPR-420)

Those above contain musical examples and verbal explanation of essential points.

Instruments of the Orchestra (Columbia, Victor, Decca). Single instruments play excerpts from symphonic literature.
Meet the Instruments (Bowmar Records with filmstrips)

Motion pictures:
Music for Young People[17]—"Introducing the Woodwinds," "Percussion, the Pulse of Music" and others

Pictures of the instruments:
Instruments of the Orchestra Charts and Handbook[18]

Learning to play an instrument is a privilege and a challenge. Of the many kinds of instruments, some are easier to learn to play than others. The ideal, most expressive "instrument" is the human voice. The musical prestige of all the other instruments is determined by how expressively and sensitively they may be played. The stringed instruments are given great prestige, for when well played they come nearest to the qualities heard in the human voice. The player "makes" the tone with his bow and his fingers and therefore has control over the finest shading of nuances in the melody. The more "automatic" an instrument is, i.e., the less *directly* its tone production is controlled by the player, the less expressive and artistic the instrument can be. For this reason accordions and electric organs have less stature as musical instruments.

CLASSROOM CONCERTS. Pupils should have opportunities to hear expressive musicians in person. When young children are close to the performer, they can see and hear him and his instrument to good advantage. Small concerts, in the classrooms or in a slightly larger room where three or four classes may gather together, are best at the primary level.

A principal and music supervisor, determined that their primary children should have music under the most favorable circumstances, planned an annual series of three concerts. These took place in the kindergarten room because it happened to be the largest space with good acoustics. In order that the intimacy of the concert might be maintained, only three or four classes at one time attended a performance.

To enable the children to center their attention on one or two instruments, only soloists and small ensembles performed. Each concert was thirty minutes long, for it was considered important that the experience be a short, successful one, which would leave the children eager to hear the next. The artists were chosen for musicianship and personality appeal. They were members of the community who were actively engaged in music, although not professional in the field, and occasional outstanding high school or college musicians. In every case the performers were delighted with their young audiences, who listened with much receptivity and enthusiasm.

All of the numbers performed were short and there was ample contrast in the program. One concert featured a pianist and a cellist. The pianist performed Mozart's lively rondo, "Alla Turca" from the *Sonata in A Major,* and followed this with the tranquil "Träumerei" of Schumann. In these two compositions the children were easily able to discern the contrasting rhythmic and tonal possibilities of the piano. Ibert's "Little White Donkey" is colorful "picture" music and, as the third piano solo, was especially appealing to the children.

To see the artist performing was a very important part of these concerts. The cellist discussed the important parts of her instrument and gave the children samples of the different techniques that would be used. Her numbers, too, were varied—"The Swan" by Saint-Saëns and then an arrangement of "Londonderry Air" in which the melody was played in both low and high registers. Contrast and a more lively technique came in the "Waltz" from *Music for Children*, Opus 65, by Prokofieff.

After returning to their classrooms, the children discussed the music and the teachers answered questions. Before the concert careful orientation in each classroom had prepared the children to meet their artist friends and to understand something about the instruments they were to play. Because many of the children had never before been to a concert, the teachers gave careful attention to a discussion of "concert manners." The children learned that one never talks during the playing of a number; they were interested in how and why they should applaud to show their appreciation. It was found that the children liked the formality surrounding the concert.

Children's concerts such as this do not just "happen." They are the result of purposeful planning. In every community there is talent that may be used for the benefit of children in the primary school. We need more teachers who will promote the experience of live music for children as a recognized part of a vital music education program.

CONCERTS FOR OLDER CHILDREN. Pupils in the intermediate grades should have opportunities to attend concerts either of a type designed especially for young listeners or of the community concert variety. While concerts at the primary level should be intimate and informal, boys and girls from the fourth grade upward should be given some large-concert experience.

A small city school district, located 200 miles from a metropolitan center, arranged a series of three annual concerts for all of the pupils above the second grade. The plan began modestly with support from a PTA concert committee and the music supervisor. Over a period of four years the children heard a fine boys' choir, a professional string-woodwind orchestra, and several soloists. They attended musical plays and performances by an established ballet company. Many of the children had no other contact with talented musicians, dancers, and actors.

The project was unusual in that *all* pupils and their teachers attended. Programs were designed on the artistic rather than on the showmanship level; much care was taken in the selection of music, and all concerts were under one hour in length. In addition, the music supervisor planned and, in some cases, presented material for preconcert orientation. Teachers, administrators, music personnel, and parents were enthusiastic; all agreed that quality in the performances and careful planning were the essential features in the series.

Many cities have their own symphony orchestras and opera companies, and often special school concerts are arranged. Key personnel in making concert attendance a successful activity are the school principal and the classroom teacher. If these people do not actively support the project, more often than not many of the children are not enthusiastic. If the concert is an all-school activity, the indifferent teacher may bring a group of children who do not know how to be members of a concert audience.

A teacher's enthusiasm for a community concert series may interest pupils so much that the parents buy tickets for them. Pictures of performing artists, newspaper clippings, and programs brought by children can be arranged on the tack board in the music center. Thus, important local musical events are brought to the attention of the class. Student reports after attendance at a concert may promote interest in future concerts.

Important musical events on radio and television should be given the same type of attention. The teacher who reads the announcements of such programs can discuss and evaluate them ahead of time with the class. A student music committee may be set up to keep the class informed on programs of particular interest during each week. Occasionally a teacher can plan preliminary classroom music activities that will increase the value of the out-of-school listening experience.

Many homes have fine collections of recorded music. As musical forms, such as marches, dances, opera, are considered in the classroom, pupils may explore their families' collections for similar or contrasting compositions. Likewise, a student who is studying an instrument with a private teacher may know a comparable march or dance which he could play for his fellow students. Much can be gained from class analysis of the musical elements in the composition played by the student. Individuals would be led to see that their "pieces" are not just collections of notes, but that those notes make rhythm patterns and melodies; the melodies are supported by harmonies and are set in certain patterns of phrases and sections, just as are the compositions heard on recordings or in concerts.

ACTIVITIES FOR COLLEGE CLASSES

A. Written Assignments

    1. List for use in your handbook, Section V-C, four compositions which you believe would be suitable background music for:
       a. quiet-time
       b. quiet activities

2. Go to a record store, hear and evaluate in terms of objectives for music education, the current new releases designed to acquaint children with the instruments. Consider such things as appeal, musical tone quality, and informational content. List significant titles and record numbers in handbook Section V-B.

3. Make a collection of pictures of the more common orchestral instruments. Outline the "family" relationships and make notes about the chief physical and sound characteristics of each.

4. Select two short character sketches in music and find poems, stories, or pictures that seem especially appropriate for use with each.

5. List in Section V-B, several examples of "character sketches" in music that would be useful in your classroom.

6. Select one short descriptive composition that you find appealing. State first the general descriptive effects which you hear in the music. Study carefully the rhythm, melody, harmony, form, and instrumentation of the composition, and insofar as possible state how the use of each contributes toward the descriptive effect.

7. Select one suite, one tone poem, or something from opera that will be appropriate for the intermediate grade of your choice. Become familiar with the music and prepare teaching notes that will enable you to present the music effectively if you are asked to do so next week.

8. In the basic song book from which you may teach, find material designed to assist in a study of one composer. Outline the information given; list suitable songs and recorded compositions available to you.

B. Classroom Projects

1. Select a short musical composition that is descriptive in nature. Listen to it a number of times and write a story based on what you hear in the music. Read your story and play the record for the class.

2. Prepare and present a musical story to the class. Use MacDowell's "Of a Tailor and a Bear" or any other short musical sketch you like.

3. Select two short contrasting compositions that may be expressed in color and design. After hearing the music, create in finger paint, water color, or crayon, your impression of each.

4. On different days, hear Ibert's "Little White Donkey" and "The Little Train of the Caipira" by Villa-Lobos. Whether you are an artist or not, give yourself the pleasure of expressing what you hear in color on paper.

5. Play for the college class your choice of a descriptive composition under No. 1 above. Through skillful questioning and rehearing of the composition as necessary, draw from the students satisfactory answers to the questions:
   a. What descriptive effects are heard in the music?
   b. How does the composer use the musical elements to achieve these effects?
   Use bodily movement or other forms of creative response that may be suitable in this study.

CHAPTER NOTES

1. "Notes for Teachers" in each album from RECORD LIBRARY FOR ELEMENTARY SCHOOLS (New York: Radio Corporation of America, RCA Victor Record Division, 1947).
2. Lillian Baldwin, *A Listener's Anthology of Music*, Volumes I and II (Morristown, N.J.: Silver Burdett Company, 1948).
3. Hazel Gertrude Kinscella, *Folk Tales from Many Lands, Tales of Olden Days*, and others from STORIES IN MUSIC APPRECIATION (Lincoln, Nebr.: University Publishing Company, 1951) [Olden Days].
4. James L. Mursell *et al.*, *Music Now and Long Ago* from the MUSIC FOR LIVING Series (Morristown, N.J.: Silver Burdett Company, 1956).
5. Lillian Baldwin, *Music for Young Listeners: The Green Book, The Crimson Book, The Blue Book* (Morristown, N.J.: Silver Burdett Company, 1951) [Gr Bk, Cr Bk, Bl Bk].
6. MUSICAL SOUND BOOKS (recordings), Scarsdale, New York: Sound Book Press Society, Inc.
7. Syd Skolsky, *The Music Box Book* (New York: E. P. Dutton and Co., Inc., 1946).
8. Irving Wolfe *et al.*, *Music Through the Year* from TOGETHER WE SING Series (Chicago: Follett Publishing Company, 1956).
9. William C. Hartshorn and Helen S. Leavitt, *At Home and Abroad, Prelude, Progress* from MAKING FRIENDS WITH MUSIC Series (Boston: Ginn and Company, 1940).
10. Lillian Baldwin, *Music to Remember* (New York: Silver Burdett Company, 1951) [Mus to Rem].
11. Hazel Gertrude Kinscella, *Music and Romance* (New York: Radio Corporation of America, RCA Victor Record Division, 1941) [M&R].
12. Gian-Carlo Menotti's *Amahl and the Night Visitors*, narrative adaptation by Frances Frost (New York: Whittlesey House, McGraw-Hill Book Co., Inc.).
13. Robert Lawrence, METROPOLITAN OPERA GUILD STORIES FOR CHILDREN (Series): *Carmen*, adapted from Bizet's opera (New York: Grosset Dunlap, Inc., 1938), *Haensel and Gretel*, the story of Humperdinck's opera (Morristown, N.J.: Silver Burdett Company, 1938), and others.
14. Opal Wheeler and Sybil Deucher, *Joseph Haydn, The Merry Little Peasant* and others, biographical series (New York: E. P. Dutton and Co., Inc., 1936).
15. Harriet Huntington, *Tune Up* (New York: Doubleday and Company, Inc., 1942).
16. Marion Lacey, *Picture Book of Musical Instruments* (New York: Lothrop, Lee and Shepard Co., Inc., 1951).
17. MUSIC FOR YOUNG PEOPLE Series (films), distributed by NET Film Service, Indiana University, Bloomington, Ind.
18. *Instruments of the Orchestra Charts and Handbook*, available from J. W. Pepper and Son, 1423 Vine Street, Philadelphia, Pa.
19. Ernest La Prade, *Alice in Orchestralia* (New York: Doubleday and Company, Inc., 1948).
20. Benjamin Britten and Imogen Holst, *The Wonderful World of Music* (New York: Garden City Books, 1958).

21. Martin Bernstein, *An Introduction to Music* (Englewood Cliffs, N.J.: Prentice-Hall, Inc., 1951).
22. Edwin John Stringham, *Listening to Music Creatively*, Second Edition (Englewood Cliffs, N.J.: Prentice-Hall, Inc., 1959).
23. Aaron Copland, *What To Listen for In Music*, Revised Edition (New York: McGraw-Hill Book Co., Inc., 1957).
24. June King McFee, *Preparation for Art* (San Francisco: Wadsworth Publishing Company, Inc., 1961).

OTHER REFERENCES

Hartshorn, William C., "The Role of Listening," Chapter XI from *Basic Concepts in Music Education*, edited by Nelson B. Henry. The Fifty-seventh Yearbook of the National Society for the Study of Education (Chicago: University of Chicago Press, 1958).

Kinscella, Hazel Gertrude, and Elizabeth Tierney, *The Child and His Music* (Lincoln, Nebr.: University Publishing Company, 1953). Chapter 3, "Dramatic Music for Children," Chapter 4, "Instrumental Music for Children," and Chapter 5, "When the Child Listens."

McMillan, Eileen, *Guiding Children's Growth Through Music* (Boston: Ginn and Company, 1959). Chapter 5, "Listening Adventures for Children and Teachers," and Appendix B, "Supplementary Materials for Listening."

Myers, Louise Kifer, *Teaching Children Music in the Elementary School* (Englewood Cliffs, N.J.: Prentice-Hall, Inc., 1956). Chapter 6, "Listening."

Sheehy, Emma Dickson, *Children Discover Music and Dance* (New York: Henry Holt and Company, Inc., 1959). Chapter 9, "Phonograph Records, Radio, Television," and Chapter 10, "Concerts."

Snyder, Alice M., *Creating Music with Children* (New York: Mills Music, Inc., 1957). Chapter 6, "Listening to Music."

Timmerman, Maurine, *Let's Teach Music* (Evanston, Ill.: Summy-Birchard Publishing Co., 1959). Chapter 5, "Let's Listen," with listings of recordings, films, and books, pp. 142-148.

Taylor, Katherine Scott, "An Autochthonous Approach to Music Appreciation," *Music Educators Journal*, February-March, 1949.

Zimmerman, George H., "Art and Music Mix Well," *Music Educators Journal*, June-July 1956.

See Appendix B for record companies and others supplying catalogues of current recordings.

CHAPTER NINE

MUSIC IN THE SOCIAL STUDIES
AND OTHER CONSIDERATIONS

We have traveled a long road in delineating the kind of education in music that should be provided for elementary school children. The challenges of the first chapter return in these final pages: a music program cannot be extracted from a textbook, but must be created by the inner promptings of teachers charged with the responsibility for it. Teachers are resourceful individuals, capable of meeting the challenges and assuming the responsibilities given them. Although the complete program outlined here cannot be awarded, like a diploma for faithful study, it can be recreated by each teacher according to the needs of his pupils, his own talents, and the reservoir of skill available in others.

Frequent references have been made to a relationship between music and the social studies. This relationship is especially important at the intermediate level where various national or ethnic groups are studied. Experience with the music of other peoples can bring an individual into dynamic association with the spirit and feelings of those peoples. Prescott says: "If we teach art subjects in such a way as to induce feelings, surely our children will understand the stream of history, will sense the on-goingness of civilization as they never can through mere verbal symbols describing those times. . . . Indeed, the aesthetic arts should render the same service of interpretation and crystallization to the point of feeling within our own culture."[1]

In planning a program in which music is drawn into the social studies the teacher must survey the available materials and evaluate them in terms of their contribution to the general study and their value as musical experiences. Some suggestions and important considerations for such a project are given in the following paragraphs.

Music in the Social Studies—
Resources and Organization

In the social studies of the intermediate grades, students are concerned with the people of their own community and with those as far distant as the Pacific Islands and Europe. Historically such studies may go back beyond the Mayflower to the earliest cultures from which contemporary society sprang. When music is related to such topics, teachers and pupils should study it from both the historical and the geographical points of view. When the pupils see how various aspects of music develop and are related down through history, they will more surely understand the close relationship of peoples. In most areas city, county, and state curriculum planners have determined the topics to be used in each grade. Once the study is limited to a region or a particular period in history the teacher may determine the values that musical resources might have within the total study. In some units the use of related music may be very worthwhile, and, for a time, the greater part of the musical activities of the class may be centered around the study.

The classified indexes of the basic music texts list appropriate songs for a variety of subjects. Some of the recent books and listings from various recording firms suggest specific recordings. No one source contains all the most desirable songs, and therefore it is advisable that a teacher provide himself with specialized supplementary books. The music consultant should be of service in gathering or recommending such materials.

The study of music related to the social studies topic need not be limited to folk music. Composers identified with a country make important contributions to the culture; pupils should hear representative instrumental and vocal music of these composers. As far as possible the pupils should understand the ways in which the composer's nationality, his time in history, and the events of his life influenced his music. Such an understanding depends on the background and maturity of the pupils and the extent to which they can understand such basic social considerations.

REGIONAL STUDIES. Fourth grade social studies often are related to the county, section, or state in which the children live, or to type-regions of the world such as the hot, dry countries or the cold countries.

Material relative to local areas is compiled in state or county courses of study and generally is not available in national publications. Often there is a shortage of good usable musical material that is authentic rather than "arranged" and adapted. Local libraries, historical societies, and museums may be sources of information having some bearing on music of the locality. Available material will center around (1) a tribe of native Indians, if any, (2) immigrants (early or more recent) who brought their folk music with them, or (3) particular historical events of local interest commemorated in song.

Some of the type-regions studied offer good opportunities for a consideration of related music. *Literature and Music as Resources for Social Studies*[2] by Tooze and Krone contains information and musical examples from most of the countries of the world. The other references listed at the end of this chapter suggest sources of information and music. Some curriculum bulletins list all of the music available on each topic, but many such listings are unselective and often include a large number of songs of little authenticity and musical value. Such lists are useful as resources, but the teacher must judge each song or musical reference by its genuine worth in the topic concerned.

In addition to musical criteria, a teacher might evaluate songs in terms of the following:

1. Is this a song actually sung by these people or is it merely composed about them?
2. If it was sung by the people themselves, of what significance is it? Does it reveal them as a particular type of people, of a particular occupation? Is it genuinely expressive of human feeling and experience? Is it a good representative of its type?
3. If the song is composed *about* the life and circumstances of a particular people, is it a good song in itself? Does its musical and poetic quality make a genuine contribution to the study of the topic at hand?

Recorded music typical of the countries or regions studied is of importance. Some valuable recordings of this nature are mentioned earlier in Chapter 3. Fourth grade children are not interested in extensive listening of this sort, but short examples designed to give them the flavor of such native music can be valuable and impressive. Someone must select the music to be heard by the class as a whole; in some cases a small committee of children can assist in determining what will be of greatest interest to the entire group.

When such music is heard it should be studied with respect to its rhythmic elements, melody, harmony or lack of it, and instrumentation. Older pupils are able to deal with these questions much more extensively than younger pupils.

MUSIC IN THE UNITED STATES. In many schools fifth grade children study the American scene from the landing of the Pilgrims to the present day and from the East Coast to the West. The musical potential of this study is rich and should comprise a large part of the musical experiences during the year. Several fifth grade song books center around songs of the United States, and therefore it is not difficult to obtain appropriate song literature.

There are several points to be noted with regard to the use of American folk music. Genuine folk music is an expression of a people; it expresses their concerns, moods, love, and relationship to their work, family, and the world. The music has lasting value as a part of American life insofar as it is truly expressive of these things.

Such music has an important place in education and should be studied in such a way that these expressive factors are brought to the attention of the students. Certainly not every cowboy or riverboat song is as important as others. Outstanding examples of each type of song should be chosen. Some songs may be included because they have an important historical significance. Others may be included on the basis of musical considerations. The teacher should endeavor to use not only those that are the best representatives of each type but also those that give the pupils varied musical experiences in melody, mood, rhythm, and accompaniment. Because the United States is a collection of immigrants from many countries, folk music of other lands has its place in a study of American music; well-known melodies of other countries complement the study of folk music in this country.

A number of important resource books are available for use by the teacher and the pupils. *Literature and Music as Resources for Social Studies*[2] devotes fourteen chapters to literature and music in various times and areas of this country. For teaching purposes the study should be divided into smaller units such as "Music of the Colonial Period" and "Music of the Western Frontier." Kinscella's *History Sings*[3] gives representative incidents and stories designed to bring readers into a close relationship with the people throughout the history of America.

Patriotic and service songs may be learned by fifth grade children. Often the occasion and purpose of a song's origin is as important as the song itself, for only in that setting are some songs fully appreciated. The children should hear recordings of fine soloists and choirs singing these numbers. The historical background of this music may be found in *History Sings*, in Lyon's *Stories of Our American Patriotic Songs*,[4] and in other sources. These books are understandable to children and may serve as references for student reports.

WIDENING HORIZONS OF PEOPLE AND MUSIC. Song books at the sixth grade level reflect a broader source of music: *Music Everywhere, Music for Living Around the World*, and *Voices of the World*. Some sixth grades study Canada, Mexico, or countries in Central and South America. Other classes look closely at the Philippines, Japan or Australia. Perhaps only one or two such topics will be considered, but the related music is plentiful and interesting. Topical indices in the basic song series suggest authentic songs; Tooze and Krone[2] give a few pertinent facts about the important characteristics of the music of any country; the Library of Congress and commercial companies such as Folkways, Columbia, and Victor have made recordings of the native music in many lands; and a number of films are available as enrichment for such a study.

Sixth grade children can be very capable musicians; when previous training has been good they can sing and play melodies and rhythms with little guidance from their teacher or the music specialist. These pupils may do research reading on selected topics and report on their findings. The extent of such activities of course depends on the resources available at a suitable reading level. Because of the relative maturity and the greater musical skills of these pupils, a study of music can have considerable significance in a social studies unit.

DEVELOPING A RESOURCE UNIT. When building a resource unit in which music is related to social studies and other classroom activities the teacher should consider the following questions:

1. In the selection of song literature, which songs are authentic and appropriate? Are there possibilities for student reports on the backgrounds of these songs? If so, what readings are available? Where?

2. Are recordings of authentic native music available? Which would be most appropriate for use with this class? Are there reliable sources of information about this music?

3. How are the character, customs, and life of the people reflected in the music? If they were a primitive tribe, were they generally peaceful or warlike, agrarian or hunters? Are religious and social customs revealed? If they were immigrants and settlers, what were their life purposes and outlook, social and religious customs, occupations, and everyday concerns with living?

4. What are the important distinctive melodic, rhythmic, and harmonic characteristics of this music? How much of this should be brought to the attention of the pupils?

5. What use of musical instruments was made in the period or region? Did instruments vary with the music and the occasion? Are similar instruments available, or can they be made by the students?

6. What possibilities exist for the use of bodily movement or playing instruments in authentic or nearly authentic ways with this music?

Teachers and pupils often arrange a culminating program around the activities of the study. Pupils sing, perform typical dances, and dramatize events related to the topic. Parents or other classes may be invited to the classroom. If these programs are closely related to the everyday studies and activities, they are quite justifiable educational enterprises, a sharing of what has been learned in a particular study rather than a "program" in the formal sense. Drama, art, poetry, music, and dance may be combined to provide a colorful and interesting presentation.

Social studies topics vary in their musical importance. Occasionally a topic may have rich musical potential and for a time little other music is studied. Other topics may offer little of genuine musical value or interest, and the attention may be focused in other directions. Certainly the teacher should explore the possibilities for musical enrichment with whatever units are used.

Talent from Varied Sources

The discussion in this book has been based on the premise that the chief motivator of music in the education of children must be the classroom teacher. When the teacher knows what kind of a music program may be developed, he can go a long way toward achieving it in spite of his own musical limitations; he may find specific music skills in others: the music consultant if he has one, the special music teacher, the classroom teacher next door, a parent, the school secretary, or an upper-grade student. Of all these people, only the music consultant is likely to know as well as the teacher what kind of music program is needed in a particular classroom. Even this expert will need conferences and visits to the classroom to work with the teacher and the class before he is able to give the best advice and assistance. Conscientious administrators provide enough music specialists to assist the general teacher with this important task.

The music consultant is an assistant, a resource person and an advisor to teachers. If a music consultant has a realistic schedule, with no more than 75 teachers to assist, he can come to each school once or twice a week and go into the rooms of those teachers who need his aid. With a schedule such as this, the music consultant who knows the teacher's abilities with regard to music is able to (1) give assistance in the planning of the music program for the class, (2) suggest and provide new and varied materials to meet specific needs in that classroom, and (3) use his own musical skills to supplement the experiences that the classroom teacher is able to provide.

If the music consultant is available but does not visit often enough to do more than assist in the planning, the teacher must find music skills in others. In one school district the music consultant had two needs in mind when she arranged to have talented fifth and sixth grade pianists aid the primary teachers in music. The teachers knew that they needed more help than the consultant could give personally, and the consultant felt that the older students needed an outlet for their musical talent and training. These students could both sing and play the piano. Although it was necessary to plan the work so that it did not interfere with their regular studies, the whole project was a challenge to the older students and very helpful to the primary teachers.

If a consultant is not available to set up such a program, an individual teacher might seek out an older student whom he knows to be musical and eager to cooperate in such a venture. By planning ahead, the teacher can utilize the student's talent for teaching new songs and for providing accompaniments for familiar songs, rhythmic activities, and dances. In such a cooperative undertaking, it is necessary that the teacher know good music-teaching techniques and that he discover how the student's talents may best be utilized to assist in effective teaching.

Many teachers find that another teacher is willing to assist in specific ways. If the two work together in planning, and if the classroom teacher himself carries on as much of the program as he is able, the specific help given can be of great value. Occasionally a parent who has special skill may be invited to come into the classroom on a more or less regular basis. He may assist in special ways, such as providing instrumental accompaniments, singing, or helping to notate original songs. The teacher does not abdicate his responsibility for the program, but plans together with the musician to use this special skill in the most advantageous ways.

In some schools, elementary teachers practice a daily exchange program wherein one teaches music while the other teaches another subject such as physical education. This exchange may provide more skilled music teaching for both classes, but it tends to isolate the classroom teacher from the musical activities and interests of his pupils. He may develop a disinterest in these activities and do little to include music in significant ways at any other time of day. In all of the situations in which the skill of another person is used, the teacher must maintain an active interest in music for his class. He must assist in planning the program and do as much as he can to increase his own music-teaching skills. Under such arrangements a great number of elementary teachers can become capable music teachers within their own classrooms.

Evaluation in Music

In the elementary school, evaluation of progress made in music is not so much a grading of the pupil as it is a grading of the program itself and the implementation of that program through effective teaching. Because of its varied, natural appeal children respond with enthusiasm to music when it is brought to them in vital, meaningful ways.

If individual evaluation reports of the children are necessary, the teacher should consider the musical potential and evaluate in terms of individual achievement. A brief written report or conversation with a parent is better than a number or letter grade in music. When grades are required, one point of caution should be observed: it is a mistake to give the highest possible grade in music to a pupil who has a limited musical potential. The highest grade should be reserved for those who both have and use their natural ability; next highest grades may go to those who have enthusiasm and who participate in spite of lower natural endowment. When a child who is not capable of doing first quality work is given the highest grade, he and his family are given the erroneous impression that he has a superior musical potential.

A failure in music can only be the result of such poor teaching that it does not find and develop whatever limited aptitude there may be. Musical activities are so varied that everyone can find some point of success and interest. If a child is disinterested, it is more a problem of relationships with the teacher and other pupils, home environment, and factors other than musical deficiency.

The teacher's evaluation of his program should be immediate as well as long range. Under each of the activities there are objectives toward which the teacher must work. A check-list of such objectives in each section of the handbook should assist in evaluating the effectiveness of the program in all of these areas. In the last analysis, evaluation of the program must be in terms of what music is doing and can continue to do for the individual. If music is to continue to have beneficial effects throughout life, there must be continuous growth in response to it, and growth in the individual's ability to participate in it in progressively more mature ways. If the prospective teacher, as a result of the studies and musical experiences suggested in this text, can objectively evaluate his own music-teaching potential he will be better prepared to assume the responsibilities assigned to him here.

A New Teacher Beginning the Year

School administrators generally are pleased to employ a teacher who is fully prepared to do all of the music teaching in his classroom, and there are a few beginning teachers who are qualified to reply unequivocally that they can do this. Many others may answer in the affirmative, but they should also inquire whether there is a music specialist who can give them advice and assistance in some areas.

When a candidate has significant limitations in this field, it is advisable that he state these when he accepts the position. If his general letters of recommendation are good this will not disqualify him but it may have some bearing upon his placement in the district and will enable the administration to provide assistance for him.

When his assignment is assured, the teacher should find out what music books are in use, what access he will have to a good record player, what records are available, and so forth. He will then make adjustments in his music-teaching handbook in preparation for this specific assignment. As he establishes himself in the classroom he can arrange different centers of activity and interest. Among these, there should be a music center where he will place a few well-chosen items: an easy-to-play instrument or two, a colorful song book, pictures or posters giving promise of musical activities to come.

It is hoped that the teacher will have a record player and some records for use the first day of school. It may be a short day, but certainly there will be a few minutes when music can be used to refresh the spirits of both pupils and teacher. The primary teacher may have a short song-story, such as "The Shoemaker and the Elves,"[5] which he would like to play for the boys and girls. If they begin to join in singing the repetitious parts of the refrain all well and good; if not, another day will be soon enough to suggest it. At the intermediate level an interesting recording of a good folk singer may serve as an introduction to a social studies unit; a descriptive composition such as an excerpt from the *Grand Canyon Suite* may reflect holiday travels.

During the first few days, the new teacher should use music informally, helping the children feel that music is a part of life in that school room. They may experiment with and play the instruments at certain times. The teacher can show an interest in their simple discoveries and listen to the songs they hum or croon at work and play. Older children may be provided with number notations for a song or two that they know. The bells or xylophone will then immediately be a playable instrument for them. Informal groups may enjoy singing with the Autoharp.

Events will occur that will suggest a song the teacher knows and can teach; a "song-story" may invite the children to sing along. If kindergarten or first grade children become tired, an action song or finger play will wake them up, or a lullaby will relax them. Soon music will have a well-accepted place in the classroom, and the teacher can begin to provide a more balanced program. He may look for a musical assistant to help in specific ways. He will begin to know the musical abilities of his children, and, thinking in terms of the first visit of the music consultant, he can jot down his musical problems and needs.

Too often the teacher does not make it easy for the consultant to help him. Either he covers up his problems when the consultant is there, or he fails to give any prior thought to assistance this person can give. If the consultant is scheduled to arrive on a particular day, the new teacher should make an effort to find out when he could have a conference with him, and what type of service the consultant is in the habit of giving. If he wants a sample lesson in a particular musical activity, he should let the consultant know a day ahead so that he might come prepared.

Whereas a music specialist may be quite successful teaching music with his voice and a pitch pipe as his total equipment, a less talented teacher will need something more. His pupils can benefit from the use of books, records, and instruments. The music consultant may be able to assist the new teacher in getting these or in setting up a systematic plan for their later acquisition. With these material helps, a judicious use of available music talent, and a keen sense of the value of music classroom teachers can do much to make music a significant part of education in the elementary school.

ACTIVITIES FOR COLLEGE CLASSES

A. Written Assignments

   1. Look back at the suggested organization of the music handbook in Chapter One. You are now be in a position to complete Section I, "The Teacher and the Program."

2. As a prospective intermediate grade teacher, determine in what grade the local county, state, or region history and society are studied. What part does music play in such a study? How significant is this music? Prepare a unit or evaluate the musical material of a resource unit on the music related to a topic of your choice. Include significant material under topical headings in your music handbook.

B. Classroom Project

With a small group, prepare a thirty-minute culminating program to be presented in the college class at the end of the term. Using drama, art, literature, music, and dance in simple but effective ways, develop a theme related to some aspect of social studies or other topic of interest at the grade level the group selects.

CHAPTER NOTES

1. Daniel A. Prescott, *Emotion and the Educative Process* (Washington, D.C.: American Council on Education, 1938), p. 225. Reprinted by permission.
2. Ruth Tooze and Beatrice Krone, *Literature and Music as Resources for Social Studies* (Englewood Cliffs, N.J.: Prentice-Hall, Inc., 1955).
3. Hazel Gertrude Kinscella, *History Sings* (Lincoln, Nebr.: University Publishing Company, 1948).
4. John Henry Lyons, *Stories of Our American Patriotic Songs* (New York: The Vanguard Press, 1942).
5. "The Shoemaker and the Elves," a song-story sung and told by Frank Luther. Decca C.U.S. 8. Also found in *Singing on Our Way* (Ginn and Company).

OTHER REFERENCES

Elliott, Raymond, *Teaching Music* (Columbus, Ohio: Charles E. Merrill Books, Inc., 1960). Part 2, "Materials," pp. 195-312.
Perham, Beatrice, *Music in the New School* (Park Ridge, Ill.: Neil A. Kjos Music Co., 1941). Pp. 35-44, "Correlation and Integration," and Chapter 10, "Evaluation."
Pierce, Anne E., *Teaching Music in the Elementary School* (New York: Henry Holt and Co., Inc., 1959). Pp. 32-34, "Evaluation of Pupils," and Chapter 9, "Music: Servant and Master."
Mathews, Paul Wentworth, *You Can Teach Music* (New York: E. P. Dutton and Co., Inc., 1953). Chapter 9, "Music Doesn't Walk Alone."
Myers, Louise Kifer, *Teaching Children Music in the Elementary School*, Second Edition (Englewood Cliffs, N.J.: Prentice-Hall, Inc., 1956). Chapter 12, "Music's Role in Understanding Other Peoples," Bibliography and Sources of Materials, pp. 338-350, annotated and under headings (1) "Background in Music" and (2) "Music's Role in Understanding Other Peoples."
Nye, Robert Evans, and Vernice Trousdale Nye, *Music in the Elementary School* (Englewood Cliffs, N.J.: Prentice-Hall, Inc., 1957). Chapter 9, "The Value of Music in Other Areas."
Timmerman, Maurine, *Let's Teach Music* (Evanston, Ill.: Summy-Birchard Publishing Company, 1958). Chapter 7, "Let's Live With Music," pp. 177-187, and suggested sources of materials, pp. 199-202.

APPENDIX A

REFERENCE MATERIAL
FOR MUSIC THEORY
AND NOTATION

I. METER AND RHYTHM

metric beat—the underlying framework of regular pulses around which the rhythm of music is organized. The beat is usually represented by one of the following symbols:

♪ = an eighth note (numerically indicated by 8).

♩ = a quarter note (numerically indicated by 4).

♩ = a half note (numerically indicated by 2).

tempo—the speed of the metric beat, designated by:
 (a) metronome marking indicating the number of beats per minute, e.g., MM = 72.
 (b) traditional Italian terms that suggest mood and type of movement as well as pace:

largo—very slow and broad	*moderato*—moderate
lento—slow	*allegretto*—moderately fast
adagio—leisurely	*allegro*—quick, lively
andante—moderate and flow-ing	*vivace*—brisk, fast
	presto—very fast

 (c) words qualifying the above and suggesting more definite expression:

dolce—sweetly	*meno mosso*—less movement
grazioso—gracefully	*molto*—very much
maestoso—majestically	*poco*—a little

 (d) simple English equivalents of the Italian terms.
 (e) variation within the established tempo indicated by:
 accelerando, accel.—increase tempo gradually
 ritardando, rit.—decrease tempo gradually
 a tempo—in the original tempo after a change
 rubato—fluctuation or not in strict time
 (f) rhythmic treatment of an individual note:

> —an accent

⌒ *fermata*—hold or lengthen

sf *sforzando*—a heavy accent

265

meter—a systematic grouping of the metric beats.
measure—one unit of metric beats.
bar lines—vertical lines to frame the measure.
meter signature—figure given at the beginning of a composition to indicate the metric organization.

simple duple meter:

which is *alle breve* (sometimes called "cut time")

simple triple meter:

quadruple meter:

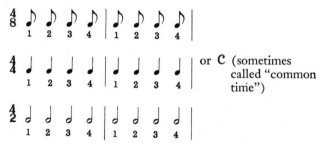

or **C** (sometimes called "common time")

duration—the length of time assigned to a note or rest.

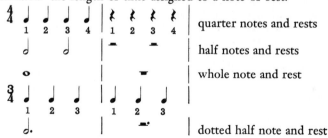

quarter notes and rests

half notes and rests

whole note and rest

dotted half note and rest

even division within the beat showing eighth (♪) and sixteenth (♪) notes with flags and beams, rhythm syllables:

uneven division within the beat showing the use of the *dot* to indicate the additional time of one-half the value of the note it follows, a *tie* binding together two notes on one pitch level, and eighth and sixteenth rests:

compound meters:

duple: $\frac{6}{8}\left(\frac{2}{J.}\right)$ ♩.

triple: $\frac{9}{8}\left(\frac{3}{J.}\right)$ ♩.

comparison of subdivided duple meter and duple compound meter:

triplet division within one beat:

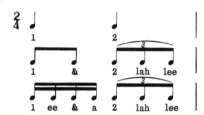

combination meters—groupings of two or three beats within one measure:

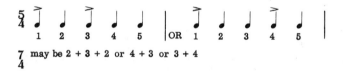

$\frac{7}{4}$ may be 2 + 3 + 2 or 4 + 3 or 3 + 4

rhythm—the flow of the tones in music in short patterns or in longer phrases toward a point of release. Rhythm is related to the underlying metric structure but is not limited to it. Whereas meter is framed by measure bars, rhythm flows across them. Rhythm patterns cutting across measures:

anacrusis—an upbeat leading to the accent:

syncopation—a shift of the accent from what would be its normal position in the underlying metric scheme. Achieved by:

(a) failure to begin a tone on the normal accent:

(b) prolonging a tone on the unaccented part of the measure:

II. PITCH

The *grand staff* and a diagram of the piano keyboard:

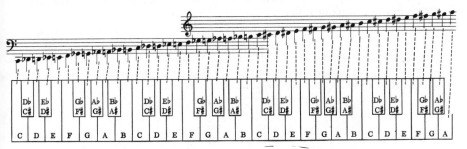

 **G CLEF** establishes the pitch for higher voices. So named because a gothic letter G was used to locate that tone on the *treble staff*.

F CLEF establishes the pitch for lower voices. So named because the gothic letter F was used to locate that tone on the *bass staff*.

staff degree—a line or space on the staff, named by one of the first seven letters of the alphabet.

leger line—a short line above or below the staff to extend the range of tones.

octave—duplication of each letter name every eighth scale degree.

half step—the tonal distance between each consecutive key (whether black or white) on the piano keyboard.

accidental—a tonal alteration of the pitch indicated by a given staff degree. Its influence lasts during the measure in which it appears and is canceled by the bar line.

   sharp (♯)—raises the tone one half step.

   flat (♭)—lowers the tone one half step.

   double sharp (𝄪)—raises the tone one whole step.

   double flat (♭♭)—lowers the tone one whole step.

   natural (♮)—cancels other accidentals or the influence of a sharp or flat in the key signature.

enharmonic tones—a single pitch notated in different ways and called by two or more different names, depending on the key in which the composer is working.

III. SCALES AND CHORDS

major scale—a group of seven different tones in a particular pattern of whole and half steps. Half steps occur between the 3rd and 4th and the 7th and 8th tones of the major scale:

1 2 3 4 5 6 7 8

key center—the tone on which a scale is built.

scale numbers—a general means of naming the tones within a scale.

sol-fa syllables—Italian syllables naming the tones within a scale.

C major scale showing number, syllable, and letter names:

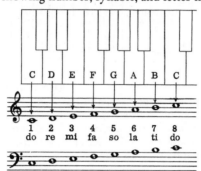

F major scale   G major scale

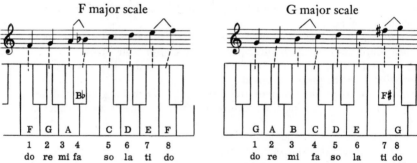

key signature—sharps or flats placed on the staff immediately after the clef sign to designate the key center and to alter the pitches of the staff degrees to provide the correct arrangement of whole and half steps:

common major key signatures (in addition to those already shown):

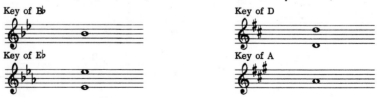

circle of keys:

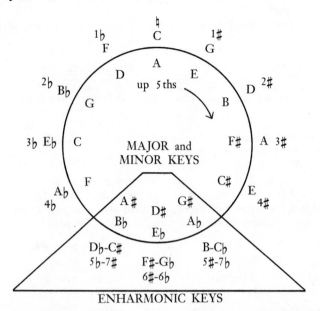

From Howard A. Murphy and Edwin J. Stringham, *Creative Harmony and Musicianship: An Introduction to the Structure of Music* (Englewood Cliffs, N.J.: Prentice-Hall, Inc., 1951). Used by permission.

chromatic scale—a group of twelve tones, all one half step apart (see grand staff under Section II).

sol-fa syllables for chromatic scale (showing ascending and descending forms):

```
              do
              ti
      ♭7 te       li ♯6
              la
      ♭6 le       si ♯5
              so
      ♭5 se       fi ♯4
              fa
              mi
      ♭3 me       ri ♯2
              re
      ♭2 ra       di ♯1   (pronounced dee)
              do
```

interval—the distance between two tones, determined by the number of staff degrees involved.

Intervals between the key tone of the major scale and each of the other tones:

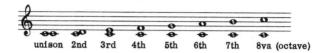

| unison | 2nd | 3rd | 4th | 5th | 6th | 7th | 8va (octave) |

Qualifying sizes of intervals in the major scale (as above):

perfect (P): unison, 4th, 5th, 8va.

major (M): 2nd, 3rd, 6th, 7th.

minor (m): one half step smaller than major intervals.

diminished (d): one half step smaller than minor or perfect intervals.

augmented (A): one half step larger than major or perfect intervals.

Other common intervals between notes of the major scale:

$$3 - 5 = m3$$
mi   so

$$5 - 8 = P4$$
so   <u>do</u>

$$6 - 8 = m3$$
la   <u>do</u>

$$4 - 8 = P5$$
fa   <u>do</u>

triad—a chord of three tones, built in thirds.

root—the tone on which the chord is built.

third—the tone of the chord a 3rd above the root.

fifth—the tone of the chord a 5th above the root.

major triad—a chord in which the lower 3rd is major and the upper 3rd is minor:

minor triad—position of major and minor 3rd reversed:

diminished chord—the triad built on the seventh step of the scale and consisting of two minor 3rd intervals.

triads of the major scale, classified as to size with scale numbers, chord numbers and names:

M	m	m	M	M	m	d	M
I	II	III	IV	V	VI	VII	I*
tonic	supertonic	mediant	subdominant	dominant	submediant	leading tone	tonic

dominant seventh chord: a four-tone chord built on the fifth step of the scale:

V7

minor scales:

natural minor—containing the same tones as the major scale but with a tonal
center a minor third lower:

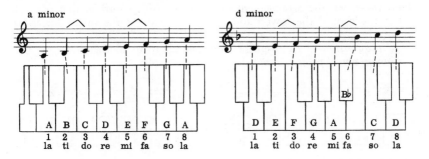

harmonic minor—same as the natural minor but with the seventh step of
the scale raised so that the following pattern is formed:

(descent is the same)

melodic minor—the sixth and seventh steps of the scale are raised in ascent
and unaltered in descent:

pentatonic scale—a scale built of five tones. The most common is that which
represents the major scale with the fourth and seventh scale steps omitted:

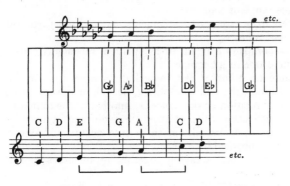

IV. ELEMENTARY PIANO ACCOMPANIMENTS

chord inversion—the arrangement of the tones of a chord so that one other than the root is the lowest tone (see III, triads of the major scale, tonic chord I*).

chord progression—the movement from one chord to another.

common chord progressions using inverted chords:

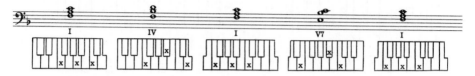

rhythmic use of chord progressions in accompaniments:

V. GLOSSARY

alto—the lowest female voice, or instruments and written parts sounding in the upper middle range of tones.

bass—the lowest male voice, or instruments and written parts sounding in the lowest range of tones.

bourdon—an accompaniment in fifths, played repeatedly, giving an effect similar to the drone of a bagpipe.

cadence—a pause or point of rest in melody, momentary or final depending upon its position at the end of a phrase, period, or musical work as a whole.

canon—the exact imitation of one voice by another at the same or at a different pitch level, with each voice starting at a different time.

concerto—a large work, usually in three movements, for one or more solo instruments accompanied by an orchestra.

counterpoint—a horizontal weaving together of melodies to form a musical texture.

crescendo, cresc., ————————-an increase in loudness.

da capo, D.C.—a return to the beginning of a composition.

dal segno, D.S.—a return to a sign 𝄋 .

diminuendo, dim.,▭▭▭▭—a decrease in loudness.

fine (pronounced *fee*-nay̆)—the end.

forte, f—loud.

fugue—a composition employing imitation, but more free than a canon. "Fugue" means "flight"; two or more parts seem to chase each other, but may diverge after each entrance.

ground bass—a bass part consisting of a few notes and used as a theme over which new melodies are created.

legato—smooth and connected; indicated by a *slur* above or below a group of notes:

mezzo—medium or half. Therefore: *mezzo-piano, mp*—medium soft; *mezzo-forte, mf*—medium loud.

modulation—moving from one key to another within a composition.

neighboring tone—the tone a staff degree above or below a tone in a chord from which the melody comes and returns:

opera—a drama sung throughout with solo voices and chorus, accompanied by an orchestra, and staged with scenery and costumes.

oratorio—a dramatic presentation for solo voices, chorus, and instruments, usually on a religious theme and presented in concert style.

ostinato—a continuous repeated rhythmic or melodic pattern.

overture—an instrumental prelude to an opera or an oratorio; also an independent one-movement composition for band or orchestra.

passing tone—a tone which is touched in passing stepwise from one chord tone to another:

period—a unit of two or more phrases which presents a complete musical idea (analogous to a sentence in language). Within a period two phrases may provide contrast and balance wherein the first serves as the *antecedent* and the second the *consequent* phrase (in a sense, "question and answer").

phrase—a short section of music with a well-defined point of arrival but not necessarily complete in itself.

piano, p—soft.

repeat—a sign indicating that the passage is to be repeated. 𝄆   𝄇

rondo—the form resulting from a prescribed repetition of different sections of a composition. Usually the first section is heard alternately with different sections: A B A C A D A *etc.*

round—a canon in which the imitation is on the same pitch level and where the identical melody is sung more than once by each voice.

sequence—the reproduction of a pattern of tones at a higher or lower level.

sonata—a work for one or two instruments in three or four movements (sections). There is a completeness within each movement but the work as a whole is balanced and the sections provide necessary contrast.

soprano—the highest female voice, or instruments and written parts sounding in the highest range of tones.

staccato—a note to be played short, not connected; indicated by dots above or below the notes:

suite—a group of related compositions. (a) The *Classic dance suite* is a group

APPENDIX B

I. BASIC SONG SERIES
(with reference code)

American Book Company, New York, 1954. John Beattie *et al.*, editors: THE AMERICAN SINGER Series
    AS—*The American Singer*, Books I-VI
        Guide and accompaniments for each level
        Pupil's books II-VI
        Recordings (78 RPM) for all books
American Book Company, New York, 1959. Richard C. Berg *et al.*, editors: MUSIC FOR YOUNG AMERICANS Series
    ABC—*Music for Young Americans*, Kindergarten Book and Books I-VI
        Guide and accompaniments for each level
        Pupil's books II-VI
        Recordings (33⅓ RPM) for all books
Follett Publishing Company, Evanston, Illinois, 1956. Irving Wolfe *et al.*, editors: New TOGETHER-WE-SING Series

MRC—*Music Round the Clock*	MAOC—*Music Across Our Country*
MRT—*Music Round the Town*	VOA—*Voices of America*
MTY—*Music Through the Year*	VOW—*Voices of the World*

        Teacher's edition for each level
        Pupil's book for each level
        Recordings (78 RPM) for all books
Ginn and Company, Boston, 1959. Lilla Belle Pitts *et al.*, editors: OUR SINGING WORLD Series, Enlarged Edition

KBk—*The Kindergarten Book*	SED—*Singing Every Day*
FGB—*The First Grade Book*	ST—*Singing Together*
SOOW—*Singing on Our Way*	SIH—*Singing in Harmony*
S&R—*Singing and Rhyming*	

        Piano accompaniments for each level
        Guide and teaching suggestions K-III
        Guide and teaching suggestions IV-VI
        Primers—*Singing as We Play, Singing All the Day, Playing as We Sing*
        Pupil's books II-VI
        Recordings (78 RPM) for all books

Silver Burdett Company, Morristown, New Jersey, 1944. Osborne McConathy *et al.*, editors: NEW MUSIC HORIZONS Series

    NMH—*New Music Horizons,* Books I-VI
        Piano accompaniments for each level
        Teachers' manual for primary grades
        Teachers' manual for intermediate grades
        Pupil's books I-VI
        Recordings (78 RPM) for all books
    ECh—*Music for Early Childhood,* 1952; Jarman and Tipton, editors
        Recordings (78 RPM)

Silver Burdett Company, Morristown, New Jersey, 1956. James L. Mursell *et al.*, editors: MUSIC FOR LIVING Series

MTD—*Music Through the Day*	**MN&F**—*Music Near and Far*
MIOT—*Music in Our Town*	**MIOC**—*Music in Our Country*
MNLA—*Music Now and Long Ago*	**MAW**—*Music Around the World*

        Teacher's book with piano accompaniments for each level
        Primers—*I Like the Country, I Like the City*
        Pupil's books II-VI
        Recordings (78 RPM) for all books

Summy-Birchard Publishing Company, Evanston, Illinois; Theresa Armitage *et al.*, editors: A SINGING SCHOOL Series (C. C. Birchard, 1949)

OFM—*Our First Music*	**WS**—*We Sing*
OS—*Our Songs*	**OLS**—*Our Land of Song*
MM—*Merry Music*	**ME**—*Music Everywhere*

        Teachers' manual and accompaniments for each level
        Pupil's books II-VI
        Recordings (45 or 78 RPM) for all books

Summy-Birchard Publishing Company, Evanston, Illinois, 1958. Marguerite V. Hood *et al.*, editors: THE BIRCHARD MUSIC Series

    BIR K *Kindergarten*
        Recordings (78 RPM)
    Books I-VI (in preparation)

Code references for song books not in the basic series:

    AFlk—*American Folk Songs for Children,* Ruth Seeger. New York: Doubleday and Company, Inc., 1948.
    SGro—*Songs to Grown On,* Beatrice Landeck. New York: Edward B. Marks Music Corporation, Music Publishers, William Sloane Associates, Inc., Publishers, 1950.

II. RECORD SERIES
    (with reference code)

RCA Victor RECORD LIBRARY FOR ELEMENTARY SCHOOLS
    Rhythmic Activities (album numbers: WE-71 to WE-76)

Volume One (**Rhy I**)	Volume Four (**Rhy IV**)
Volume Two (**Rhy II**)	Volume Five (**Rhy V**)
Volume Three (**Rhy III**)	Volume Six (**Rhy VI**)

Listening Activities (album numbers: WE-77 to WE-82)

Volume One (**Lis I**)   Volume Four (**Lis IV**)
Volume Two (**Lis II**)   Volume Five (**Lis V**)
Volume Three (**Lis III**)   Volume Six (**Lis VI**)

Singing Activities (album numbers: WE-83 to WE-86)

Primary Grades   Volume Five
Volume Four   Volume Six

Special Activities (album numbers: WE-87 to WE-91)

Singing Games   Music   for   Rhythm   Bands
Music at Christmastime   (**Rhy B**)
Music of American Indians   Patriotic Songs
(**Ind Alb**)

ADVENTURES IN MUSIC, A New Record Library for Elementary Schools, RCA Victor Recording Corporation

Grade One (in preparation)   *Grade Four* (in preparation)
Grade Two (in preparation)   *Grade Five* (in preparation)
Grade Three, Volume One (**A in**   *Grade Six, Volume One* (**A in M,**
M, III-1) album number LE-   **VI-1**) album number LE-1009
1002

MUSICAL SOUND BOOKS, created by the Sound Book Press Society, Inc., Scarsdale, N.Y.

Music for Young Listeners
Green Section, MSB 78001-78018
Crimson Section, MSB 78019-78038
Blue Section, MSB 78039-78051
Tiny Masterpieces for Young Listeners, MSB 78301-78320

III. RECORD COMPANIES AND SOURCES OF CATALOGS FOR EDUCATIONAL USE

Bowmar Records, 4921 Santa Monica Blvd., Los Angeles 29, Calif.

Children's Music Center, 2858 W. Pico Blvd., Los Angeles 6, Calif. Recommended books and records for the elementary curriculum.

Children's Reading Service, 1078 St. John's Place, Brooklyn, N.Y. Annotated list of phonograph records.

Columbia Records, Inc., Educational Department, 799 Seventh Avenue, New York 19, N.Y.

Decca Records, 50 West 57th Street, New York 19, N.Y.

Educational Records Sales, 146 Reade Street, New York 13, N.Y. Phonograph records for classroom and library.

Folkways Records and Service Corporation, 117 West 46th Street, New York 36, N.Y.

Greystone Corporation, Educational Activities Division, 100 Sixth Avenue, New York 13, N.Y. Affiliates: Children's Record Guild and Young People's Records.

Mercury Record Corporation, 35 East Wacker Drive, Chicago 1, Ill.

Phoebe James, Creative Rhythms for Children, Box 904, Mentone, Calif.

Rhythm-Time Records, P.O. Box 1106, Santa Barbara, Calif.

Ruth Evans, Childhood Rhythms, Box 132, P.O. Branch X, Springfield, Mass.

Sound Book Press Society, Inc., P.O. Box 222, Scarsdale, N.Y.
RCA Victor Record Division, 155 East 24th Street, New York 10, N.Y.
Vox Productions, Inc., 236 West 55th Street, New York, N.Y.
Whitney Records, 150 Powell Street, San Francisco 2, Calif.

IV. FILMS, LISTINGS FOR EDUCATIONAL USE

Library of Congress, Washington, D.C.: Catalog to Motion Pictures and Film Strips.
Music Educators National Conference, 1201 16th Street N.W., Washington, D.C.: Lilla Belle Pitts, "Handbook on 16mm Films for Music Education."
H. W. Wilson Company, 950 University Ave., New York 52, N.Y.: "The Educational Film Guide," Eleventh Edition, 1953; annual supplements.

V. COMPANIES SUPPLYING CLASSROOM INSTRUMENTS

Conn Corporation, 1101 E. Beardsley, Elkhart, Ind. Distributors of rhythm band equipment, accessories, and educational aids.
Educational Music Bureau, Inc., 30 E. Adams St., Chicago 3, Ill. Representative for Sonor school glockenspiels and xylophones.
Grossman Music Corporation, 740 Bolivar Rd., Cleveland 15, Ohio. Flutophones and school materials.
Harmolin, Inc., P.O. Box 6157, San Diego 6, Calif. Resonator Bells, Zylo Bells, Harmolin, Psaltery, etc.
B. F Kitching & Co., Inc., 9047 Monroe Ave., Brookfield, Ill. Mallet-played instruments for school use.
Wm. Kratt Co., 988 Johnson Place, Union, N.J. Chromatic pitch pipes.
Lyons Band Instrument Company, 223 W. Lake St., Chicago 6, Ill. Rhythm band equipment, Autoharps, Tonettes, bell sets, etc.
Pan American Instrument Company, Elkhart, Ind.
Peripole Products, Inc., 2917 Ave. R, Brooklyn 29, N.Y. Rhythm, melody, and harmony instruments.
Oscar Schmidt-International, Inc., 19 Ferry St., Jersey City 7, N.J. Manufacturers of the Autoharp.
Walberg and Auge, 86 Mechanic Street, Worcester 8, Mass. Manufacturers of percussion and educational instruments.

INDEX OF SONGS AND DANCES

INDEX OF SUBJECTS

Bodily movement, 190–218 (*see also* Creativity)
  for ballads, 213–214
  breaks, analysis of, 206
  costumes for, 201, 209
  creative, 191–195, 198–199
  for dialogue songs, 213–214
  holds, analysis of, 206
  impersonation, 191, 201
  in the intermediate grades, 208–218
  interpretive, 195–201 (*see also* Interpretation)
  listening program, use in, 210–211, 227–228
  marches, 208–209
  in melodic movement analysis, 205
  in music analysis, 205–207
  pantomime (*see* Pantomime)
  physical arrangements for, 198–199
  pictures and, 200
  poetry and, 200
  props for, 209
  records for, 210–211
  retards, analysis of, 206
  with singing, 192–195
  in song interpretation, 213–218
  stories and, 200
Bongo drums:
  description and source, 56
  with Latin-American songs, 70
  with orchestral compositions, 76–77
Books:
  social studies resources, 255, 257
  song, 137–141, 277–278
Bourdon:
  definition, 274
  for harmony study, 113
Boys' voices, 30–32
Brass wind instruments (list), 245
Breaks, bodily movement in analysis of, 205–207
Breathing, 30
Broudy, Harry S., 5–6
Buchtel, Forrest L., 98

C

Castanets, 55, 56, 57
Catalog sources (list), 279–281
Cello:
  in harmony study, 112
  orchestral listing, 245

Chants:
  in melodic improvisation, 94–95
  in singing instruction, 144–146
Character, music and, 5–6
Character sketches, 232–234
Children (*see also* Students):
  boys' voices, 30–32
  comprehension level, 224–225
  creativity of (*see* Creativity)
  dance innovation by, 191–195
  evaluation of progress of, 260–261
  "gifted" voices, 34–35
  individual instruction, 29
  out-of-tune voices, 21, 25–29
  personal enrichment of, 5–6
  remedial work with, 32–34
  self-expression, 6–9 (*see also* Creativity)
  singing practices of, 20–22
  skill variations of, 20–22
  tone quality of voices, 22–23
  vocal imitation by, 20, 22
Chinese woodblocks, 56
Choral work, 35–37
Chording, 101–113 *passim* (*see also* Chords; Harmony)
  by ear, 144–145
Chording instruments:
  and principals of harmony, 167
  influence on melody of songs, 161
Chord inversion, 111
  definition, 274
Chord progression, definition, 274
Chords (*see also* Scales):
  characteristics of, 105–108
  intervals, 175–176
  inversion of, 111, 274
  names of, 105–108
  reference material for, 270–273
  as singing accompaniment, 152, 154
  in singing instruction, 144–146
Chromatic scale, definition, 271
Clarinet in singing instruction, 122
Classic dance suite, 240–241
Classroom:
  background music in, 225–227
  concerts in, 246–247
  performances in, 258
  singing situations in, 24–25
Classroom teachers (*see* Teachers)
Claves, 55–56, 70–71